HOW TO BE YOURSELF

HOW TO BE YOURSELF

Quiet Your Inner Critic and
Rise Above Social Anxiety

ELLEN HENDRIKSEN, PH.D.

St. Martin's Press
New York

This book is dedicated to
(and couldn't exist without)
Nicolas.

www.stmartins.com

The Library of Congress Cataloging-in-Publication Data
is available upon request.

ISBN 978-1-250-16170-3 (hardcover)
ISBN 978-1-250-12223-0 (ebook)

Our books may be purchased in bulk for promotional,
educational, or business use. Please contact your local
bookseller or the Macmillan Corporate and Premium Sales
Department at 1-800-221-7945, extension 5442, or by
email at MacmillanSpecialMarkets@macmillan.com.

First Edition: March 2018

10 9 8 7 6 5 4 3 2 1

Contents

PART 3

Heading Out into the World

PART 4

Busting the Myths of Social Anxiety

PART 5

All You Have to Be Is Kind

Prologue

Moe could fight injustice like a cornered tiger on one condition: as long as he didn't have to speak.

A lawyer by training, Moe was whip smart and had a reputation for being genuinely respectful. Despite his mild-mannered appearance—diminutive, skinny, and balding, with two perfect circles of wire-rimmed glasses perched above a trim little mustache—his commitment to social causes like the rights of the elderly or the protection of vulnerable women was fierce. His experience spanned the globe—at this point in his career, he had already worked in three different countries on three different continents.

As part of his idealistic crusade for justice, however, he often found himself in the most unidealistic of settings: meetings. It was at these meetings, in community centers and church basements with folding chairs and a lingering smell of old coffee, where Moe's story played out. He told it like this: "The other day I was at a meeting and one of the organizers turned to me and said, 'You know, Moe, when it's just you and me you talk totally fine, but you're so quiet at meetings. I don't think I've ever heard you open your mouth.'"

Moe was mortified. He knew, deep down, that his colleague spoke the truth. Moe was always attentive, always pleasant, but it was true—he never said a word. And now it was confirmed to Moe that his silence was obvious—that he couldn't simply hide in plain sight.

"It's not that I don't want to say anything; I just don't know how to say it," Moe said. "Everyone else seems to feel so comfortable, so confident. But as soon as I work up the courage to speak, the topic has changed. That happens *all* the time."

Not knowing what to say doesn't happen only to Moe. It happens to so many of us, particularly in today's world of cryptic, how-do-I-answer-this text messages and gotta-be-right Instagram captions. If you're wired or were raised like Moe—more on this distinction shortly—technology and the internet ensure you have a million reasons to second-guess yourself. Plus, you still have to battle the anxieties of *in-person* social interaction.

Like Moe, you may know firsthand the excruciation of teetering on the edge of speaking. It's like standing at the end of a ten-meter diving platform, your heart pounding at the prospect of leaping in. Remaining silent invites frustration—"I *knew* that was the answer," or, "Dammit, that was *my* idea," but the thought of jumping into the abyss of conversation is paralyzing. But after his colleague's comment, Moe decided it was actually worse to remain silent than to say something. Ongoing silence weighs a person down like a slowly accumulating pile of bricks in the lap. A few moments of silence can easily be shaken off, but hours of silence are nearly impossible to break, particularly without causing turned heads, exclamations of surprise, and crushingly offhand comments of, "Oh, I forgot you were there!"

So Moe decided to try to speak sooner rather than later: "So I showed up to the next meeting with some notes jotted in my phone. I thought it would be easier if I wrote out what I wanted to say. But I couldn't do it. The worst part is that the guy next to me took my phone and read my notes to everyone. I think he thought he was doing me a favor, but I wanted to die. What kind of man can't read his own notes?"

Once humiliated, twice shy. It took Moe a while to work up the courage to try again, but he did. Before the next meeting, he gamely typed out some more notes, but he still couldn't manage to say anything. "I tried," he said, "but my vision got blurry; I started to shake. It was horrible. Why does this keep happening to me? What the hell is wrong with me? Why can't I do what other people can do so easily?"

From working in politics, Moe was used to having to try again. So he decided to push himself—to try one more time. "I had a dinner to go to—just friends—so I thought I'd try giving a toast," he said. "I rehearsed it over and over in my head, but when I stood up I couldn't get past the first sentence. I had even worked a joke into it, but once I got past the first line I couldn't remember the rest of the joke, much less what else I wanted to say, so I just said, 'Thanks for coming,' and sat down. And I thought, 'Oh my God, what an idiot.'"

Moe's experience is so common it has a name: social anxiety. Social anxiety is self-consciousness on steroids. First there is a sense of being conspicuous, of sticking out like a sore thumb. There follows an urge to hide, to conceal, sometimes by staying away altogether, sometimes by showing up but remaining silent or staring intently at the floor. We worry we'll say the wrong thing, do something awkward, and get roundly, deservedly criticized for it. Therefore, so many of us feel stressed in class, at parties, in groups, at work, with strangers, on social media. We are convinced we are too much of something: too weird, too awkward, too annoying. Or that we are not enough of something else: not confident, not socially skilled, not competent.

Finally, our bodies betray us; we are sure everyone notices our graceless blushing, sweaty palms, or trembling hands.

This may all sound familiar. Did your eyes light up in recognition at Moe's story? Did you find yourself nodding your head as you read? Something else you and Moe have in common, I'll wager, is that at some point along this awkward, anxious journey—perhaps before a date, an interview, or a first day of school—a supporter has offered you some time-honored advice: "Just be yourself!"

This phrase is always well meant but can be phenomenally irritating. It seems so simple, but in the moment it feels impossible. Anyone who has been in Moe's position knows how difficult it is to think through the buzz of anxiety—how it hijacks our ability to think, speak, and respond. Also, "just be yourself" implies you hadn't thought of that option. "Oh, is that all I have to do? Silly me."

But despite all this, it's also sound advice. Your true self is the self that emerges when you are with close friends, trusted family, or in blissful solitude. Underneath all that anxiety, you're equipped with everything you need. There's nothing you need to fake, no image to manufacture. You are enough just as you are. Indeed, imagine if *that* self showed up at work, in relationships, and in the world. What would be possible? You could share your ideas and opinions. You could finally feel at ease. You'd have more bandwidth to deal with the world. You could feel comfortable in your own skin. You'd feel that home-sweet-home comfort, connection, and closeness wherever you went.

Therefore, in *How to Be Yourself* you'll learn (finally!) how to put that advice into action. You'll learn *why* you feel the way you do, but more than that, you'll learn *what to do about it,* and finish the book with a toolbox full of shiny new tools to try out. We'll debunk myths you didn't even know you believed and break habits you didn't even know you had.

There are so many of us who feel socially anxious that standardized questionnaires have been developed to measure our experience. If you think you may have a touch (or more) of social anxiety, check out the following twenty-five situations cribbed from two widely used social anxiety questionnaires.* The more items you agree with, the more social anxiety you likely carry with you as you travel through life.

1. I get nervous if I have to speak with someone in authority (teacher, boss, et al.).
2. I have difficulty making eye contact with others.
3. I become tense if I have to talk about myself or my feelings.
4. I find it difficult to mix comfortably with the people I work with.
5. I feel tense if I am alone with just one other person.
6. I worry about expressing myself in case I appear awkward.
7. I get anxious returning an item to a store.
8. I find it difficult to disagree with someone else's point of view.
9. I find myself worrying that I won't know what to say in social situations.
10. I am nervous mixing with people I don't know well.
11. I feel I'll say something embarrassing when talking.
12. When in a group, I find myself worrying I will be ignored.

---

* I've rendered these scales unofficial by editing some items to avoid repetition and have updated others with the language and technology of our time.

13. I am unsure whether to greet someone I know only slightly.
14. I feel uncomfortable making a phone call when others can hear me.
15. I feel awkward or anxious eating or drinking in public places.
16. I feel anxious acting, performing, or giving a talk in front of an audience.
17. I feel uncomfortable working, writing, or calculating while others watch me.
18. I get anxious calling, emailing, or texting someone I don't know very well.
19. I have difficulty speaking up in class or at a meeting.
20. I feel anxious using a public bathroom (shy bladder).
21. I have difficulty talking to people I find attractive.
22. I feel anxious taking a test or exam.
23. I get stressed and anxious when hosting a party or event.
24. I find it difficult to resist a salesperson or solicitor.
25. I dislike being the center of attention.

These are just twenty-five examples, but there are many, many others. For instance, those of us who feel socially anxious would rather get a bikini wax and dental work done simultaneously than work the room at a networking event. We might ask our colleague at the next desk, "Can you look over this email and tell me if anything sounds weird before I send it?" We might get a little antsy at the gym, the grocery store, in line, or wherever people might be inspecting us. We've been known to rehearse our food order before we get to the counter, our customer service request before we pick up the phone, and the story we're planning to tell at the party later that night. And of course, we try to sneak out of the same party without saying good-bye.

And this is just IRL. If social anxiety was at a slow burn a few years ago, technology poured gasoline on the fire. Why? Anxiety is rooted in uncertainty, and what's more uncertain than modern communication? "Why did those three dots appear and then . . . nothing?" "Why did my boss reply with a one-word email?" "Why did she text 'Can I call u?'" "Um, why did he text 'I am Batman'?"

Social media makes things even worse. A study out of the University of Pittsburgh surveyed almost two thousand young adults ages nineteen through thirty-two and found that the more social media platforms they used, the greater their anxiety. And it wasn't the amount of *time* they spent on social media—there was something unique about social media itself. What exactly? Well, social media is social judgment *in public,* complete with a quantitative count of others' approval. Especially for teens and young adults, the tasks of identity formation and solidifying self-esteem are tough enough, but having your friends observe and comment 24/7 makes the world of social media a tough place to grow up.

Whether we're feeling social judgment online or in the real world, we find ourselves doing one of two things: *avoiding* or *enduring.* Unlike most psychological jargon, both these terms mean exactly what you think. *Avoidance* is the equivalent of sticking our fingers in our ears and singsonging, "I can't heeeeear you!" Avoidance can be a lot of work—faking an illness means remembering to have a lingering cough the next day, walking the long but less crowded way around wastes time, and showing up to a meeting at the moment it begins so you don't have to make small talk takes exhausting precision. Avoidance can be overt:

WHERE YOU WILL FIND ME AT PARTIES...

YOU'RE SO PRETTY!

COOL PEOPLE

MAKING FRIENDS WITH THE RESIDENT ANIMALS, LIKE A DRUNKEN SNOW WHITE.

GEMMA CORRELL

not showing up at the party, letting our calls go to voicemail. But avoidance can be covert, too—we may not even realize we're doing it. Not making eye contact is the classic. Or we may go to the party but spend most of our time petting the host's cat or checking text messages on the balcony before sneaking home to watch Netflix and eat a bowl of cereal. But while avoidance offers immediate relief, it's almost always followed by a bitter aftertaste of guilt, shame, disappointment, or frustration.

Enduring, however, is white-knuckling it through an office team-building event, presentation, or wedding reception. God help the well-meaning bridesmaid who tries to pull us onto the dance floor—we would rather stab her with a dessert fork than have to YMCA. Those of us who endure usually get home with jangled nerves, a mysterious stomachache, and sore cheek muscles from continuous smiling. Or we get drunk, but more on that later.

Most of us have felt this way for a long time. For 75 percent of people who experience social anxiety, this long, awkward trip all started somewhere between the ages of eight and fifteen, allowing us many future decades to scroll through our phone rather than make conversation. For many of us, it's as much a part of us as our brown eyes or curly hair. It's what we remember from Day One.

By now, you may have noticed that I say "we." In academia there's a saying: "research is me-search." Many scientists choose their field because their subject matter rings true to them and their lives. The grit researcher bounces back after any setback. The trauma expert survived a life-threatening experience. The ADHD researcher works surrounded by teetering stacks of paper. For me, it is telling that I work at Boston University's storied Center for Anxiety and Related Disorders, or CARD. If anxiety were a religion, CARD would be the mother church and I would be a lifelong congregant.

My very first memory reveals how my brain is wired: I'm three and at preschool, resting alongside fifteen or so other kids on mats on the floor. It is the early 1980s and my teacher, Mrs. Fish, has long, center-parted brown hair and plays the guitar—quiet songs like "You Are My Sunshine" and "Hush, Little Baby"—to lull us into a few moments of stillness. This is what I remember: I open my eyes to Mrs. Fish leaning over her guitar, looking intently at me with a smile on her face. She had clearly been watching me for a while. "There she is!" she says. "Good morning, sweetheart!" As I sit up and rub my eyes, I realize with a shot of adrenaline that every single kid is looking at me. I freeze like the proverbial deer in the headlights. Some of the kids laugh—none in a mocking way, but still, to a sensitive three-year-old it is a Tinkertoy through the heart. I am still dazed from my accidental nap, which just makes the humiliating feeling of being laughed at that much worse. I want the eyes off me, so I squeeze shut my own, mortified in the darkness behind my own eyelids.

It is striking, I think, that this is my first memory, and not, say, feeding my little brother's popcorn to the ducks at the local lake or the knock-on-doors-equals-candy revelation of my first time trick-or-treating. Instead, my anxious brain decides to remember feeling humiliated by a friendly teacher and amused classmates after an innocent snooze.

It goes on from there. In first grade, I remember going to bed with a stomachache and a gnawing feeling "that I was forgetting something," not having the vocabulary to label feeling overwhelmed by a busy classroom day in and day out. In third grade, I knew my multiplication tables by heart but put off reciting them to my teacher until I was the very last in the class to do so. Middle school—that perfect storm of profound self-consciousness and desperation for peer acceptance—was the deepest pit in social anxiety hell, but that's no surprise. In high school, I came into my own with a solid circle of friends and some leadership roles, but then came the shock of college. While other students attended the infamous Naked Party and argued with intellectual luminaries in seminars, I avoided eye contact at fully clothed parties and raised my hand a single-digit number of times in four years.

However, over many years and a Ph.D. in clinical psychology, something slowly changed. Today, not only can I speak in a meeting; I can also lead one. I host a mean dinner party, lecture to a room full of students with confidence, and actually look forward to dancing at wedding receptions. Alongside my clients, I have done all sorts of embarrassing things in the name of social anxiety practice: asked for lemongrass in a hardware store, deliberately spilled my coffee in a crowded Starbucks, asked for directions and walked the opposite way. When I disclose my anxious past, I get incredulous looks—"I never would have guessed!" "But you're so comfortable." Today, I can say wholeheartedly I am comfortable in my own skin, even if it wasn't always this way, and I know you can, too. How did I get there? And how can you get there? I'll share all the answers with you in the pages ahead.

I still have my moments, to be sure. I do my fair share of public speaking, but my tears well up—sometimes very subtly, sometimes overtly—whenever I have to speak to more than a handful of people at a time. I've learned to think of this as the anxiety leaking out. I blubbered my way through my grandmother's eulogy, which you could argue was appropriate. I was sad to be sure, but I was mostly terrified of all the eyes on me. But I also got misty during my master's thesis defense. Appropriate? Not so much.

My Achilles' heel is being on camera. I subtly lean out of the scene when my kids record a video on my phone. I hate FaceTime. When the videographer at my brother's wedding jumped in front of me, camera running, and asked, "And what words of wisdom do you have for the bride and groom?" I must have looked like the Road Runner—a circle of legs and puffs of smoke emanating from under my floor-length gown. I left her with mouth agape and eyebrows somewhere close to her hairline. That little red light on her camera might as well have been a barrel of a loaded gun. Suffice it to say, I'm still working on that.

But that's the point: you can work on it. It can happen. You can feel comfortable in your own skin, comfortable talking, comfortable being seen, comfortable with your fellow humans. It will get easier. So much of anxiety is learned, which means it can be relearned. And you don't need decades and a slog through

grad school to outgrow social anxiety. I did it the hard way, but
that's why you've got this book.

How to Be Yourself is for all of us—and we are many—who find
ourselves tangled in social anxiety from time to time, or virtu-
ally all the time.

Indeed, there are levels. Social anxiety falls along a wide
range. The first and most common occurrence along the social
anxiety spectrum is socially awkward moments. Even the smooth-
est among us feel awkward or embarrassed at least sometimes.
These are the moments we say, "You, too!" when the waiter
says, "Enjoy your meal." Or we accidentally end up with a handful of breast while hugging a woman. Or we say a heartfelt good-
bye to a friend, only to realize we're both walking the same
direction. I've done all three of these things more than once.
These moments may be cringe worthy, but they're inescapable,
plus they make for a good story and a laugh later.

The next level is what is often called *shy*. I call this everyday
social anxiety. If you felt a spark of recognition at the word "shy,"
How to Be Yourself is for you. So many of us can relate: we stick
tight to our partner or best friend at parties; we eat lunch at our
desk; we don't raise our hand even if we know the answer. We
all have the thing we hate doing: making small talk, sharing an
elevator with the boss, or asking someone to continue his cell
phone conversation outside the movie theater. Left to our own
devices or with a few familiar people, we feel totally fine, but
our heart pounds when all eyes in the conference room focus
on us, we suddenly lose the ability to calculate the tip while our
friends finish their drinks and watch, we get sweaty and flustered
when we attempt to parallel park outside a crowded sidewalk
cafe. We worry we'll come off as inappropriate or incompetent,

and then get frustrated at our own worry: *This is stupid! Why can't I be more confident? What's wrong with me?*

Finally, like Moe, at some point in life 13 percent of Americans will consider themselves what your grandma called painfully shy, but what I call capital-S Socially Anxious. Social Anxiety is the fear of being scrutinized, judged, and found lacking in social or performance situations that gets in the way of doing the things you want or need to do. It has the dubious distinction of being the third most common psychological disorder, after the big boys of depression and alcoholism. Social Anxiety crosses the line from an annoyance to a problem if it causes *distress* or *impairment,* which is the technical way of saying it freaks you out or stops you from living the life you want. Distress, for example, is obsessing for weeks over a presentation, including losing sleep and fantasizing about whether you could escape out through your workplace's bathroom window. Impairment is when you turn down a promotion that would require you to lead meetings or supervise others, effectively stopping your career in its tracks. It's when you consciously decide to take a 20 percent hit to your grade by foregoing class participation. It's when your best friend asks you to speak at her wedding and you can't muster the courage, which breaks both your hearts. Or, for the 21 percent of capital-S Socially Anxious folks for whom nerves manifest as anger and irritability, impairment means sarcastic comments and critical judgment. It means losing friends and relationships by striking out in anger.†

Now, if you know you're solidly in the capital-S Social Anxiety distress or impairment zone *How to Be Yourself* is absolutely

---

† Common pushback to "be yourself" is "But what if your true self is an asshole?" I maintain that assholery is driven by fear and insecurity. When the fear goes away, so does the jerkitude.

for you, but don't stop there. You deserve even more. A thoughtful cognitive-behavioral therapist can customize a program just for you. A good therapist is like a good bra: they'll both push you and support you into the best shape possible.

But no matter where in the range you find yourself, social anxiety—whether for a moment or a lifetime, whether cowering in a corner or picking a fight—is the fear that people will see something bad about you and reject you for it. No matter how it manifests, social anxiety holds us back in our work, keeps love and friendship from deepening, and leaves us miserable and lonely.

What does this loneliness cost us? Way more, it turns out, than a few Saturday nights with the shades drawn. Loneliness turns out to be toxic. Loneliness is a perception: you can feel connected even when alone or desperately lonely even when surrounded by people. A lot of people, it turns out, perceive the latter: up to 15–30 percent of the population find themselves chronically isolated.

Loneliness is thought to be as fundamental a drive as hunger or thirst: the feeling tells us we are lacking something vital for survival and exhorts us to search out connection. Unchecked, loneliness makes us feel desperate and unsafe. It kills our sleep quality, our mood, our optimism, and our self-esteem. Chronic loneliness has been linked to an increased risk of heart disease, Alzheimer's disease, even mortality. The take home: Social connection is vital. Our very lives, it turns out, depend on it. Anxiety can't kill you. But loneliness can.

Now, if you're less socially connected than you'd like to be that's an intimidating thought. Conquering social anxiety may seem overwhelming or impossible. But let me assure you, you have a lot going for you. How do I know? As decades of research stack up, it's clear that social anxiety is a package deal. It comes bundled with powerful skills. With social anxiety come traits and tendencies that will serve you well in a culturally diverse twenty-first-century world (and won't disappear, even if your fear and awkwardness do).

Indeed, the research—as well as my experience working with many shy and socially anxious individuals—demonstrates we are often:

- Careful thinkers—we consider what we're going to say
- Conscientious, with a robust inner guide and strong work ethic
- Gifted at remembering faces
- Deeply empathetic
- "Prosocial," meaning positive to others, helpful, and altruistic
- Considerate of the rights, needs, and feelings of others

How does this manifest in our lives and the world? Those of us who experience social anxiety often:

- Omit needless words—in a world full of shouting and mugging for attention, we rise above the "more is better" approach to speech
- Work hard to ensure others feel comfortable
- Look and listen closely—a near-lost art in today's look-at-me culture
- Hold high standards, which lead to exemplary work
- Respect other cultures and backgrounds—we are the diplomats and ambassadors of the world

Sound familiar? Many people who experience social anxiety also rack up these strengths. Even if you're one of the 21 percent of capital-S Socially Anxious folks for whom anxiety manifests as sarcasm and criticism, I know that underneath all your prickles you likely have many of these qualities, too. Like a puffer fish, you're prickly only because you're scared.

Check out that list again. These are twenty-first-century skills for an increasingly interconnected and global society. Many of us socially anxious souls navigate a multicultural world with sensitivity and care. Indeed, those who don't care what others think squander potential relationships by disregarding the rights and feelings of others. You may already do many of the things on the list naturally, and with some practice you can do them while simultaneously feeling comfortable in your own skin.

Next, you're in good company. Fully 40 percent of people consider themselves to be shy, which is a shorthand way of saying socially anxious. Expand the question and ask people if they've *ever* been dispositionally shy at some point in life and the percentage skyrockets to 82 percent.‡ What's more, a whopping 99 percent of people feel socially anxious in particular situations. Only 1 percent of people (I'm looking at you, psychopaths) have never experienced social anxiety. With statistics like these, everyday social anxiety is, dare I say, *normal*. These experiences of yours are more common than you ever dreamed, despite sometimes (or even continuously) feeling awkward and conspicuous.

But despite the normality of social anxiety, you're holding this book because social anxiety has gotten in the way of your life in some respect. It may be circumscribed—agonizing over how

---

‡ Why? Time is on our side. Social anxiety declines steadily with age. We can't avoid everything and everyone. As people grow older, they naturally worry less about what other people think. But why wait for time to take its course when we can help it along?

to word a text, praying the teacher doesn't call on you. Or there may be a specific consequence you dread—you're afraid you'll offend someone or that your mind will go blank. Or you may feel all but paralyzed. No matter the shape of your social anxiety, there is hope.

Consider *How to Be Yourself* a path to change—to shed the outer layers of nervousness to reveal the comfortable, confident core of who you are. No matter what you're currently showing the world—sarcastic and tough, ultra-nice and agreeable, high-strung and awkward—I know your best "you" is in there. It's the you that surfaces around people with whom you are comfortable—your confidants, your closest family—or when you're savoring your solitude. That's the real you. So when I say "be yourself," I mean that *true* self. *The self you are without fear.* And believe it or not, it's safe to show that real self to the rest of the world. But I can't just tell you that. Instead, in the coming chapters we'll shine a bright light inside that brain of yours, keep what's working, discard what's not, and load you up with tools to nudge you in the direction you want to go.

"Yourself" is always changing. You're a living, breathing entity, and you're not the same person at ten or twenty that you are at thirty, forty, fifty, and beyond. You've changed over the years, and you will continue to change. But here's the thing: you get to choose the direction. Now, I will not promise a "new you," because, believe it or not, there's no need to change your personality. You just need to see that who you are is already perfectly sufficient. Fundamentally, social anxiety is *seeing our true self in a distorted way and believing the distortion to be the truth.* We magnify (or even flat-out imagine) our bad points. We worry about our perceived flaws, all while completely forgetting the myriad gifts we have to offer. You don't need to co-opt someone else's confidence when you can discover your own. All you need to grow is a willingness to try.

Learning how to be yourself and rising above social anxiety will improve every area of your life—your work, your relationships, even just going to the grocery store. Being the true, authentic you, even if just standing in the checkout line, shaking hands at a party, or sitting in your Thursday afternoon seminar, will help you make the most of this messy, imperfect, but glorious life you have been given. If there's one thing I know deep in my heart, it's that nothing is wrong with you. I repeat, *nothing is wrong with you,* even if you think you're the lone exception to this sentence. This book will help you feel comfortable when you're caught being yourself. Where you take it from there is limitless.

As you start learning how to be yourself, let's glean some inspiration from the best of them: a man who inspired revolutionary change and spoke to huge crowds as no one other than himself. In his quiet way, Mahatma Gandhi shook the foundations of British imperialism, led India to independence, and inspired movements for civil rights across the globe. He has much to teach us.

In 1930, in one of his greatest acts of civil disobedience, Gandhi led a march to protest the British colonialist government's monopoly on salt, a necessary household staple. At the time, Indians not only had to buy salt from the government at exorbitant prices but also paid a huge tax, a burden that fell heaviest on the poor. As Gandhi began his 200-mile protest march to the Arabian Sea, he gathered his few dozen followers around him to offer some words of wisdom, a call for peace and nonviolence that concluded with a simple statement: "I wish these words of mine reached every nook and corner of the land."

Day after day, as Gandhi marched and word spread, more supporters began to join the ranks. For three and a half weeks they walked, gathering hundreds, and then thousands of followers. When finally, at the edge of the sea, Gandhi waded out to the mud flats and scratched together a symbolic handful of salt, thousands of supporters looked on.

Not that many years later, Martin Luther King Jr. would write that Gandhi's quiet civil disobedience provided "the method for social reform that I had been seeking." Gandhi's methods led directly to King's leadership in the campaign for desegregation in Birmingham, the bus boycott in Montgomery, the March on Washington, and ultimately catalyzed the Civil Rights Act of 1964.

Gandhi's message of nonviolence indeed reached every nook and corner of the land, from Ahmedabad to Alabama to Washington, D.C. But he hadn't always wished to be heard and seen by thousands. Remember Moe from the beginning of the chapter? "Moe" is short for "Mohandas," as in "Mohandas Gandhi." In his autobiography, Gandhi devotes an entire chapter to his social anxiety, my adaptation of which you read at the beginning of this book. He wrote that as a young man, "I hesitated whenever I had to face strange audiences and avoided making a speech whenever I could." And his anxiety wasn't limited to public speaking: "Even when I paid a social call, the presence of half a dozen or more people would strike me dumb." Gandhi, who earlier in life couldn't even give a toast, would, in 1947, give a speech to a live audience of more than twenty thousand people.

Looking back on his life, Gandhi wrote: "I must say that, beyond occasionally exposing me to laughter, my constitutional shyness has been no disadvantage whatever. In fact I can see that, on the contrary, it has been all to my advantage. My hesitancy in speech, which was once an annoyance, is now a pleasure."

Social anxiety a pleasure? At first there may seem to be no redeeming value in caring what others think of us. But let's think about it. Gandhi is right. There is true power in holding on to just enough social anxiety to give weight and regard to the beliefs and perspectives of others. Call it empathy, respect, or equality—whatever you call it, especially at this point in history, it's never-more-crucial care and concern for our fellow human travelers.

In his autobiography, Gandhi wrote of his social anxiety, "It has allowed me to grow. It has helped me in my discernment of the truth." I hope this book will help you in your discernment of truth. The truth is already in you. You are enough. Together, let's rise above social anxiety and discover the power of being yourself.

PART 1

I Thought It Was Just Me!
Introducing Social Anxiety

1

The Root of It All:
How Social Anxiety Takes Hold

Jim never missed Sunday night at the dance studio.

Outside, a few late-fall leaves still clung to the trees, blazing orange and trembling in the New England wind. Inside, the vast hall looked like a wedding reception, but in inverted proportions. Off to the side stood a few round banquet tables covered with linen tablecloths and scattered with half-finished glasses of water, but most of the room was given over to the expansive, gleaming hardwood dance floor. Marvin Gaye's "How Sweet It Is" rang out from the sound system.

The room was busy—perhaps twenty couples stood in loose lines, practicing the East Coast swing under the tutelage of Tomas, the studio's stately Brazilian owner. Every Sunday evening, Tomas held a group lesson that morphed into a social dance—he called it a practice party. Tomas manned the music system, announcing with each song, "Ladies and gentlemen, it's a foxtrot!" or, "Next up, let's rumba!" Students asked each other to dance. As they practiced their steps, instructors circulated, dispensing guidance and adjusting posture—a hand on a shoulder here, a raising of the chin there. In the four years since taking up ballroom dancing, Jim, fifty-six, with the trim build of a runner and neatly cropped red hair that reflects his Irish ancestry, had become a regular.

That evening, as the last notes to Harry Connick Jr.'s "A Wink and a Smile" wound down and couples slowed their foxtrots, Tomas leaned into the microphone. With a gleam in his eye, he asked, "Okay, can everyone clear the floor except Mayumi, please?" Jim was puzzled—Tomas usually linked the songs one after another to keep everyone out on the floor. But tonight something was different. Mayumi was Jim's instructor, so he clapped politely, then turned and headed for a folding chair. But Tomas continued, "We have a surprise performance for you all tonight—a birthday dance!" Jim froze. Today was his birthday. How on earth did they know? He hadn't told anyone. He turned back to the dance floor and looked past the dozens of people. In an otherwise empty circle of onlookers stood Mayumi, a smile on her face, her hand outstretched toward him.

What a difference time and practice make. Four years previously, never in his wildest dreams would Jim have imagined himself at any kind of party, much less a dance party where he approached women, busted out a cha-cha, and did it all surrounded by mirrors and dozens of others.

Jim grew up in the sixties and seventies in the Irish-Catholic section of Dorchester, a working-class neighborhood in the heart of Boston. Jim's father, a calm and even-keeled man, worked as a groundskeeper at Harvard for thirty years; Jim's mother was a secretary for an insurance company. Jim and his kid brother, Ryan, grew up on the second floor of what in Boston is known as a triple-decker, their apartment sandwiched between two identical others, fronted by a stoop of wooden stairs. After school, Jim and Ryan roamed the streets with the neighbor kids, many of whom were their cousins. Except when winter snowdrifts clogged the streets, the boys would play street hockey, lobbing friendly insults and taking turns fishing the puck from under boat-sized cars with vinyl roofs. Between games, they trooped back and forth to the variety store on the corner, using the change from running errands for Mom to purchase their near-daily installments of Mountain Dew and Twinkies.

The neighborhood was close, both literally and figuratively. "I could have jumped from my bedroom window into the window of the house next door if I wanted to," Jim remembers. "The houses were that close together." But the tightness of the houses reflected the tight-knit community. If a stranger appeared in the neighborhood, locals would take notice and approach, asking, "May I help you?" There were eyes on the street, eyes on the kids. "It was so safe," remembers Jim. "Though sometimes it would get me into trouble. My brother and I would go out to play, and our mother would tell us not to go past Linden Street. And of course we'd go past Linden Street. So when we got home she'd ground us. I'd say, 'How did you know?' And she would say, 'Mrs. O'Neill saw you and called.' We couldn't get away with anything. But it meant we were safe no matter where we went. I wouldn't have wanted to grow up anywhere else."

But while the Irish eyes peering from the triple-decker windows meant safety for Jim and his friends, for Jim's mother, Maeve, they meant something entirely different. Whether Jim and Ryan were headed to school, church, a family gathering, or just outside to play hockey, before they ricocheted down the stairs and out the door Maeve would put them through her usual paces. Jim remembers, "She'd say, 'Come here, let me look at you.'" She'd peer at them, giving the boys the once-over from head to toe, smoothing unruly hair and spit-shining smudged faces. "We had to look good," Jim said. "There was always a fear. A fear of being judged. Fear that the neighbors would talk. That the ladies would get together, shake their heads, cluck their tongues, and say, 'Oh my goodness, did you see those Nolan boys the other day?'"

When the boys came home, there was another ritual. As they rifled through the cabinets for a snack, Maeve would ask: Did you run into anyone? Did you see any of the neighbors? Jim remembers, "There was just a sense of being in a fishbowl. Of always being scrutinized. She lived in fear that a neighbor would see one of us playing in the dirt or being disrespectful or who knows what. But she could never articulate it."

Maeve got more self-conscious when she went out herself. "Standing in line at the bank with her was the worst," remembers Jim. "Because she was trapped; someone might see her and she couldn't do anything about it. It was like being on display between those red velvet ropes leading to the teller window." Over the years, her discomfort grew, and eventually Maeve took to staying home. She would make Jim and Ryan go to church, but she never went herself. Jim explains, "I think she was too scared to go to church and see people, so she sent us as stand-ins so the neighbors wouldn't talk. Over the years, in trying to understand, I've tried to be generous, thinking maybe she was just proud, but I know it was fear."

Anxiety is unquestionably genetic. If you have a first-degree relative—in Jim's case, a parent—with an anxiety disorder, you have a four- to sixfold increased risk of having the same disorder. But psychological genetics is a puzzle, a maddening Rubik's Cube for even the most dedicated scientist. Why? First, unlike

Huntington's disease or sickle-cell anemia, anxiety isn't controlled by a single gene. But it's unclear whether anxiety is a result of the large effects of a few genes or the small effects of many. There's also another problem called *phenotypic complexity*, which means that anxiety is like the mythological hydra, with many different heads. Social anxiety qualifies as "anxiety," to be sure, but so do manifestations as diverse as OCD, panic attacks, and even fear of spiders. It can be difficult to imagine how such different flowers can sprout from the same genetic seed.

Next, anxiety isn't an objective condition—at least not yet. There's no lab test for anxiety. We can't look at Jim's or Maeve's blood under a microscope and see anxiety. For now, it's all based on self-report. Although our genes have expressed anxiety for millennia, Social Anxiety Disorder, the capital-*S* version of social anxiety, was first described in the literature in 1966 and has only been a distinctly defined disorder since 1980. As such, it's unclear if our modern, man-made diagnoses would even match up with our ancient genomes.

A final complication is the impossible-to-separate, coffee-and-cream swirl of genetics and experience. Our temperaments drive our day-to-day choices, but does a preference to stay in and read reflect a particular genetic constellation or do we like it because we're well practiced? In short, *whether* anxiety is genetic is clear as day, but *how* anxiety is genetic is clear as mud.

In addition to genetics, the seeds of social anxiety are also sown through learning. At some point, like Jim, we learned to fear the judgment of others, learned to conceal what was potentially humiliating. This lesson might have been seared into us through a discrete experience, like throwing up in front of the whole school during an assembly or having a panic attack in a crowded restaurant that resulted in a well-meaning waitress summoning the entire fire department. It might have been a horrified witnessing, like seeing a friend destroyed by bullies or a classmate demeaned, day after day, by a bad apple of a teacher. It might have come from growing up in an insular family that didn't see the point of socializing. However the lessons of social anxiety were learned, they created a fear of being caught doing something stupid or inappropriate—of being revealed. The lessons are often subtle and impossible to pinpoint; for me, like many others, there was no real beginning—it just always was.

With Jim, Maeve's lessons that he was being watched and judged everywhere he went, combined with confirmation from the Mrs. O'Neills of the world, shaped him over the years like a stream wearing a groove in the bedrock. Fifty years later, he says, "I always had the sense that people were watching. That they'd see something wrong. She drilled it into my brother and me."

Like sponges, we absorb our families' lessons, without quite realizing that a core belief is crystalizing inside us. In other households, very different lessons may be modeled; for example, that chatting on the stoop with neighbors is the ideal way to spend a weekend afternoon or that showing off your moves at the center of a dance circle is exhilarating rather than a crisis. My husband grew up thinking it was mandatory to invite the roofers or the plumber to stay for dinner. But if we grow up in a house like Jim's, or even a subtler version thereof, we learn to expect that people will not only judge us, but judge us harshly. And this fear feels like a fact. We think it's just how the world is. And that world makes us feel surrounded by judgment, yet alone in our fear.

This fear costs us: it makes it hard to meet people, get close to them, and have a good time. It makes it hard to ask for what we need. It can make others think we're snobby, unfriendly, or cold, when really we're just nervous. At its worst, it can leave us depressed and isolated. And of course, the fear gets in the way of being ourselves.

One hot summer day when Jim was fourteen, the call went out. In a neighborhood of 90 percent boys, a family with two girls had moved in down the block. Deena and her sister had arrived. Deena was also fourteen, with long brown hair and a wide, open smile. She was strikingly pretty, and, as the boys in the neighborhood (ahem) quickly noticed, well developed beyond her years.

Deena's house was on the corner, the last on the block before the main drag. It was also right across the street from Jim's cousin Rosaleen's house. For Jim to get anywhere—to school, Rosaleen's, the variety store, or back home again—he had to walk right past Deena's front steps, where she and her younger sister would often sit, their stork-like legs folded under them. While Jim was as intimidated as most heterosexual boys would be, walking past them five or six times a day meant eventually saying hi to the friendly Deena and her kid sister. Subsequent trips back and forth eventually led to pointing out his blue triple-decker down the street and joking complaints about cantankerous neighbors. One day, Deena's eyes were red—her grandmother had fallen and broken her hip. Jim listened intently to Deena's scared and worried rush of thoughts, not knowing what to say, but wishing he could make things better for her. As the year went on, they fell into a kind of ease—the most at ease one can feel during the turmoil of puberty and desperate desire to fit in that comes with being fourteen.

"And then one day," Jim remembers, "one of my friends at school turned to me and said, 'You know, Jim, Deena really likes you.' And that was the beginning of the end. I didn't know what to do or say. From then on, every time I saw her, I'd hide. Behind bushes or a car—it didn't matter. I avoided her at every turn. I had never avoided anyone until her. Because of her, I taught myself avoidance."

It was the defining moment. If genetics and learning had loaded the gun, Jim's friend had inadvertently pulled the trigger. Now, we've all had that stomach-dropping, cheeks-are-burning, surge-of-adrenaline moment of social mortification. But what turns that onetime jolt into social anxiety that burns on and on? Avoidance. Simply put, avoidance is turning away from what makes you anxious in an effort to feel better. And herein lies the rub: avoiding *does* make you feel better, at least in the short term. Avoidance makes the anxiety go away temporarily; in Jim's case, it subsided until the next time he spotted Deena down the block and crouched behind the nearest Chevy Chevelle.

But long term, avoidance is disastrous. It is enemy number one of emotional well-being and perpetuates all anxieties, not just social. For social anxiety to become a problem, genetics and learning aren't enough—the anxiety has to grow and be carefully maintained. Avoidance does just that, and does it perfectly.

Of course, a teenage boy wouldn't be expected to know the long-term effects of avoidance. Jim just knew it delayed the moment he would have to tell Deena he really, really liked her, too. It delayed the awkwardness of first love. And most important, it delayed the possibility that if she truly got to know him she would, as Jim feared, realize she had made a terrible mistake and grind his heart into the Dorchester sidewalk.

This fear is the core of social anxiety. It's the sense that something embarrassing, deficient, or flawed about us will become obvious to everyone. Jim feared what I call The Reveal. Social anxiety isn't just fear of judgment; it's fear the judgers are *right*. We think there is something wrong with us, and we avoid in order to conceal it. In our minds, if The Reveal comes to pass we'll be rejected, humiliated, or exposed.

But what exactly are we afraid of? Dr. David Moscovitch, a deep-thinking psychologist at the University of Waterloo, theorizes that The Reveal falls into one of four categories:

1. **Our anxiety.** First, we might be afraid people will see the physical signs of anxiety itself—we'll sweat through our shirt, blush as if Grandma just caught us watching porn, or stammer like a beauty pageant contestant failing the onstage question. Thus, our closet is filled with turtlenecks; our medicine cabinet is stocked with clinical-strength antiperspirant. We won't use a laser pointer or drink from a glass in public because we don't want people to notice our hands shaking. We never let 'em see us sweat, but that's only because we never take off our blazer. Or we pop a benzo.

2. **Our appearance.** Second, we might think there is something shameful about how we look—we're not attractive enough; we're dressed inappropriately; our hair is weird. We're too fat. Everyone will notice our blemishes or think that we look strange. However we slice it, our looks don't measure up.

3. **Our character.** This is a big one. We might be worried about our whole personality: we're not cool, not funny, stupid, a loser, an idiot, crazy, unqualified, inadequate, incompetent, or defective. We may mutter to ourselves in moments of angst, "What the hell is wrong with me?" Answer that question and you'll find your core fear. Whatever it is, The Reveal will show everyone we're fundamentally deficient.

4. **Our social skills.** This is another big one. We might think

that we have no personality or are embarrassingly awkward. We worry we won't have anything to say, we won't make sense, our mind will go blank, we're too quiet, too boring, we'll get emotional, we'll be confusing, or no one will understand what we say, and after staring uncomprehendingly, they will ask us to repeat ourselves in a tone used when talking to a three-year-old.

So rather than risk The Reveal, we hide. Sometimes it's overt, like Jim's diving for the shrubbery. But sometimes it's covert: we stare into our phones, avoid looking at people, or sit silently as friends chatter over us.

For Jim, hiding from Deena taught him two things: one, that interacting with Deena was risky—dangerous, even. There was danger of humiliation, the possibility that they would start something and she would lose interest, leaving Jim in the swirling agony of teenage heartbreak. And while this was absolutely *possible,* by staying far, far away he never got to confirm that things weren't guaranteed to end up that way.

The second thing avoidance taught Jim is that he couldn't handle Deena's interest. Avoidance is your brain's equivalent of a fussy mother hen—it means well, but in protecting you from a situation it inadvertently sends the message that you can't deal. In shielding you from threat, avoidance keeps you from learning "Hey, that wasn't so bad," or, "Wait, nothing terrible happened," and blocks the resulting confidence that comes with succeeding in ever-larger challenges.

In sum, each time we avoid heading to the bar with co-workers after work (*Nah, I've gotta finish this—don't wait for me*), avoid telling the woman cutting our hair we didn't actually want it *that* short (*I don't want her to be offended—she's armed with scissors!*), or avoid returning those king-sized sheets when we meant to get queen (*Maybe I can return these online*), it underscores to our brains that this conversation, this event, these people, are secretly but truly dangerous, plus we can't handle it. To compound the problem, we lose out on gathering evidence to the contrary. We never get to discover that despite an awkward silence or two with our co-workers at the bar, they like us just fine. We sit in appalled silence while we calculate how long it will take to grow out our bangs. We end up lying on uncomfortably bunched-up sheets, rolling our eyes at our own ridiculousness. To an anxiety-prone brain, these costs are a small price to pay to avoid danger and rejection. But when they are paid over and over again, we rack up a debt of experience and confidence, not to mention lots of lousy haircuts.

After a year or so of Jim's taking the long way around the block and ducking behind cars, a neighbor kid told him that Deena and her family had moved away the previous weekend. Jim was relieved but also, to his surprise, deeply disappointed. Disappointed in himself and disappointed that this was—he thought—how the story ended. And now that he had discovered avoidance, it would become his go-to for the challenges of adolescence and early adulthood. His genetic inheritance, combined with the lessons of Maeve and amplified with avoidance, had settled in Jim's brain for the long haul.

Fast-forward almost forty years. Just after his fiftieth birthday, Jim hit a low point: after a long but fitful marriage, Jim's wife packed her bags and moved in with another man, leaving Jim alone with his anxiety. "She used to call my anxiety 'Your Thing,'" he remembers. "She would yell at me, 'You need help!' but when I finally saw a doctor, she hated the fact that I had to see someone." After the divorce, Jim worked and ran necessary errands, but that's about it. He would stay inside from the end of the workday on Friday until Monday morning. He read historical novels, somewhat because he liked them, but mostly because he was scared to do anything else. He would show up to the occasional family gathering—a christening, a wake—but from the moment the invitation came, two or three weeks before, he would start to worry and obsess about what he'd say, how he'd feel, how it would go. The day of, sometimes he'd cancel, fake-coughing into the phone, saying he was ill.

Jim's cousin Rosaleen noticed his absences and was concerned. She told him he had to get out or he would rot. She encouraged him to join a church, so he went to please her but stopped after a few weeks. Then she pushed a book club. "But you love to read," she said when he shook his head. "You need to get yourself out of the house." So he started going to the family lake house on weekends when no one else was using it. By himself at the lake, he'd people-watch but spoke to no one. Rosaleen rolled her eyes. This was not what she had in mind.

Many of us have a Rosaleen in our lives. Encouragement for the socially anxious among us runs from the slightly patronizing (*You can do it!*) to the threatening (*Do you want to die alone?*). But in trying to remedy an underwhelming social life stunted by overwhelming unease, socializing because "it's good for you" takes on all the appeal of eating your vegetables. Even if we have a nagging feeling that indeed we should "put ourselves out there," the more others push, the more we dig in our heels. Plus, it doesn't seem worth it. Why would we relent and go to a meetup, a party, or a volunteer event? To sweat bullets and feel awkward? We breathe sweet relief when we finally come home, thankful it's over.

But one weekend, Jim—Rosaleen's admonitions in his head—

reluctantly went to her house for an evening barbecue. As he sat on the couch in the living room, people circulated around him, chatting, holding paper plates of hamburgers and potato salad. Kids chased panting dogs and younger siblings. Someone walked behind him. The person stopped. After a beat, a woman's voice asked, "What are *you* doing here?"

Jim turned. It was Deena, all grown up. His eyebrows shot up. The old urge to dive behind a bush kicked in, but instead he heard himself blurt, "Rosaleen's my cousin—what are *you* doing here?"

"I used to live across the street from Rosaleen, remember? We're friends." She walked around the couch and sat beside him, balancing her paper plate on her lap.

They caught up—the usual—what are you doing now, where are you living, how long has it been, how time flies. The years had been hard on Deena, but now she had a steady job at the local transportation authority and was in a relationship, a good guy after a string of bad boyfriends. Jim told her about his divorce.

"I'm so sorry," she said. Then, "Before you leave, can I talk to you in private?"

Jim felt his heart in his throat. "Sure," he croaked.

They moved to the front steps and sat side by side in the waning light. She lit a cigarette and politely blew the smoke away from him. After a moment, she said, "You know, I thought you didn't like me. It hurt me, because I thought you were a really great guy and I liked you. I wasn't stupid—all these guys would come along, all these older guys, who wanted one thing. I had guys hitting on me all the time. It bothered me. But I knew I could talk to you. You actually listened, you were a gentleman, and that's what I wanted. I knew you were the one for me."

Jim was speechless.

"You thought I didn't like you?" he said eventually. "It was the opposite."

Deena turned and looked at him for a long time. Then she smiled and gently punched his arm. She took a long drag from her cigarette. "What could have been."

I met Jim at Boston's sprawling Massachusetts General Hospital on a crisp February day. Months of kicking himself after the barbecue at Rosaleen's had spurred him to make an appointment. Jim easily could have continued on as he was—lost love, failed marriage, emerging from his home after a weekend to squint in the bright sun of yet another Monday morning. But after his conversation with Deena, he decided enough was enough. It was time for a change. When he told me the story, I asked Jim what he thought would have happened with Deena under different circumstances. He chuckled and gazed out the window. "If I had done the opposite all those years ago we might be coming up on our thirtieth anniversary. I want to feel less anxious so I can live my life," he said.

"Absolutely," I said. "We'll do that, but how about in a different order? You'll feel less anxious *by* living your life."

I wish I could shout that last sentence from the rooftops. With a bullhorn. Over and over again. It's almost impossible to retreat from the world and reemerge transformed, like a cocoon transforms a caterpillar into a butterfly. Instead, humans learn and change on the job. Put another way, rather than reading about how to ride a bicycle, we have to get on the bicycle. It is wobbly at first. We fall. But eventually our muscles and mind learn. And after that, we never forget. So Jim and I got to work.

If this were a movie, this is where we'd expect a transformation montage of sweaty training scenes set to "Eye of the Tiger." But while working on anxiety takes equal commitment, it looks very different. In our movie, we'd see Jim doing ordinary things like hanging out in the heavily trafficked copy room at work to practice small talk, running on a treadmill to practice feeling his heart race, sitting down for lunch with his co-workers, and walking through the doors to his first ballroom dance lesson. All these things seem mundane but are actually profound. Zoom in on his brain and we'd see radical shifts—a rewiring of the lessons of 1970s Dorchester, newfound faith in himself, and, best of all, the desire and confidence to build a community of friends.

To be absolutely clear, Jim's path to change was not magically conjured up by me—I and other anxiety specialists of today stand squarely on the shoulders of giants. Diligent, dedicated researchers have plugged away for decades—in the lab, in the clinic—and their discoveries change lives. These days, devoted, hardworking scientists, many of whom you'll meet in the pages ahead, are soldiering through funding crises, ever-increasing regulatory documentation, and a relentless pace of work unrecognizable to the scholars of yesteryear. Despite all this, the newly minted knowledge that comes out of their labs is nothing short of priceless. Neuroscientists, using ever more powerful technology, peer inside socially anxious skulls to watch networks of neurons flare and quell like fireworks. Evolutionary psychologists theorize why social anxiety stretches back over thousands of generations. Developmental psychologists venture everywhere from maternity wards to college dorms and beyond to chart the course of social anxiety over a lifetime. And of course, clinical psychologists continue to discover what to do with our thoughts, our actions, and our bodies to reclaim lives, including Jim's, one at a time.

Back at the Sunday night dance party, Mayumi waited on the dance floor, her hand outstretched. Jim politely shouldered his way through the ring of people and onto the dance floor. A few years ago, Jim wouldn't have walked through his front door on a Sunday, much less a crowd of people. Not on his life would he have asked unfamiliar women to dance surrounded by studio mirrors and the gazes of others. But this wasn't a few years ago. This was now.

Jim paused beside Mayumi and offered his hand. She took it. Tomas hit a button and "Moon River" poured from the speakers. A waltz. One-two-three, one-two-three, Mayumi and Jim danced. As they circled around the floor, forty pairs of friendly eyes followed and one heart—Jim's—warmed with pride and contentment. When the music stopped, there was raucous applause. Someone whistled. Another called out, "Happy birthday, Jim!" and the circle closed in around them. Jim was swept up in a tide of friends' handshakes, hugs, and slaps on the back. Tomas called over the system, "Beautiful! Happy birthday, Jim! Okay, ladies and gentlemen, let's cha-cha!" As couples paired off, Jim found his way to a table and sank onto one of the folding chairs. He thought, *I've met more people in the past four years than in the previous fifty-two.* He looked around with a deep exhale and thought, *I still can't believe I'm here.*

If you've never wanted to ballroom dance, no problem—the activities aren't the point. The point is internal—to grow the skills and the willingness to try whatever it is you hunger to do. To know, deep in your heart, that you are fine just as you are, even in the moments when anxiety might try to convince you otherwise. You can have the option to take a spin on the dance floor, the option to speak up in a meeting, the option to talk to whoever you choose, and the strength to know that even if things don't go as expected you can handle it.

Like Jim, you can challenge the lessons you learned growing up and rewire those old well-worn neural ski slopes in your brain. And here's the paradox: you can grow and stretch without changing who you are. You'll remain the same person and retain all the qualities that make you, you. Jim never once changed his fundamentals; he is still the guy who listens to your worries when Grandma takes a fall, is curious what's beyond the Linden Streets of this world, and cares deeply about those close to him. The only thing that's changed is fear.

The other night, Jim was watching the TV show *Modern Family*. Gloria, Sofia Vergara's character, was consoling Ty Burrell's character, Phil. Phil was mopey and disappointed in himself. After a public snafu, he tried to redeem himself by playing the superhero but just made things more embarrassing. Gloria said to him, "The point is that you're comfortable with yourself and you make people around you feel comfortable. They feel they can talk to you. That's your superpower."

"And I realized," Jim said, "now that's me."

Jim had always been comfortable with a select few—his brother, his cousin Rosaleen. But there were many more people he was comfortable with now—people at work, at the gym, at the dance studio. And as his comfort grew, so did his circle. But the reverse was also true—the more people Jim engaged, the more comfortable he grew with himself.

Does that mean he never gets anxious? Of course not. Does that mean he is confident in every situation? Not on your life. But does it matter? Again, let's ask Jim.

"Every time I walk out of the house I still feel that old twinge in my stomach," he says. "It was so drilled into me. But I know I can get nervous and still do whatever I want."

The goal is not to dance on the bar or wear a lampshade on your head, but to challenge yourself a little, on your own terms. You will start off by living the life you want *with* anxiety—by carrying it along with you. And as you do, surprisingly, the anxiety will ebb away.

Nothing will change. And everything will change.

Jim came down with pneumonia during the infamous Boston winter of 2015. Locals called it the Worst Wicked Wintah Evah. Images of roof-high snow and stressed city officials were all over the national news. Rosaleen and a set of snow tires got him to the doctor. In the office, after listening to Jim's lungs and peering down his throat, the doctor inquired about the pace of his life.

"Wait a minute," the doctor said. "You're telling me you're fifty-six, you work all week, you go to the gym every day, and you dance all weekend with dozens of women?"

Jim had never thought about it like that. "Um, I guess so."

The doctor looked at him. He said something to Jim about listening to his body, but Jim was busy experiencing The Moment. I promise this—The Moment—to clients. I've seen it happen time and time again. It works like this: as you grow and practice and challenge yourself, you won't notice your anxiety changing in real time. Only after your transformation can you look back and realize something is different. The Moment is when you realize, *Huh, I would never have flagged down the waiter for another napkin before,* or, *Wait, I just went to a holiday party without thinking of a million excuses to stay home,* or, *Hey, I can't remember the last time I stayed in all weekend.* Or a doctor looks at you with a raised eyebrow and tells you to take it easy, tiger.

2

Social Anxiety Is Like an Apple Tree (or, Why Social Anxiety Has Stuck Around for Millennia)

A stammering man is never a worthless one. Physiology can tell you why. It is an excess of sensibility to the presence of his fellow creature that makes him stammer.

—THOMAS CARLYLE, IN A LETTER TO RALPH WALDO EMERSON, 1843

Social anxiety may seem like it serves no purpose except to boost antiperspirant sales and at-home *Saturday Night Live* viewership. But sheer numbers—remember, 40 percent of us consider ourselves "shy" and 13 percent of us will have capital-*S* Social Anxiety at some point in life—tell us social anxiety isn't an oversight of evolution. Nature is trying to tell us that the wallflowers and shrinking violets among us are a necessary and beautiful part of this bouquet of humanity.

Judging from the pictures popping up in my Facebook feed every September, those of us who live in New England and have little kids are mandated to make a fall pilgrimage to a "pick your own" apple orchard. As part of this demographic, I've spent my fair share of autumn afternoons pondering apple trees.

You'd think the bigger and more verdant the tree, the more fruit it would bear. But that's not the case. Apple trees are notorious for requiring pruning, and lots of it. Each and every year, beginning early in the tree's life, the tree must be cut back. You might think aggressive pruning would stunt its growth, but the opposite is true: pruning lets in air and sunlight and leads to a bountiful harvest. By contrast, let the tree overgrow and it stops bearing fruit.

Why am I telling you this? Let's call the ability to gauge the emotions, beliefs, and intentions of others and to respond accordingly social awareness. Social awareness is necessary and good. It's the closest we come to mind reading. Properly pruned, social awareness yields social payoff. But if social awareness grows wild and unchecked, instead of merely being aware, we get hyperaware. We over-read social situations, think the spotlight shines too brightly on us, and get a wee bit paranoid. We take every look and gesture personally. We see threat in every interaction, which makes us duck out or stand silently. In short, it overgrows into capital-S Social Anxiety. And there, like the overgrown apple tree, the payoff stops.

All in all, social anxiety isn't helpful, but the traits it stems from are: this thing we're calling social awareness, and even behavioral inhibition, a term I'll talk about shortly. These core traits are so important that evolution has ensured that a sizeable percentage of the population is born with the tendency for them to overgrow.

So what kind of a personality blooms from those seeds? Why are the core traits so important? And like the apple tree, what happens when the core traits overgrow, and what happens when they are pruned back? To answer those questions, let me start by telling you a story about Cynthia.

It is February 1980 and Cynthia is a graduate student at Harvard's oldest-in-the-nation psychology department, founded over one hundred years prior by none other than William James, the father of American psychology. A pretty brunette originally from Puerto Rico, Cynthia has come to Cambridge, Massachusetts, for her Ph.D., which is still about a year's worth of midnight-oil-burning work away. In her junior year of high school, Cynthia took a psychology course and knew, like the flip of a light switch, that she had found her life's work. Tomorrow she has a meeting with her advisor, the eminent developmental psychologist Dr. Jerome Kagan, where she will update him on data collection for her dissertation. She's looking forward to telling him her data file is growing; she has run a number of subjects since the last time they met.

And now, today, it is time for another. Twenty-one-month-old Jennifer, bundled in a bright red snowsuit and holding Mom's hand, appears in the lab's doorway. Cynthia's work is in child development, so while most of the other psychology grad students study rats or, for the sake of convenience, Harvard undergrads, Cynthia's subjects are painstakingly recruited from local Boston-area hospitals at birth. Jennifer is one of these babies, now a toddler of almost two. Cynthia greets Mom and Jennifer warmly, crouching to meet Jennifer on her level. As Cynthia smiles at her, Jennifer is having none of it. She turns and buries her head in her mom's leg. Cynthia isn't finished with data collection yet, but as she kindly regards the back of Jennifer's snowflake-flecked head she intuits what she'll find today.

Over some quick paperwork, Cynthia explains to Jennifer's mom the purpose of her study. "We're going to have Jennifer try out some age-appropriate challenging experiences," she says. "It's nothing she wouldn't experience in real life—you and she will play in a new space, see some new objects, meet a new person. The experiences will slowly get more demanding. We're interested to see how Jennifer will respond." Mom nods in agreement. She's as eager as Cynthia to learn about her child. Cynthia leads Mom and Jennifer down a hall to a cheerful playroom well stocked with dolls, play food, utensils, stuffed animals, and a mysterious curtain drawn across one corner.

Over the course of an hour, Jennifer is introduced to novelty after novelty. First Cynthia models playing with the new toys as Jennifer, who has elected to stay in Mom's lap, watches wide-eyed. Cynthia sets up a table and serves play food, with great ceremony, to two dolls. "And here is your fried egg, my friend! Would you like some toast? Or maybe an apple?" She gathers three stuffed animals together and pantomimes that it has begun to rain. "Oh my!" she exclaims. "I hope we don't get wet, friends!" She holds a palm upturned, frowning upwards as if at a disobedient gray sky. She pulls a baby blanket over herself and the stuffed animals, protecting everyone from a certain, if imaginary, drenching. Throughout it all, Jennifer watches with a serious but riveted expression. Her eyes follow every motion, absorbing Cynthia's breakfast scene and rainstorm like a sponge. Her body is still, but deep within her you can tell wheels are turning. There is great activity, but it is all internal.

Then the task changes. Cynthia introduces Jennifer to a new person, a friendly grad student who invites Jennifer to play, enticing her with a pegboard and pink puzzle. Jennifer hesitates for a long while, then finally pulls Mom along with her, keeping her within arm's reach as she tests what puzzle pieces go where.

And then a final task: when the mysterious curtain is drawn back, Jennifer is introduced to a new object—the crown jewel of the protocol—a two-foot-tall robot made of tin cans, with Slinkys for arms and a head adorned festively with Christmas tree lights. Jennifer is intrigued but cautious. Cynthia encourages her to approach. "Look, the robot has lights on his head. Isn't that silly?" she says. "And you can turn them off and on with this switch here." Emboldened, Jennifer reaches out and flips the switch. The lights go on and she smiles. She flips the switch back and forth, back and forth, delighted with the result. But then, suddenly, the robot starts to speak. "Hello," says a man's recorded voice. "Would you like to play with me? Look at my eyes—they light up, too." Instantly, Jennifer shrinks back. Cynthia encourages her to flip the switch again, but now Jennifer is wary. She has ventured out, and now returns to the safety of Mom.

All in all, Cynthia will perform this scene 117 times. She will serve the egg, pantomime the rainstorm, and reveal the robot for 117 different children. Of the 117, approximately one-third will behave as Jennifer did. But another third will look very different—they will run straight into the playroom and explore, join Cynthia and the stuffed animals under the blanket when it starts to rain, talk a blue streak to the grad student with the pink puzzle, and squeal with delight when the robot starts talking. Over the course of 117 kids, Cynthia will witness both caution and boldness, shy and social, yin and yang.

What specifically did Cynthia see in Jennifer's behavior? When, in 1984, Cynthia published her findings from the 117 kids in the prestigious journal *Child Development,* it marked the scholarly debut of the term *behavioral inhibition,* a tendency to withdraw from unfamiliar situations, people, and environments. Today, behavioral inhibition is a defined personality trait, at the heart of which lies an individual's degree of caution when faced with new people, places, and events.

Behavioral inhibition goes way beyond toddlers, of course. In any organism, from bacteria to lizards to Jennifer to you or me, when faced with something new—a new environment, a new food source, a job offer, or a stranger with a pink puzzle— behavioral inhibition tells us to stop and consider. It makes us look before we leap. It's designed to keep us safe from risk.

Evolution keeps behavioral inhibition around because, kept well pruned, it helps keep us safe. Same goes for social awareness. So even though social anxiety isn't pleasant or useful, its roots absolutely are.

Allow me to take this even further. Even social anxiety itself, *in small amounts,* is helpful. What in the world might social anxiety buy us? Through the wide lens of evolution, it buys us quite a bit. Humans are social animals. Unlike, say, tigers or bears, we are designed to live as part of a group. During humankind's hunting and gathering days, we relied on the group for food, shelter, finding water, making tools. It took a village not only to raise a child but also simply to keep everyone alive, which ensured the group could reproduce and carry on through the ages. Therefore, it was essential to avoid conflict and be seen as a contributor. The way to stay in good standing was to work hard, make friends, and be liked. A little social anxiety helped ensure that happened by buying two things.

The first thing social anxiety buys is *group harmony*. We are wired to be aware of others' judgment of us because just enough social anxiety maintains social cohesion, and a cohesive group that avoids time-and-energy-consuming internal conflict is more nimble and durable than one weighed down by infighting. Over time, a harmonious group will outcompete other, more fractious groups. Therefore, playing well with others is a smarter evolutionary strategy than letting the one asshole drag down the whole group.

The second thing social anxiety buys us is *individual security*. Because what happens if you're that asshole? Call it ostracization, exile, banishment: No matter the name, cutting off those who threaten the group's hard-earned harmony has been used across time, culture, and even species (I'm looking at you, chimps, lions, and wolves).

In the early days of humanity, banishment meant certain death. The Bible, for example, is filled with stories that end in the punishment of exile, of a wrongdoer being "cut off from his people." Being left alone to fight off the jackals was the ultimate punishment. Therefore, what could be more useful than a cognitive system that keeps us from being thrown out in the cold?

These days, it's easiest to see the function of exclusion in circumscribed, tightly knit communities where there is a clear distinction between "us" and "out there." The Amish, for example, call it shunning. If you have transgressed and are shunned, all social contact with you is ceased until you confess your error.

Others will neither eat with you nor speak with you. As an Amish leader in the PBS documentary *Shunned* neatly sums up, "If we lose obedience, we lose the church."

But modern exile is not exclusive to traditionalist religions. It happens officially in sports: Pete Rose, Donald Sterling. It happens unofficially in politics: Anthony Weiner, John Edwards. It is litigated in business: Jeffrey Skilling, Bernie Madoff. And even today, despite on-demand potable water and online grocery delivery, we all still need the group to provide the necessary intangibles of community and love.

Speaking of love, a little bit of social anxiety makes us a better mate: more aware, more thoughtful, more cognizant. Now, you might be thinking, *Wait a minute. Social anxiety makes me act all weird and awkward. It's basically a mate repellent.* I hear you. Social anxiety doesn't feel useful when you're making awkward small talk on a first date, but in Darwinian terms it's the cat's meow. Social awareness and behavioral inhibition are such useful traits in maintaining harmony and security that to Mama Nature it's worth the risk of sometimes going overboard. After all, this is Darwinism, and *reproduction always wins out.* The awkwardness of social anxiety may be uncomfortable, but in the grand scheme of things it's a small price to pay. Our genes have a greater chance of getting passed on if we have a highly sensitive social smoke detector. A false alarm—detecting social threat when there is none—doesn't cost us anything genetically, whereas missing a true social threat means we get thrown to the wolves and our genetic lineage meets its lip-smacking end. In other words, social anxiety triumphs as an evolutionary advantage because the costs are low and the benefits are high.

To sum it all up, social anxiety has stuck around through the millennia because evolutionarily it buys us more than it costs us. It keeps social groups running smoothly. It ensures we remain part of a group, which, even in the age of Seamless and Amazon Prime Now, is necessary for companionship and belonging. And the self-awareness, empathy, and consideration it confers make us a solid long-term partner, which ensures our genes are passed on.

If you have too much of a good thing—too much behavioral inhibition, too much social awareness—take heart. Too much is way better than too little. Remember the apple tree. Better to have an apple tree that grows abundantly and requires pruning than one that withers away and dies. Better to have an "excess of sensibility" to the presence of your fellow creature, as Thomas Carlyle points out in this chapter's epigraph, than to be found lacking.

So what's the social anxiety equivalent of the expertly pruned apple tree? Where do those of us wired for excess social awareness and behavioral inhibition find our sweet spot? To find it, let's look again at Jennifer and her 176 cohort-mates.

Longitudinal research is rare in science, but the Kagan lab continued to follow Jennifer's cohort for years after Cynthia collected her dissertation data. In the early 1990s, when the kids reached the age of thirteen, some were invited back to the lab for an interview about their adolescent fears, from fear of spiders to fear of making new friends. They came from opposite ends of the temperamental spectrum—roughly half had originally been categorized, as Jennifer had been, as inhibited, the other half as uninhibited. The results were remarkable. While you might think that the inhibited kids would be afraid of everything and the uninhibited kids would be afraid of nothing, that wasn't the case at all. Indeed, there was zero difference between the groups when it came to classic phobias like fear of heights, elevators, or dentists. In contrast to a decade prior, there was no difference in clinginess to parents, otherwise known as separation anxiety.

The only true difference between the inhibited and the un-inhibited? Social anxiety. Of the kids who were inhibited as tod-dlers, a full 34 percent were capital-S Socially Anxious. Of the uninhibited group, 9 percent were. And while it may seem that even 9 percent is high for the uninhibited group, remember that age thirteen is perhaps the most awkward age of one's life. A thirteen-year-old is equally overgrown and immature, desper-ately horny, and wildly self-conscious. Through this lens, it's no wonder a significant proportion of the uninhibited kids were im-paired by Social Anxiety.

But more striking is the gulf between the groups—more than triple the number of inhibited kids were suffering. These are the overgrown apple trees. A behaviorally inhibited temperament, while useful in many respects, is more likely to set the course for a socially anxious journey through childhood.

But what was happening with the 66 percent of inhibited kids who weren't suffering? What did it look like to have behavioral inhibition deep in your marrow but feel good and do well? Herein lies the sweet spot. Thanks to a groundswell of quiet empower-ment over the last few years, these people have a name: introverts.

At long last, introverts are having their day. Over the last few years, being quiet and inner directed has become not only ac-ceptable but also downright trendy, with candidates as unlikely as Amy Schumer, Guy Kawasaki, and Kim Kardashian claim-ing the introvert mantle. Personally, I remember reading Susan Cain's 2012 bestseller, *Quiet,* and feeling astonished. How did she know I preferred reading to partying and working alone rather than in forced collaboration? To be sure, I enjoy social gatherings, but I have to recharge afterwards. I need to interact with people throughout the day to keep from getting bored and lonely, but I much prefer one-on-one to a big mix.

You may be a *non-anxious introvert.* You may love solitude

and intimate gatherings but still be comfortable in the presence of others, including strangers and authority figures. You may dislike big parties or receptions because they sap your energy, not because they make you want to hide under the buffet table. You are quietly confident and quietly comfortable in your own skin.

You may also be a *socially anxious extrovert,* one of the 9 percent of the uninhibited kids in the Kagan lab's follow-up study. This is exquisitely torturous—imagine getting your energy from people while simultaneously being afraid of them. For example, you may really want to go to the bar with your co-workers but worry they don't want you there. Or you may love parties but obsess about saying something stupid. You may feel pulled to the microphone but petrified by the crowd. You may be psyched for weekend plans with friends but get overwhelmed and cancel at the last minute, leaving you with a reputation for being flakier than a croissant. To top it off, while the introvert finds time alone refreshing, the extrovert finds it draining; indeed, too much time alone leaves an extrovert with the energy and motivation of a slug. The no-win choice? Feel lonely and sluggish or awkward and scared.

While being an anxious extrovert feels like being stuck between a rock and an angsty place, no one mistakes extroversion for anxiety. With introversion and social anxiety, however, it's fuzzier. Because it's common to be a *socially anxious introvert,* the two terms often get used interchangeably. Sometimes social anxiety is even thought to be a more extreme form of introversion. But while the root of behavioral inhibition gives rise to both introversion and social anxiety and the two often manifest together in the same people, the concepts are actually quite different. Far from being a psychological tomato-tomahto, introversion and social anxiety are more like apple and orange.

So what's the bright line between an introverted temperament to be honored and social fear to be challenged? Four things.

First, introversion is born, while social anxiety is made. Both Jim and Jennifer came out of the womb with behavioral inhibition, but remember, two things were necessary to trigger Jim's social anxiety. Let's say it together: learning and avoidance.

For your own learning, maybe getting bullied taught you that peers are mean and critical. Maybe you learned never to ask for help because, your parents warned, people would think you're weak. Maybe living in a Western culture that idealizes extroverts taught you, as Susan Cain puts it, that your quiet temperament fell "somewhere between a disappointment and a pathology." However social anxiety worked its way into your brain, you somehow learned to believe that people would judge you and find you lacking.

And of course, just like Jim hiding from Deena, you learned to avoid. Maybe being the center of attention as a kid made you so uncomfortable you've avoided it ever since and never had the opportunity to learn you could handle it just fine. Perhaps you bolt at the end of the meeting to miss the ensuing small talk, feign illness so you don't have to go to the holiday party, or stare at your phone whenever you feel nervous, all of which inadvertently keeps you stuck. You don't get the chance to discover this social stuff isn't as bad as you think and maybe, just maybe, you got this.

Second, with introversion, solitude makes you feel good. But with social anxiety, it just makes you *less anxious*. It's a fine distinction—feeling less anxious feels good, too—so let's look a little closer. Introverts gain energy by being alone, one-to-one, or in a small group of trusted confidants. If you're an introvert, being in solitude is refreshing and recharges your batteries. By contrast, with social anxiety being alone makes you less anxious,

which might feel good, but it's more a sense of relief than contentment. You may tell yourself, "I don't care," about missing
the reunion or turning down the invitation to karaoke, but deep
down, avoiding people leaves you lonely or filled with regret.
But the drive to make anxiety go away is strong. So you may
avoid events you'd otherwise love to attend because you're worried about making a fool of yourself, getting rejected, or feeling
awkward. We might say to ourselves, "Parties freak me out,"
"I'm worried I'm going to say something stupid," "I always feel
like I have nothing to say," while the non-anxious introvert simply says, "It's not my scene," "It's not my style," and then invites
a friend over to hang out the next day.

Third, social anxiety thrives on perfectionism. We'll cover
this one in chapter 13, but here's a sneak peak. With perfectionism, far from fifty shades of gray, you think your social performance is black or white. As you see it, only a flawless social
showing can stave off harsh criticism. You're either perfect—you
come off as witty, articulate, and cool as a cucumber—or you're
a stammering idiot whom everyone sneers at and turns their
backs on. And that kind of pressure is paralyzing; we think we'll
be rejected unless we come off as the paragon of effortless social
banter, which instead just makes us clam up.

By contrast, with non-anxious introverts (or non-anxious
extroverts, for that matter), perfectionism isn't an issue. Why?
There's no performance involved. And without a performance,
judgment is moot. You can pause during your presentation, lose
your train of thought in conversation, not be 100 percent prepared to talk about any given subject, and it doesn't necessarily
mean anything bad about you, nor is there anything at stake.
Some conversations are absorbing and flow easily. Others may
be graceless or banal, *but that doesn't mean you are, too.*

Finally, introversion is your way; social anxiety gets in your way. In one of the few negative side effects of the introvert revolution, some introverts took the label as permission to avoid. But using introversion as a reason to avoid isn't simply introversion anymore. For instance, a client of mine named Sanjay came to see me after he accidentally lost most of his friends. He identified as an introvert, which was true, but we discovered he would also put off returning calls and texts, dreaded getting together in groups, and would often cancel at the last minute, saying he wasn't well or had had a long week, all with the rationalization that he was an introvert and needed to recharge. He was indeed an introvert, but he was also avoiding his friends. He found out the hard way that if you say no over and over eventually people stop asking. Thankfully, he reeled them back in and now has, as he says with a roguish grin, "a raging introverted social life."

Remember, social anxiety is fear of The Reveal and the things we do to avoid The Reveal are what get in our way. You worry it will be revealed that you turn lobster red when you try to speak, so you stay silent. You think it will be revealed that your hands shake like James Bond's martini, so you keep them firmly crossed over your chest in a posture that broadcasts *go away*. Fear of The Reveal makes us slip out of the graduation party early because we're convinced we're weird, we think we won't have anything to say, or we're suspicious that dancing might be imminent. But then we miss the cake, but more important, we miss the shared moments. We miss out, either because we're physically absent or because we're stuck in self-monitoring mode, worrying that we've said something stupid or that we've screwed up. This is how social anxiety gets in the way of living the life we want to live.

By contrast, with non-anxious introversion you feel good and confident overall about yourself and how you present. You can turn "on" and be social if you need to. And even though it might take some effort to be "on," you can recharge by reading a book on the couch the next day or going out to brunch with your best friend. There's no fear of The Reveal because there's nothing to hide.

Now, a non-anxious introvert may leave the party early, too, but there's none of the self-criticism and self-consciousness involved. Many of us would really, honestly, like to go home and read, practice guitar, or putter in the kitchen. No judgment, no self-flagellation, no convincing ourselves we don't care. We choose to walk out the door; fear doesn't choose for us.

If you're still not sure where you fall, try this: picture what your social life would be like if you felt comfortable and confident. If you picture something different from what it is now, the cause is likely anxiety, not just introversion. But social anxiety doesn't doom us to stay stuck. Like Jennifer, we may come out of the womb with a predetermined temperament, but that doesn't mean we can't change: like the apple tree, we can prune back our overzealous social awareness. We can bring out the best of ourselves—our conscientiousness, our empathy, our deep thinking and feeling, our high standards—through a willingness to try new things and, vitally, some support along the way.

I know this firsthand. I was lucky enough to get some support from the woman who started it all: Cynthia.

Today, Cynthia is Dr. Cynthia Garcia Coll, a distinguished developmental psychologist with a thirty-plus-year career as professor of education, psychology, and pediatrics at Brown University. As of this writing, she is the editor of *Child Development,* the same scholarly journal in which her groundbreaking 1984 paper on Jennifer and the other 176 kids was published. Dr. Garcia Coll is a pioneering scholar, but her work isn't restricted to journals; as I discovered firsthand, she brings her care and understanding for those of us with some behavioral inhibition everywhere she goes.

In the fall of 1998, my senior year in college, Dr. Garcia Coll was the professor for a class I took on the history and theories of child development. Ostensibly a seminar, the class, at least in my memory, was big—thirty or so students. Undaunted, the teaching assistant arrived early and dragged dozens of desks into a huge circle around the room, giving each of us a front-row seat. I remember feeling conspicuous, usually preferring a spot in the middle of a lecture hall. Dr. Garcia Coll would breeze into class and perch confidently on an empty desk, arranging an elegant scarf over her suit. The air around her crackled with intelligence. She lectured without notes, citing studies as easily as if listing what she had for breakfast. I watched and listened, fascinated, but never raised my hand, a fact that weighed increasingly heavily on my shoulders as the semester wore on.

In the last few weeks of the semester, Professor Garcia Coll announced at the end of one class, "If you have trouble speaking in front of a group, come to office hours and let me know." I was astonished. I had never encountered this from a professor before. She gave no further explanation. I wasn't sure if I would receive a free pass or an ultimatum, whether I would be told not to worry about it or that I had better speak up soon. All I knew was that she meant me. So I went.

Despite the early December chill, I felt hot, as if I had been caught with my hand in the cookie jar. I arrived at office hours and hovered at Professor Garcia Coll's door. She motioned for me to come in. After I mumbled my reason for being there, she took off her glasses and looked at me. "Okay," she said, after a moment. "Thanks for letting me know." I'm sure she also asked me about how the class was going or what I was going to do for my final research project, but I don't remember. What I do remember is that through my anxious filter I thought she was disappointed in me or annoyed that I couldn't muster the courage to speak up. Now I know better.

It wasn't until researching this book, discovering Dr. Garcia Coll's research roots, and interviewing her directly that I learned why she invited me (and others—though at the time it felt like me alone) to disclose my difficulty. Simply put, she understood. When she took off her glasses and looked at me, I now realize, it wasn't a look of accusation. It was recognition. It was understanding. I could very well have been Jennifer, retreating to her mother's lap.

What I know now is that after I left Dr. Garcia Coll's office that December day, she looked more carefully at my work. "There are people who cannot raise their hand or speak freely in a group," she told me when I interviewed her and recounted my story. "I need to assess their interaction and involvement in a different way." Rather than docking my grade, she evaluated my understanding of the material through my writing, my exams, and my final project. She knew I was watching and listening like a sponge, just like Jennifer drinking in the scene of the dolls sharing breakfast.

Many of us change naturally over time; think of the 40 percent of people, myself included, who refer to themselves as "formerly shy." Temperament isn't infinitely stable. Genetics isn't destiny. As Dr. Garcia Coll's dissertation advisor Dr. Jerome Kagan himself has written, "Genes, culture, time, and luck make us who we are."

Here's an analogy: think of temperament as an anchor, but with a long chain attaching it to our boat. Temperament doesn't keep us static; instead, it provides a surprisingly wide range in which our boat can travel. Positive experiences can propel us to one end of our range, while fearful beliefs and avoidance can keep us bobbing fitfully on the opposite end. Jennifer may grow up to be introverted without being anxious. She may psych herself up to be "on" in social situations but then relish recharging in solitude. She may not choose a career as a cruise ship activities director, but she doesn't need to—leave that to the kids who bounded into Cynthia's playroom and were enthralled with the robot. Indeed, in the constant interplay between genes and environment the environment is always changing, the waves rolling and churning. Jennifer and the millions of us like her can use the environment to experiment, to practice living without fear, and, ultimately, to stay true to ourselves while becoming who we want to be.

The conclusion? Social anxiety is changeable. And change on the social anxiety front won't alter your introverted (or extroverted) personality; indeed, it doesn't need to. As you continue on, you won't become less yourself; you'll just become less anxious. So let's lose the social anxiety that's getting in the way and keep the personality that fits. We won't change *you*. We wouldn't want to, anyway.

Don't believe me? Let's ask the brain scientists.

3

Your Brain on Social Anxiety

As you forge ahead in your own journey of growing and stretching, you'll start to make changes in your life. You'll surprise yourself by speaking up in class, asking a stranger where she got those fabulous shoes, politely disagreeing with your father-in-law's political rant, or telling everyone in the office it's your birthday instead of silently hoping no one remembers.

Which begets the question: As we stretch and grow, what will happen inside our brains? It has been established that anything you do frequently can change your brain, from driving a taxi to playing the violin to watching porn to, as luck would have it, practicing social confidence.

But wait. Didn't we just spend a chapter establishing that social anxiety is written in our very genes? Didn't we just learn that natural selection has cemented the place of social anxiety in our species? How could striking up a conversation with your Uber driver counter the twin forces of genetics and evolution?

Remember: genetics isn't destiny. The brain, with its genetic programming and evolutionary shaping, influences behavior, but it goes both ways: behavior also influences the brain.

This is all very good news. It means that through practice

and a little help from the principles of cognitive-behavioral ther-apy* you can rise above your social anxiety and be yourself—your true, authentic self.

Case in point: a few years ago, a group from Stanford Uni-versity published a series of studies that found that cognitive-behavioral therapy for capital-S Social Anxiety fundamentally changes connections across areas in the brain, thus underscor-ing the idea that brain wiring doesn't seal one's fate.

But how? How is a socially anxious brain different from a non-anxious brain in the first place? What happens in the brain as we nudge ourselves to the top of our temperamental range? And who exactly is in this neural cast of characters?

To answer those questions, picture yourself arriving at a house party. Before you left home, you struggled mightily in deciding whether or not to go. You almost texted your friend, the host, with regrets, but instead you dug deep, busted out a Won-der Woman power pose in front of your bedroom mirror, and strode purposefully out the door.

But now, as you enter the party and look around, you won-der if you're in the right place—you don't see anyone you know. Your stomach sinks. Finally, you spot your friend. Her eyes brighten when she sees you. She comes over, takes your coat, and gives you a hug. But then she steers you to the kitchen, points out the drinks, and trots off to deposit your coat in another room, retreating, it feels to you, like the last lifeboat off the *Titanic*. You are left in a sea of strangers. You shimmy around people (*Sorry, sorry, pardon me . . .*) to the kitchen counter and pour yourself a

---

* *How to Be Yourself* is solidly rooted in cognitive-behavioral principles. Cognitive-behavioral theory is based on the idea that how you think and how you act affect how you feel, so by changing our thinking patterns and trying out new behaviors we'll feel differently—less anxious, more will-ing—in situations that previously gave us the heebie-jeebies.

stiff one. And it is here, next to a platter of chips and seven-layer dip, that the battle in your brain plays out.

Just as all flavors of ice cream, from plain vanilla to wasabi-bacon, are made from the same base of cream-eggs-sugar, all flavors of anxiety, from fear of the dark to panic to social anxiety, are made from the same overshot fear response in the brain. As you stand beside the seven-layer dip feeling like you have nothing to say and fighting the urge to leave, your synapses are lighting up like Times Square on New Year's Eve. Where exactly? And to what effect? Let's peer inside and take a look.

Imagine a line bisecting your head from ear to ear. On that line, behind each of your eyes, lie a pair of neural nuggets collectively known as the amygdala. The amygdala is surprisingly versatile—more little black dress than, say, cummerbund. It's part of the eating system, sex system, addiction system, and while it is not the only part of the brain responsible for handling fear, it is the linchpin of the fear system. It receives sensory information—the sight of a snarling dog, the sound of a bus hurtling toward us—and jump-starts a reaction. It's our fire alarm, designed to detect and respond to threats.

However, imminent threats to bodily harm aren't the only kind of threat for which the amygdala sounds the alarm. Change the snarling dog to a snarling stranger and our sirens blare just as loudly. For those of us vulnerable to social anxiety, the stranger doesn't even have to be snarling—she simply has to be a stranger.

Indeed, the last time the Kagan lab followed up on Jennifer and the other inhibited and uninhibited kids, rather than twenty-one months old they were twenty-one years old, the same age I was when I sat sweating in Professor Garcia Coll's seminar. But this time around, into the MRI scanner they went. The goal was to peer into their brains, to see what structures and functions, if any, might differentiate the inhibited and the uninhibited. In order to test this, the team created a slide show of sorts—a parade of faces, shown one after another on a screen. In the scanner, grown-up Jennifer and others saw portraits of stranger after stranger flash by. But then some of the faces began to repeat themselves. The same portrait might be shown two, three, or more times—eventually, strangers no longer. When they saw these familiarized faces, the kids' inhibited and uninhibited brains reacted the same way, which is to say, they didn't react. But when a truly novel face suddenly appeared on the screen, uninhibited kids' amygdala remained calm while the inhibited kids' amygdala lit up like a pair of headlights. A new person— whether a stranger with a pink puzzle or a portrait in an MRI scanner—was threatening, according to their inhibited amygdala.

So are those of us prone to social anxiety doomed to walk through life with blaring amygdala-induced alarms? Not always. Put your hand on your forehead as if checking for a fever. Directly beneath your palm is your prefrontal cortex, the part of your brain responsible for, well, responsibility, and higher-order thinking in general. It plans ahead, works toward goals, makes decisions, and suppresses unacceptable, NSFW urges. What's more, specific areas of it can talk the amygdala down from its social freak-outs.[†] It can help your amygdala realize that your boss is grumpy because she's under a deadline, not mad at you, that there are other fish in the sea even if your date just wasn't that into you, or that lots of people like you even if your amygdala is screaming otherwise.

But for us socially anxious types, our prefrontal cortex isn't as adept as our non-anxious friends' at shutting off the alarms.

---

† Since you asked, they are the dorsomedial and dorsolateral prefrontal cortex—affectionately known as the DMPFC and DLPFC.

For starters, our brains take a little longer. Let's pretend a friend hasn't texted you back. In a non-anxious brain, immediately after the amygdala screams, *She hates me!* the prefrontal cortex is recruited to calmly propose that she was probably just busy and will get back to you soon. The socially anxious brain can do this, too, but it takes longer—only three or so seconds longer, but those seconds add up to a major difference in how we interpret the world and the intentions of others. Life, as they say, is in the details.

Then, once the socially anxious brain recruits the prefrontal cortex, compared to a non-anxious brain the response is weaker. Indeed, in both speed and magnitude the response of a socially anxious prefrontal cortex never quite reaches the level of the non-anxious. When the amygdala sounds the alarm, it's as if the non-anxious brain dispatches a fire truck to the scene immediately, but the socially anxious brain sends a guy on a bicycle with a bucket of water.

But that doesn't mean your life is doomed to end up a smoldering pile of social wreckage. Enter Dr. Philippe Goldin. Before getting into clinical neuroscience, Goldin spent six years in India and Nepal studying Buddhist philosophy and even served as an interpreter for a handful of Tibetan Buddhist lamas. But after trading the Himalayas for the hills of San Francisco, he turned his attention to social anxiety.

Over four years, Goldin and his team at Stanford University painstakingly recruited seventy-five people with capital-S Social Anxiety Disorder. To make the study as personal and powerful as possible, they asked each participant to write out their four most cringe-worthy memories of socially anxious moments: that job interview where they felt woefully unqualified, that time they skipped their daughter's soccer game to avoid small talk with other parents, that painful date where they weren't sure which was worse—feeling lonely or desperately trying to keep the conversation going.

After their stories were written, everyone took a turn in the scanner. As the scanner whirred and clicked, taking pictures of their brains, their stories flashed at them from a screen, one sentence at a time. To further amp up the anxiety, the researchers embedded in the story each participant's personal hot-button beliefs: "I'm a failure," "I'm weird," or "No one likes me." In all caps, their belief literally flashed in front of them for nine excruciating seconds, each flash hammering home their personal Reveal: NO ONE LIKES ME, NO ONE LIKES ME, NO ONE LIKES ME. The whole ordeal was designed to send their social anxiety off to the races.

While in the scanner being pummeled by their own stories, participants were asked to handle their anxiety in one of two ways. During some stories, they were asked simply to *react*—to pretend their "no one likes me" belief was true, signed, sealed, delivered. But with other stories, they were asked to *reframe*—to think differently, to "actively reframe the belief" and make it "less negative and toxic for you." Having had no training in how to do this—yet—everyone bumbled through as best they could.

Once out of the scanner-slash-social torture chamber, the group was divided in half. For the next four months, one half twiddled their thumbs, but the other half got weekly cognitive-behavioral therapy where they learned to challenge their anxious thoughts and face their fears.

Four months later, everyone went through the whole scanning process again: same four stories, same all-caps flashing of anxious beliefs. But this time things were different. After four months of practice, when asked to reframe, the group armed with newfound cognitive-behavioral skills was able to think their way out of social anxiety much more successfully than the group who languished on the wait list. This time, NO ONE LIKES ME was quickly countered with "Well, that's not the case," "I can name a bunch of people who like me," or, "Hey, just because that's flashing in front of me doesn't mean it's true." Even when the CBT group was instructed to revert to their old habits and react, their changed brains couldn't help but think differently.

What's more, the scans confirmed this. Remember how the socially anxious brain's response to social threat is both slower and weaker than that of the non-anxious brain? In both magnitude and speed, the CBT group's new abilities were visible in their brains. CBT helped narrow the gap on those few seconds of delay and less-than-robust response in recruiting the neural architecture. Dr. Goldin summed it up perfectly when he said to me, "Those seconds can powerfully steer one into trouble or into freedom."

Let's revisit you at the house party and offer some motivation and encouragement for the future. As you grip your glass, it's no wonder you're feeling anxious—you're surrounded by strangers, your amygdala is freaking out, and your prefrontal cortex is taking its sweet time to help. You promise yourself never to do this again. But this time you make yourself a new promise. Rather than avoiding the next party, you vow to make some changes. Things can be different. Here's why: A socially anxious brain, physiologically, is exactly the same as a non-socially anxious brain. The architecture is all there. You have the capacity; it just takes some practice to strengthen the ability that's already innately there. CBT activates brain networks that are already present. And just like a commitment to working out strengthens the body, a commitment to practicing thinking and acting differently strengthens the brain. What's more, other studies have concluded that CBT leads to visible brain changes—Goldin's results aren't just a happy fluke.

The conclusion? When we challenge our socially anxious habits, over time we can break free of our well-worn neural pathways. By the time the next party rolls around, you and your brain can be ready. Pass the seven-layer dip.

It's tempting for those of us punished by social anxiety to think we need a drastic change—to turn our personalities inside out like a tube sock or to shake our brains clean, Etch A Sketch style. But it turns out the drastic opposite end of the spectrum isn't the goal, either.

What's the opposite of social anxiety, anyway? Fearlessness? At first, total lack of behavioral inhibition sounds great—no more dread, no more getting stuck in our own heads. But wait. Be careful what you wish for.

While you might guess the opposite of social anxiety is confidence, that's not quite right. The only people who have attained the dubious achievement of a total lack of social anxiety are the approximately 1 percent of the population who are psychopaths. But just like a tendency toward social anxiety is a package deal, so is psychopathy. You are indeed confident, but you're also irresponsible, grandiose, impulsive, shallow, remorseless, and deceitful. Psychopaths may make compelling fictional characters, from Hannibal Lecter to Cartman from *South Park* (chili made from Scott Tenorman's parents, anyone?), but in real life their existence, to steal from Thomas Hobbes, is nasty, brutish, and (often) short. Not exactly what we're going for.

A study by Dr. Niels Birbaumer and his team at Germany's University of Tübingen put criminal psychopaths and capital-*S*

Socially Anxious individuals through an MRI scanner and found an overactive frontolimbic circuit in the socially anxious and the exact opposite—an underactive frontolimbic circuit—in the psychopaths. This, along with additional studies, hints that psychopathy and social anxiety lie at opposite ends of the neuronal spectrum. If in socially anxious brains the circuitry is overactive— our smoke alarm goes off when there is no threat—when the situation is reversed, when there is smoke but no alarm sounds, what happens? The psychopath's house burns. Again, not exactly the goal.

So if you don't need a personality inversion, what does your brain need? Luckily, nothing so drastic. Instead, all you need is a series of nudges.

Remember, it goes both ways: the brain influences behavior, but behavior also influences the brain. So let's start making some changes. The next two chapters introduce some new ways of thinking and new strategies for taking on the world out there. Remember the range around the anchor? You can gently nudge yourself to the top of your brain's range. Just as individuals who are not athletically gifted can become fit, those of us wired for social anxiety can become more comfortable.

But wait, the analogy extends. Just as reading a book about getting in shape probably won't fit you into those skinny jeans, simply reading *How to Be Yourself* won't make you comfortable and confident. Over the next thirteen chapters, you'll learn tools that will spark a social workout with the power to change not just your brain but also your life. So go out and give them a test drive. Do. Stretch. Grow. You won't magically morph into a gregarious spotlight hog (and certainly not a psychopath), but you don't need to. You won't lose your ability to pay attention to others, to listen, to empathize, to care. You—and that glorious brain of yours—will only gain comfort and confidence.

PART 2

Looking Inside Your Head

4

How Our Inner Critic
Undermines Us

So how do we rewire to live with less anxiety? First, like a debater studying both sides of an issue, let's invest in listening to our antagonist and get to know the critical voice in our head. That voice may be soft or loud, but it exists for every single person on this earth; we're all human, and for better or worse, we always will be. I have the critical voice, too. And though my social anxiety is a faint echo of its former self, I still have moments when that voice re-ignites like a trick birthday candle.

I'll give you a recent example. My four-year-old attends a cooperative preschool. Every family has a co-op job, and ours is food shopping. So every few weeks, my partner, Nicolas, or I plow through the grocery store, clearing out the stocks of sunflower butter and string cheese for a horde of hungry preschoolers.

For lots of people, grocery shopping squarely presses their social anxiety button. There's the sense of being in the way, worry that people are evaluating the contents of our carts, or reluctance to chat up the cashier. For me, grocery shopping doesn't typically trigger any anxiety since videographers seldom jump out from behind the seedless grapes. So when I signed up for the food committee I didn't think anything of it.

However, the first time I found myself in the grocery store with the co-op's five-page shopping list, I realized I would need two carts, which in retrospect made sense for a week's worth of twice-a-day snacks for fifty children. I wheeled the first cart around the store, loading it to the brim, and then dropped it off at Customer Service while I set out with the second.

But when I looked at what remained on the list and realized my new cart would contain nothing but ten gallons of milk, forty bananas, and thirty apples, I felt that old sensation start to rise. As I maneuvered the cart over to the dairy section, I got stuck in my own head. I couldn't help but imagine what other people would think: *Well, she sure has a limited diet, Just buy a cow, lady,* or, *A little thirsty, are we?*

One by one, I hefted ten gallons into the cart, then pushed my considerably heavier load over to the produce section and topped it off with forty bananas. I don't think I'd ever bought forty of *anything* before. Finally, as I was self-consciously bagging thirty apples, imagining the obnoxious things people might say, a man approached me. "Nice apples," he intoned. I startled. In a flash, my adrenaline jolted—it was The Reveal.

But when I looked up, I saw an old friend grinning back at me. I can guess what my face looked like because his expression quickly changed to alarmed and chastened. "Sorry I scared you," he said.

"No, no, it was totally me," I said truthfully. "I was in my own world." Pleasant small talk ensued, and he said nothing about the contents of the cart. I don't think he even noticed.

To be stuck in your own world of possible judgments, or stuck in your own head judging yourself, is not fun. For me, it kept me from being where I actually was—in the produce section of a busy grocery store on a Sunday afternoon—and instead put me in a self-generated world of judgment that *wasn't even real*. It kept me from looking around at the good people of the grocery store—young couples debating coffee brands, dads with toddlers, white-haired women sniffing melons—and realizing that not one of them was eyeballing me or my cart.

After my friend rolled his cart away, I felt a resolve come over me. I decided to look at people, not put my head down. I looked at every single person as I push-pulled my two over-flowing carts to the checkout stand. Some people were looking at labels, some at the food on the shelves. And yes, some looked back at me. But no one said a word. Even if they had, what would be so bad? I'm not weird, I'm doing my co-op job, which just happens to involve a lot of milk and bananas. Exactly zero people raised an eyebrow at my carts. And even if they had, I could handle it.

That day at the grocery store, I took home a lot more than bananas. I took home a little booster shot reminding me of what it took years to learn: my anxiety is not credible. Seldom does anyone actually say, "Wow, you sure seem uncomfortable. You're weird and don't deserve to be here." Or, "That's it. You've paused in conversation one too many times—we're all going to turn our backs on you now." Or in my case, "Ma'am, is there a problem? The volume of milk in your cart clearly indicates you're a freak." Even if someone did, it would be the accuser who was unrea-sonable, not me. And if someone actually said to me, "You only eat milk and bananas! Wow, you have *problems*!" I could wave it off as the grumblings of a judgmental curmudgeon. I might even smile and offer them a banana.

MEET YOUR INNER CRITIC

Like in the grocery store, my social fear still pops up from time to time, but it used to be much more persistent. Why does our social fear endure over years and decades when no one actually says anything? Well, someone does say something. It's that voice in my head, that voice in your head. Call it insecurity. Call it self-criticism. For the purposes of this book, we'll call it the Inner Critic. We all have one.

But for those of us who experience social anxiety, the Inner Critic, rather than whispering in our ears, instead wields a megaphone. It attacks us with critical labels and embarrassing predictions. And then? Fight or flight is the response to all attacks, whether physical or emotional, whether from others *or from our own heads.*

Ironically, the Inner Critic thinks it is being helpful. In its own harsh way, it is trying to keep us safe. Think of the Inner Critic as a helicopter parent, swooping in to save us from any upset. It tells us we can't do it, we might get embarrassed, that it's too much for us. *Just sit this one out so you don't make a fool of yourself,* it instructs. *Don't risk it because people might notice.*

But at the same time, the Critic expects only the best from us. Just as the helicopter parent thinks their child is a special snowflake destined to rule the world, so does your Inner Critic expect great things from you. Only the best performance will do. The Critic wants you to do better, to be perfect, so it pushes you to perform while at the same time undermining your faith in your ability. Your flawless social performance is somehow supposed to emerge effortlessly and fully formed, like Athena from the head of Zeus. The Inner Critic's good intentions try to keep us safe but instead leave us floundering, pressured, and insecure.

THE REVEAL

So that brings us to the question: What are we social anxiety–prone folks really afraid of? Is it social situations? Not quite. It's not as if we're allergic to people. Most of us are totally comfortable hanging out with our nearest and dearests. Okay then, is it fear of embarrassment? Not quite: embarrassment is more the consequence of having our fear come true. Close, but no banana.

According to Dr. David Moscovitch, whom we met in chapter 1, what we're really afraid of is The Reveal. Ultimately, social anxiety is the fear that whatever we're trying to hide will be revealed to everyone like a gust of wind sweeps away a bad toupee. We *think* there is something wrong with us and therefore try to conceal it. But importantly, "think" comes with a big asterisk. Why? Even though our perceived flaws *feel* so real, they are either not true or only true to a degree no one cares about.

When we're alone or with people we trust, we feel comfortable. Our perceived flaws don't even cross our minds. Indeed, with the exception of when I buy thirty apples I don't walk around thinking I'm weird. It's only in a public context that these mistaken beliefs become salient—heck, that's why it's called *social* anxiety. If there were no witnesses, I could have bought three hundred apples and not given two, well, apples about it. This makes sense: without a potentially critical audience, there is no chance of The Reveal. But leave us alone with the boss, make us train a new colleague, or expect us to chitchat with a drugstore clerk (*What do you mean there's no self-checkout?*) and we start to doubt ourselves.

Put another way, social anxiety is about concealment. It's less about fear and more about shame, a word that can be traced to the Indo-European root *skam,* meaning "to cover." In short, shame makes us want to hide. Watch your body for signals. Just as sadness is heavy and fatiguing and anger is tense and agitating, social anxiety feels like an urge to seek cover.

Each of the four core fears from chapter 1—our anxiety, our appearance, our character, our social skills—lends itself to a different self-concealment strategy. If we're anxious about appearing anxious—say, blushing—we might cover our face and neck in makeup or wear turtlenecks. If we're anxious about our appearance, we might not talk to people we find attractive. If we're anxious about our social competence, we might carefully rehearse our stories for Friday night's party until we think they pass muster. Finally, if we're anxious about our personality, we may ask a million questions to deflect attention away from ourselves. *How was that new restaurant? What did you order? I remember you were going to take your mom there when she was in town. How's she doing? And your sister? Really? Tell me more.* (Stage whisper: *Just don't make me talk about myself.*)

HOW THE INNER CRITIC
DRIVES AWAY YOUR BEST SELF

In 1999, Dr. David Clark, a pioneering psychologist and professor at Oxford, dreamed up a creative way to demonstrate how the Inner Critic operates. The study participants were individuals from opposite ends of the social anxiety continuum—the highest quartile, who would have overthought a cart full of milk and bananas, and the lowest quartile, who could have wheeled around a cart full of bat guano with a cherry on top without blinking an eye. These men and women were shown a variety of words, one at a time, that described personality. Some were positive, like "relaxed," "poised," "witty," and "confident." Others were negative, like "awkward," "foolish," "annoying," and "pathetic."

Then half the participants were told they would now have to give a two-minute speech on camera. To make things worse, they were also told the speech was specifically an assessment of their social skills and public-speaking ability and that later some "expert psychologists" would watch the video and rate them. To top it off, the poor participants wouldn't be given the topic of the speech until thirty seconds before it was to begin. The other half of the participants? They got to just sit and hang. No speech, no worries.

Since only half the participants had to give a speech, there were now four groups: high anxious anticipating a high-pressure speech (*Eek!*), high anxious who didn't have to give a speech (*Whew!*), low anxious anticipating a speech (*Sure, no problem*), and low anxious who didn't have to give a speech (*Man, this study is easy money—can I sign up for another one?*).

But the speech didn't happen right away. After being scared— or not—by the prospect of giving a speech, everyone was asked how many of the positive and negative characteristics they could remember. Tellingly, the anxiety-prone folks who were stressed about the speech recalled fewer positive words. They simply could not bring to mind words like "articulate," "thought-ful," and "dynamic." However, they could remember negative words like "stupid," "ridiculous," and "failure" as if they were written on the back of their hand. Something about the immi-nence of The Reveal had flattened their ability to access posi-tive qualities but did nothing to slow their access to negative qualities. In short, the Inner Critic pulled out the megaphone, driving away their best selves.

This explains a lot. When it comes to social anxiety, bad is stronger than good. This makes sense: preparing for good stuff isn't crucial to survival, but anticipating bad stuff is. We orient toward threat because not doing so could cost us dearly. But unfortunately, this means we enter situations—the reception, the crowded room, the negotiation—already distressed. Our Inner Critic is whispering in our head, telling us things will go badly and everyone will see. That we need to do well, but we don't have what it takes. That we must either find a way to hide or face The Reveal.

Whatever your fear, it boils down to one thing: *I am not good enough.* And furthermore, everyone will see.

Many people know precisely what they're afraid will be revealed. But for others it's not as clear—there's just a vague sense of feeling out of place, of feeling the heat begin to rise. If you're not sure exactly what you fear or what will be exposed once your cover is blown, try this: Remember the old fill-in-the-blank game of Mad Libs? Social anxiety works the same way. Each one of us has the same basic story but fills it in differently. To use an example from Dr. David Moscovitch, if I'm concerned about my appearance, sitting alone in my car stuck in traffic might make me feel like I'm trapped in a Toyota-sized fishbowl. But if I'm concerned about my social skills, sitting alone in traffic might be one of the few places I find peace.

Try it for yourself. Think of a scenario that gives you the social heebie-jeebies. Then let Social Anxiety Mad Libs help you fill it in:

When _____,
       (SOCIAL SITUATION WHERE I FEEL ANXIOUS)

it will become obvious that I am

_____
(WHAT MY INNER CRITIC SAYS IS WRONG WITH ME).

Jim's might have gone something like this:

When I get in a relationship with Deena *(SOCIAL SITUATION WHERE I FEEL ANXIOUS)*, it will become obvious that I am a total loser in way over my head *(WHAT MY INNER CRITIC SAYS IS WRONG WITH ME)*.

In the grocery store, mine went this way, which shows the Inner Critic doesn't always have to strike to the soul, nor does it have to make rational sense:

When I am wheeling a cart full of milk and bananas around the grocery store *(SOCIAL SITUATION WHERE I FEEL ANXIOUS)*, it will become obvious that I am a weirdo *(WHAT MY INNER CRITIC SAYS IS WRONG WITH ME)*.

There are as many examples as there are ways to pretend to be absorbed in your smartphone:

When I am speaking up at a meeting at work, it will become obvious that I am incompetent.

When I am talking to the new intern, it will become obvious that I have no personality.

When I am at Lauren's birthday party, it will become obvious that I have no social skills.

When I am on a first date, it will become obvious that I am unattractive.

When I am at the job interview, it will become obvious that I am speaking with a trembling voice.

When I am <u>telling a story at brunch</u>, it will become obvious that I <u>am unable to express myself.</u>

When I am <u>forced to make small talk with more than one
person at a time,</u> it will become obvious that <u>my mind is
going blank.</u>

So think about the last time you pulled at your shirt collar
and thought, *Is it hot in here?* Fill in your Mad Libs here. Repeat
as often as necessary.

When _____,
        (SOCIAL SITUATION WHERE I FEEL ANXIOUS)

it will become obvious that I am

_____
(WHAT MY INNER CRITIC SAYS IS WRONG WITH ME).

THE INNER CRITIC, BEFORE AND AFTER

But the Inner Critic doesn't just pop up in the moment. It's present before and after a social moment as well. It's there in the
anticipation and in the aftermath. But don't just take my word
for it. Take my former client Loren's:

On this Thanksgiving Weekend, Loren is strangely thankful
for the I-95 traffic in which he and his girlfriend, Sarah, now
sit. Loren is exhausted. He's been "on" all weekend, having met
Sarah's parents and sister for the first time, not to mention her
grandmother, several aunts and uncles, and a multitude of cousins
whose now-jumbled names all seemed to start with *J*. His cheeks
hurt from smiling. He's grateful that the fragrant pumpkin pie

Sarah's mother insisted they take back to campus doesn't expect him to engage in small talk.

He drums his fingers on the steering wheel. "Do you think that went okay?" he asks Sarah. "I'm not sure if they liked me."

"Are you kidding?" says Sarah. "That went great. Everyone loved you. They were so happy to meet you."

"Really? I felt like I was too quiet. I should have talked more. But every time I thought of something, I felt like the conversation had moved on."

"Seriously? That never even occurred to me. You were so nice to everyone—I saw you and my dad talking for a long time during dessert."

"Yeah, he kind of cornered me," says Loren. "We talked about beach cleanups and how plastic is choking the ocean."

"How cheery. But the fact that he cornered you tells me he likes you."

"Maybe. Or maybe he just wanted to scope me out. See if I'm worthy of his daughter."

"I don't think he was testing you. He just wanted to talk with you. I told him you were an environmental studies major and that we went sea kayaking, so he probably put two and two together and came up with ocean garbage."

"Oh, great," says Loren. "Now when he thinks of me, he'll think of garbage."

"How should this have gone?" Sarah asks, getting a little exasperated.

"I don't know. Better."

What Loren doesn't say is, *My heart shouldn't have been in my throat the whole time; my voice shouldn't have been shaky; my brain should be capable of handling a simple conversation. Why in the world did I let us talk, literally, about garbage?*

"Better? But what went wrong?" Sarah asks.

"I don't know. I just should have talked more. It didn't go well."

"You did great. What are you so worried about?"

"I'm not good at this stuff. I should have told some stories at the table. Made everyone laugh. Or come up with something more cheery to talk about than pollution. I just feel like it was a missed opportunity to make a good first impression."

"You're totally overthinking this," declares Sarah.

Call it overthinking. Call it obsessing. Call it rumination. Call it the self-rated performance review from hell. Researchers call it *post-event processing*. Whatever you call it, it's a postmortem review of the bloopers reel of your social performance. As post-event processing expert Cyndi Lauper sings, "You can look and you will find me." So we do: the Inner Critic looks and finds the imperfections—the awkward silence in conversation, the answer that didn't come out quite right, the time someone laughed at the wrong point of our story—and strings them together into a Möbius strip of lowlights.

And it's this focus on the lowlights that keeps social anxiety going strong over years and decades, despite nothing horrible actually happening or even despite things going well. It's a vicious cycle: by focusing on the stuff we think went wrong, we conclude, as Loren said, we're not good at this stuff, which just restarts the dread next time around. It is, according to Dr. Richard Heimberg of Temple University, the father of social anxiety research, "snatching defeat from the jaws of victory."

But it's not just after the fact. The Inner Critic gets cranking well before the social moment, too. Indeed, the lead-up is where it does its best work. Remember Jim, the ballroom dancer? He felt it before big family get-togethers. Our partygoer by the seven-layer dip felt it before heading to the party. The enormity of the anticipation is what makes us throw in the towel, hide, or call in sick. Researchers call it *anticipatory processing,* though the best word to describe it is simply this: dread.

For Loren, what he doesn't tell Sarah is that his worry didn't start there on I-95. Indeed, he's been dreading meeting her family ever since he and Sarah made their Thanksgiving plans. For the past week, it's been his mental screen saver, popping into his head whenever he wasn't focused on something else. A couple times this week, he's been so busy silently rehearsing what he was going to say that he missed his stop on the campus shuttle.

Of course, some anxiety before a big moment or a big change is normal and expected—who isn't nervous starting a new job or going on a first date? It would be weird not to be anxious. You want to make a good impression, you want things to go well, so of course you have the jitters. But here's the thing: anxiety should *match* the task at hand. Anxiety before presenting to a crowd of thousands? Sure. But the same level of anxiety before joining a new Pilates class? That's a mismatch.

There's often a mismatch in the amount of time we spend anticipating, too. Sometimes it's a few minutes or a few hours. But in capital-S Social Anxiety, the nervousness extends for days or weeks leading up to an event. During his years of staying in all weekend, Jim remembers his anticipatory anxiety would roar to life, like pulling the cord on a lawn mower, whenever he received an invitation and would continue all the way up to the christening or cookout. Carissa, a former client, remembers being tapped in September to be a student speaker at her high school graduation that coming June. She reports, "I was anxious for an entire year. Whenever I thought about it, my stomach would flip-flop. It was awful."

In order to soften the dread, we often rehearse the upcoming situation in our heads, trying to find an answer for everything that could possibly happen. *What if the AV equipment doesn't work? What if she ignores me? What if someone asks a question I can't answer?* Most of all, we think: *How can I get out of this?* We fantasize about our escape. *Maybe there will be an earthquake and I won't have to present! Maybe the bubonic plague will make a comeback and the party will be canceled!*

What's worse is that freaking out doesn't even help. In 2003, David Clark, whose positive and negative adjective experiment we read about earlier, and his colleague Dr. Hendrik Hinrichsen tried to create a perfect storm of anticipatory anxiety in people vulnerable to social anxiety and their more resistant counterparts, and man, did they hit it on the nose. The unfortunate undergrads who took part in the study were told they would have to make a brief speech in twenty minutes' time. In order to ramp up the nervous anticipation, they were told the speech would be videotaped and rated by experts and, by the way, the participants wouldn't receive their topic until just before they had to begin. This setup was topped with a cherry of stress when they were told, "I would like you to try to make a particularly good impression."

Then, as a distraction, half the participants watched a twenty-minute movie about bugs and rated which bugs they found most appealing (ladybugs, clearly). The other half, however, were asked to spend twenty minutes freaking out. They were given the following instructions; if the Inner Critic had a recipe for anticipatory anxiety, this would be it:

1. Try to think of a social situation that did not go well, where you felt uncomfortable or others formed an unfavorable impression of you.
2. Try to imagine how you appeared in that situation. How do you think you looked to others?

3. Now try to imagine how you will appear during the speech you are about to give. How will you appear to others? What will they see?
4. Try to analyze in as much detail as possible what could go wrong while you are giving the speech.
5. Try to anticipate the worst thing that could happen while you are giving the speech.
6. Try to think about what you would have to do if you made a fool of yourself.

The poor participants were asked to spend a few excruciating minutes on each of the six steps. If they finished before the twenty minutes were up, they were instructed to rinse and repeat with a different epic social fail. You can probably guess what happened. Freaking out did nothing to help them prepare. In fact, it only made them feel bad.

Interestingly, this happened *regardless* of whether the participants were socially anxious or not. Indeed, these instructions would have made even Snoop Dogg into a nail-biting mess. Clark and Hinrichsen concluded that the main difference between high and low socially anxious individuals is not the *effect* of anticipatory processing—that's the same no matter who you are. The difference is that the socially anxious among us are more *likely* to engage in it.

To sum up, if the Inner Critic's cherry-picking of past lowlights happens *before* a big moment it's called anticipatory processing. If it's after the fact, it's post-event processing. Either way, it's hyper-focusing on stuff gone wrong. In each case—before and after—the Inner Critic puts us under the magnifying glass. But it's a magnifying glass that not only enlarges; it also distorts. It makes us interpret the neutral as negative. Ultimately, in one of the cruel ironies of social anxiety, all our preparatory freaking out and after-the-fact self-flagellation not only doesn't help; it actually sets us back, which is the exact opposite of what we were going for.

But guess what? Crucially, the Inner Critic isn't as confident and iron-fisted as we might expect. It actually waffles more than a Belgian politician. In 2006, Drs. Judith Wilson and Ronald Rapee, two distinguished Australian psychologists, ran a study much like David Clark's 1999 adjective study. They also showed folks with and without capital-S Social Anxiety words that described personality. Again, half the words were negative, like "boring," "ignorant," "lazy," and "selfish," while the other half were positive, like "admirable," "competent," "intelligent," and "warm." Importantly, the words had nothing to do with anxiety; they deliberately left out words like "nervous," "shy," and "calm." Then, just like in the Clark study, the researchers asked the participants to rate the words in terms of how well they described themselves. But then Wilson and Rapee made things more complex: in addition to measuring the degree to which participants thought the characteristics described themselves, the researchers also measured how long it took participants to make their decision about each word.

What happened? Not only did the socially anxious participants replicate Clark's findings, agreeing more often for the negative descriptions like "dull," "inadequate," and "tactless" and disagreeing more often for the positive ones like "competent," "successful," and "worthy," but also, as Wilson and Rapee discovered, they took longer to decide than the non-anxious group. In short, the Inner Critic wasn't sure. It had to think, *Is this me? Is this who I am?* That hesitation may have been a split second, but it indicated an uncertainty. There was doubt. And this uncertainty, this doubt, is the heart of *all* anxiety. Whenever we get nervous, it is because there is something we don't know. Something that's unsure. Something uncertain.

This also means there is a crack in the armor of the Inner Critic. In trying to keep us safe, it thinks we can't do it, but it's not sure. It tells us we don't measure up, but it has to think about it. Rather than being definitive and all-powerful, our Inner Critic is more like the all-too-human, not-so-great-and-powerful man behind the curtain in *The Wizard of Oz*. The Inner Critic is well intentioned but flawed and fallible. But you know what? Its insistence that you are not enough isn't just shaky; it's a full-on distortion. In fact, I'd argue that you are enough just as you are. That others would agree you're adequate and capable. And that would mean there was nothing to be afraid of and you could be, simply, yourself.

The Inner Critic is already uncertain. Let's show it that it's actually wrong. It underestimates you. You are stronger, more capable, and more likable than the Critic has ever given you credit for.

HOW'S THAT WORKING FOR YOU?

Occasionally, I'll work with a client who is reluctant to let go of the Inner Critic. "Freaking out makes me feel like I'm doing something," they'll say. "Worrying makes me feel like I'm on top of things." "If I didn't get anxious, I wouldn't get anything done." They'll defend the self-flagellation: "Being hard on myself helps me work out what went wrong. It will help me do better next time." I had one client, Rosa, who was particularly reluctant to let go of anticipatory anxiety. Just hearing the paces she put herself through was exhausting: "Whenever a presentation comes up, I start to plan," she said. "I try to picture everything that can go wrong so I can figure out how to react. I look back on all my past embarrassing moments and try to figure out how to keep them from happening again." But then she stopped. "This doesn't actually work, by the way," Rosa said, clarifying. "I just get exhausted." In her heart, Rosa knew all her planning was actually anxious anticipation gone haywire.

Let's see what it's doing for you. Is freaking out beforehand helpful? Is kicking yourself afterwards useful? No matter what you think of Dr. Phil, he's onto something with his catchphrase, "How's that working for you?" If you're not sure, try a two-day experiment: On Day One, punt all your anxiety to the next day. Then, on Day Two, let it all hang out. Anticipate and ruminate like it's going out of style. After you've recovered, ask yourself: Which day was more pleasant? Which day was more productive? I'll bet you a kangaroo that Day Two wasn't one you'd want to repeat.

From me at the grocery store to post-Thanksgiving Loren on I-95 to the undergrad research participants who were taught to freak out before their speech, it's been proven again and again that the Inner Critic doesn't actually prepare or improve anything, from speeches done for course credit to life in general.

So let's tackle the root of the problem: the Inner Critic. Ready? Here we go.

5

Think Different: Replace

There is nothing either good or bad, but thinking makes it so.

—SHAKESPEARE, *HAMLET*

There's a courtroom in your brain. You wouldn't expect that all that dark wood paneling, a judge's bench, a jury box, and a guy who looks like Bull from *Night Court* could fit, but there we have it. What's more, there's a trial under way. It's actually been going on for years. It's a trial to determine whether your fears will come true or not—that you'll sweat through your shirt and people will slowly back away, that everyone will stare at you in bewilderment as you speak, or that people would rather watch C-SPAN 2 than listen to your stories. The prosecution's star witness, of course, is the Inner Critic. It's been up there on the stand for years, yammering away, and frankly, it's time for it to be cross-examined—its annoying voice has been slandering you big time, and to quote the esteemed legal scholar Twisted Sister, we're not gonna take it anymore.

In order to challenge the Inner Critic, the plan is to shift how you respond to the Critic's admonishments—to change how you think when the Inner Critic gets loud and obnoxious. As the iconic, if ungrammatical, late-'90s Apple ads remind us: think different. To do that, we'll use two tools. These two tools are very different, but they both serve the same purpose: to respond to the Inner Critic rather than letting it convince us that hiding behind a bush or in the bathroom is the best option. Consider them the first of your new collection of tools.

The first tool is called Replace. Here, in chapter 5, we'll argue back to the Inner Critic (or at least be politely assertive—confrontation isn't my style, either) with the goal of *changing* its threats. Then, in chapter 6, I'll introduce another tool that falls under a different category: Embrace. There, rather than fighting with the Critic, we'll make peace with it. We'll extend ourselves some of the compassion we're so adept at offering everyone else.

In order to start off Replace with some finely honed arguments, let's bring in our defense attorney. She (or he—you choose) is fresh faced and, truth be told, a bit green. She hasn't really had much experience at this, but she's eager and hungry and it's time to let her test her chops. Maybe, just maybe, she has some moves that can slow the rush of the Inner Critic's criticism to a trickle.

Importantly, she's not here to think positively—positive thinking or positive affirmations don't get you far in the courtroom of your brain. Indeed, reassurance like, "You'll be great! Just be yourself!" feels like a lie. So this ain't no pep talk. Instead, our defense attorney is here to help us think *clearly*. So let's help her face down our Critic for a bit, shall we?

The defense attorney walks nervously before the bench and looks around. The Inner Critic is sitting in the witness stand like it owns the place. *Wow,* the defense attorney thinks, *the view is different from up here after waiting on the sidelines for so long.* She coughs nervously but then squares her shoulders and gathers her courage.

SPECIFY, SPECIFY, SPECIFY

The defense attorney looks at the Inner Critic, who grins obnoxiously back at her. It's been up here a long time and it's comfortable, thank you very much. But she knows the power of what she's about to do. She clears her throat and says, "First question: *What's the worst that can happen?*"

The Inner Critic laughs. "Seriously? That's the best you can do? What's the worst that can happen?"

"Yes."

"What is that, a rhetorical question?" the Critic scoffs.

"No, no," says the defense attorney. "It's a genuine question to be answered. What *specifically* is the worst that can happen?"

"That's easy: everyone will think I'm weird."

"No, see, that's what I mean," she says. "*Everyone* will think I'm weird—that's so vague. That could mean anybody. Who *specifically* will think that?"

The Inner Critic looks confused. It's never thought about things this way. "I don't know. Everybody."

"No, not everybody," says the defense attorney. "Name names."

This is the first tool for that shiny new toolbox: specify. Just like the mantra of real estate is location, location, location, the mantra of overcoming anxiety is specify, specify, specify. Why? Anxiety is often vague: Everybody *will think I'm weird!* Something *bad will happen!* People *will judge me! I will do* something *stupid!* Anxiety would make a great horoscope writer. It's hazy enough that we can read just about anything into its predictions.

Watch for the red flags of imprecision—"always," "never," "everybody," "nobody."

Anxiety can also be vague when it's less of a fully formed thought and more of a reptilian-level reflex—a lurch in the stomach, a jolt of adrenaline, the impulse to keep on driving past your cousin's wedding reception site. The Inner Critic sends you a strong feeling, and that feeling *feels like a fact*. Because we *feel* inadequate, it must be true. Because we *feel* like a loser, we must be one. Because we *feel* the heat, we must be turning an Elmo shade of red, and what's more, everyone must be judging us for it.

If your Critic is more of a feeling, in order to specify, specify, specify, try this: ask what that lurch in the stomach would say if it could talk. What would the urge to skip out on the wedding reception tell you if it was translated into words? Think of yourself as a cartoon character and ask what the thought bubble coming out of your head would say. Once the thought is verbal, it has a form, which means we can challenge it.

So get specific. *What* exactly *is the worst that can happen? What* particular *stupid thing do I expect I will do? Who,* precisely, *do I expect is going to judge me?* As the defense attorney says, name names.

> *Everyone will hate me* turns into *My boss will hate this particular presentation.*
> *Everyone will think I'm a freak* turns into *The five or six people I talk to at the party might notice my hands shaking and think something is wrong with me.*
> *People will think I'm ugly* turns into *Mackenzie and Carmen will be judgmental of my outfit and hair again.*
> *I'll screw this up* turns into *The customer service guy won't*

understand what I need and we'll get into a long, awkward misunderstanding.

Something bad will happen turns into *I'm worried I won't know where to stand or how to position my body during the meet-and-greet.*

Sometimes we get lucky and specify, specify, specify is enough to quell the anxiety right away. Once our specific fear is solidified, we recognize it for what it is. When *Something embarrassing will happen* is specified into *I will go fetal and mute in front of the whole staff meeting,* we realize it's about as realistic as Barbie's high-heeled feet.

But more often, specify, specify, specify is the first step. After we've pinned down the Inner Critic's worst-case scenario, we can start to challenge it. So let's check back in the courtroom and see how our defense attorney does this.

THE MAGIC QUESTIONS

Next up, a set of magic questions. The defense attorney looks squarely at the Inner Critic and lets loose the first: **"How bad would that really be?"**

The Inner Critic scoffs again. "How bad would that really be? Bad! Really bad! People will reject me! Or ignore me! Or think I'm stupid! You can't tell me those things aren't bad. You've got nothing."

"Okay, it wouldn't be pleasant," allows the defense attorney. "But would any of those *truly* be a disaster of epic proportions?"

"Totally disastrous!"

"Would anyone die? Would you be irreversibly broken?"

The Critic pauses. "Does dying inside count?"

"No."

"But those things would totally suck!"

"Yes, they would suck, but would they be *disasters*? Would they be worth getting really worked up over?"

For the first time, the Critic's voice gets a little softer. "They'd still be bad," it insists.

The defense attorney smiles, clasps her hands behind her back, and rocks on her heels. She may actually be enjoying this.

Okay, what's our defense attorney up to here? She's doing what's called *decatastrophizing,* which is like declawing a lion. It's bursting the bubble of the worst-case scenario. Don't get me wrong, the problem is still there—someone out there indeed might momentarily think we're weird, unattractive, or stupid. But how bad is that *really*? How bad is a little bit of judgment? Could we handle it? The consequences get put in perspective.

But then the Inner Critic gets an idea and is reinvigorated. "But lots of things *would* be disasters! I'll make a mistake in my presentation and get fired! I'll sweat through my shirt and my co-workers will think I'm an anxious freak! I'll make a fool of myself on this date and be alone forever!"

You have to give it to the Critic: this is quite the talent—the ability to take a situation that's ambiguous to slightly threatening and forecast a really huge catastrophe. "Ha! Try that! *Those* are actually disasters," says the Inner Critic. It folds its arms, smug.

The defense attorney is ready. "Yes, those would all be bad. But tell me: **What are the odds?** What are the odds you'll really get fired for making a mistake in your presentation? What are the odds that every single person will conclude you're an anxious freak because you're sweaty? What are the odds that one date will doom you to be lonely forever?"

"Really high."

"Seriously? One mistake equals getting fired? *Every single person* will think you're a freak? You'll be lonely for the remainder of your days on earth?"

Where is the defense attorney going with this one? She's reeling back our brain's tendency not only to jump to the worst-case scenario but also to convince ourselves it's definitely going to happen. Sometimes this ability to forecast social catastrophe is useful—you see a drunken crowd armed with rotten tomatoes at Amateur Night and decide to debut your interpretive dance another time. But more often, we foresee big consequences in small things: We'll go momentarily blank during a presentation at work (small thing) and get fired (big consequence). Sweatiness (small thing) means everyone will see and recoil in horror (big consequence). One date goes sour (small thing) so we'll be alone forever (big consequence).

The odds are low that the worst our brain can conjure actually happens. Let's take the presentation example. Is it more likely that you'll be fired or that people will notice something's off, feel a little pity for you, but then go back to mentally calculating their Weight Watchers points for the day? What are the odds everyone will think you're an anxious freak? Is it more likely that one or two people will notice your sweaty shirt but assume you're just overly warm? Or even that you're nervous, but they'll feel compassion for you? What are the odds you'll *actually* be lonely forever? Would it be more likely that you just didn't click with this person? Or that even if you never find a partner, you're not doomed to cry into your knitting on Friday nights for the rest of your life?

At least one of these questions, if not both—"How bad would that really be?" and "What are the odds?"—will take some of the edge off pretty much every socially anxious thought.

The Inner Critic is starting to look nervous now.

The defense attorney leans in and asks her last question: **"How could you cope?"**

We get anxious when we think we can't deal. It makes sense: anxiety makes us doubt our own abilities. Again, our fear feels like a fact. We *feel* incapable, so we must be. We *feel* overwhelmed, so we must be in over our heads. But think of all the resources you could gather—your friends, your family, your inner strength, your faith, your mojo, that coupon for a free yoga class in the back of your desk drawer—to help you deal if your fear came to pass. Spell it out: How would you cope? How would you take action?

For example, if you actually got fired, what could you do? Seriously, what *could* you do? You could look for another job. You could tighten your budget for a while. You could ask friends and family if they can connect you anywhere. It wouldn't be a cakewalk by any means. It would be really hard. But it wouldn't be hopeless. You'd make it through. And that's the point: even if your worries seem overwhelming, you can cope with pretty much anything life throws at you, from curveballs to screwballs to a few dates with oddballs.

Back to the courtroom. The Inner Critic is squirming. The defense attorney turns on her heel with a smile. "No further questions."

To sum up, when your Inner Critic kicks the anxiety into gear, first ask, "What's the worst that can happen?" Answer as precisely as possible; remember: specify, specify, specify.

Then ask:

"How bad would that really be?"

"What are the odds?"

"How could I cope?"

These questions will have you covered for almost every socially anxious thought. You'll replace your worst-case scenarios with something less heart-pounding and more realistic. Now, I know it might not *feel* true yet, but remember, your defense attorney just got started with this "Replace" business. Social anxiety took a lifetime to entrench itself. And while it won't take another lifetime to unwind, our next tool, the notion of "Embrace," can help you speed up the process.

6

Think Different: Embrace

You're driving to the local pool to pick up your kid from swim lessons. You pull into the parking lot, head inside, and say hello to the bored-looking college student at the front desk. You amble over to the pool and try not to get splashed by kids holding on to the wall, kicking up a froth. The air smells like chlorine, which you are thankful for as you realize, judging from the number of little kids in the pool, what percentage of the water is probably pee. In the pool are several groups of kids, each working at a different level with their own coach. You scan the water, looking for your kid's group. But then you hear an adult's voice booming over the chatter and the splashing.

"No! Not like that, you idiot! What are you thinking? I can't believe you're kicking like that. You look like a drowning chicken. Are you kidding me? Swim like that and everyone will laugh at you."

You look, horrified. A coach is standing over a kid bobbing in the water. The kid starts to cry, tears slowly filling the inside of her goggles. "Don't bother coming back next week," snorts the coach. "These other kids don't want you here, anyway."

You're aghast. You look around to see if anyone else is

witnessing this. Doesn't this count as child abuse? You make a mental note not to let your kid within a mile of this guy.

While you're thinking about what to tell the front desk, another lesson starts in the pool, just a few feet from where you're standing. The kids are working on kicking, just like the other group. While most of the kids happily kick away, the water churning behind them, one kid is struggling; his legs slap the water haphazardly. "Hey, buddy," says the coach. "You're working so hard—nice job. Tell you what—try keeping your legs straight; you want the kick to come from your hips, not your knee. Then your whole leg will help you kick and you'll go superfast! Can I see you try? . . . Good, you're almost there. Try it again. . . . Nice—keep practicing and you'll be faster than a fish! High five."

Okay, let's bring ourselves back to dry land, metaphorically. Which coach will make his kids better swimmers? Duh, the second one. But why? Why doesn't the harsh approach work? What effect does the criticism have? Does it motivate? No, of course not. Have you ever been yelled at by a parent, teacher, or boss and thought, *Wow, they really have a point. I'll definitely try harder next time. Thanks for showing me the error of my ways!*? No way, unless your sarcasm was so acidic it could eat through the floor.

Instead, harsh criticism does two things to the first kid: first it shames, which is bad enough, but it also makes her not ever want to try again, which robs her of the opportunity to learn. That first kid's parents will find her goggles in the trash tonight, I guarantee. She'll tell them she hates swimming and doesn't want to go back. She'll dig in her heels and cry when they try to get her in the car next week. Not to mention she'll lie in bed tonight imagining all the ways the coach could die a grisly, humiliating death.

By contrast, the second coach not only will get his kid to

come back next week but also will turn him into a good swimmer. The coach is supportive but not just an empty cheerleader. He took the time to correct him when he was doing something less than effective, and did it in a supportive way. There was encouragement to practice, an understanding that skill takes time, and a clear and positive regard for the kid. The supportive coach is not only more pleasant to be around; he's also much more effective. And therein lies the crux of the next tool: we are much more likely to reach our goals in a supportive environment than a punitive one.

The first coach sounds surprisingly like the Inner Critic. It's as if they both went to the University of Mean. Yet we talk to ourselves this way all the time. Somehow we think harsh criticism will motivate us, convince us to change, or that it's necessary to punish ourselves into some sort of submission. And while we instinctively know the coach insulting the kid is wrong, it's not so easy to realize the Inner Critic is wrong, too. Not only wrong, but ineffective. Telling ourselves we can't do it, that we don't have it in us, that we shouldn't bother trying only makes us want to hide. To conceal. To avoid.

So how should we talk to ourselves instead? In short, like the second coach. If arguing with our Inner Critic and changing our dire thoughts and fears was Replace, creating for ourselves a supportive environment from which we can try hard things is Embrace. This time, we don't challenge the thoughts head-on. Instead, we acknowledge them for what they are and give ourselves the psychological equivalent of a warm, supportive hug. Here's how to do it.

As a guy named Ringo once asked, *What would you do if I sang out of tune? Would you stand up and walk out on me?* In the face of lyrical anxiety, Ringo comes up with a good idea: *I get by with a little help from my friends.* With Embrace, you get the same effect, but instead of from your friends, it comes from within. Your friends may not be available 24/7, after all, but you are.

This is self-compassion. At its essence, Embrace is simply giving yourself the same support, warmth, and kindness you would get from a good friend or that you would offer a good friend. It's a little help when you need it the most.

Now, "self-compassion" might make visions of patchouli incense dance in your head, but it's actually a very practical tool. Some, especially those raised in an overly strict or critical family, may object at first, maintaining that self-compassion is indulgent, weak, or lets you off the hook. But when I spoke with Dr. Kristin Neff of the University of Texas, a pioneering researcher on self-compassion, she offered a good way to filter out what self-compassion is not. "Put it in a context," she suggested. "Would a compassionate mother let her child eat all the candy?" No, of course not. Instead of allowing her child to be indulgent and undisciplined, she would acknowledge that candy sure is tempting and then kindly encourage a healthier choice. Self-compassion is about creating that same sort of supportive, kind, encouraging environment from which you can gather the courage to choose wisely. In short, self-compassion is the opposite of self-judgment. Self-judgment looks for what is vulnerable inside us and pounces, whereas self-compassion looks for what is human and meets it with understanding, graciousness, appreciation, and encouragement.

According to Dr. Neff, self-compassion has three components: mindfulness, self-kindness, and an awareness that we are all in this together, or what she calls our common humanity. The first, mindfulness, you've undoubtedly heard of, but like ozone or gluten, the precise definition can be hard to pin down. Therefore, let's start with a quick and dirty crash course.

While challenging our thoughts ("How bad would that really be? What are the odds? How would I cope?") requires climbing into the ring for a few rounds with our negative musings, mindfulness calmly watches from outside the ropes. Mindfulness, simply, is paying attention to the present moment on purpose, without judgment. In her book *Self-Compassion: The Proven Power of Being Kind to Yourself,* Dr. Neff presents the best explanation of mindfulness I've come across thus far. Picture yourself in a movie theater, she writes. A movie is playing on the screen, and you're wrapped up in the story. You jump when the bad guy attacks, bite your nails as the forces battle, gasp as plot twists are revealed. But then, the person next to you sneezes. The reverie is broken. Suddenly, you are back in your seat with your popcorn, and you remember, *Oh, I'm watching a movie.*

In other words, mindfulness is not your *actual* thoughts or experience. Rather, it is a method for *watching* your thoughts and experience. It is the realization: *Oh, I'm thinking X, I'm hearing Y, I notice Z.* What's more, you can choose where you direct your attention. You can watch your thoughts, your breath, or the snaps, crackles, and pops of your own body. Just as you watch the image projected on the movie screen, you watch your thoughts or sensations float and dart across the field of your consciousness.

Using this technique, you can watch your anxious thoughts without getting tangled in them. For example, bring to mind a memory of a recent humiliating moment. Now think to yourself, *I really screwed that one up big-time.* You probably feel some embarrassment, guilt, or shame. Now shift things a little and think to yourself, *I'm having the thought that I really screwed that one up big-time.* It's subtle, but different. With the second example, there is distance, there is awareness. Just as when our fellow moviegoer sneezes, our attention shifts from being absorbed in the movie as if it were reality to being aware of the movie as not reality. And guess what? Just as the movie isn't reality, neither are our thoughts. That's a little freaky, huh? But it's also freeing. Remember, feelings aren't facts. Thoughts are transient, not truth. Just because our Inner Critic is throwing harsh, anxious expectations of failure at us doesn't mean we have to get tangled up in them. Instead, we can just watch the Inner Critic heave those thoughts and we don't have to catch them.

What's even more freaky is the realization that, up until now, the thoughts of *I'm socially incompetent,* or, *I'll have nothing to say,* seemed as real and concrete as, *I have brown eyes,* or, *I am thirty-nine years old.* But on the movie screen of mindfulness, thoughts like, *I'll look stupid,* are just beliefs. Just thoughts. With an existential sneeze, we shift from *I am not good enough,* to, *I hold a belief that I'm not good enough.* And that difference is everything. In one astonishing moment of clarity, we shift from absolute truth to merely a thought. And thoughts? They can be changed. Or, to stick with the spirit of mindfulness, simply watched.

To demonstrate the power of mindfulness on social anxiety, a 2011 study trained folks with capital-*S* Social Anxiety for just ten minutes in either mindfulness, distraction (paying attention to something unrelated to the task at hand), or nothing at all. The mindfulness training taught participants to focus on their breath and to gently bring their mind back when it wandered away (as minds tend to do—indeed, when you first try to be mindful, you will find your ability to focus falls somewhere on the spectrum between "untrained puppy" and "toddler"). In the study, the instructions to the mindful group concluded, "The purpose is to be aware of your thoughts and feelings and accept your experience in the present moment." After the training, participants were put to the test. They were asked to remember a recent experience where they felt really anxious, awkward, or embarrassed in a social situation like a party, meeting, presentation, or date. They were instructed to bring it to mind as vividly as possible and then were left alone to stew in the juices of their humiliating memory for five minutes. The participants rated how upset they were and then applied their new thinking strategy—mindfulness, distraction, or nothing—for five more minutes and again rated how upset they were. As you might guess, mindfulness won out. In the mindfulness group, distress went down steadily and significantly over the five minutes. In the distraction group distress didn't go down at all, and in the control group it actually went up. And remember, this was after just ten minutes of training.

If you're a beginner, here are three mindfulness exercises to try, each of which only takes a few minutes.

5-4-3-2-1. This is a use-anywhere little exercise that can pull you out of worry and ground you in reality. Here's how to do it: Work your way through your five senses. First, look around and name five things you can see. For me, I see my laptop, a mug of Earl Grey tea, an ornery printer, a stack of blue sticky notes, a biography of Albert Ellis. Next, name four things you can hear—a car outside, a bird chirping, the neighbor's air conditioner, water running somewhere. Next, three things you can touch—my feet in my shoes, my back against my chair, the keyboard keys against my fingers. Two things you can smell—the aroma of the tea, the musty smell of the biography. And finally, one thing you can taste—for me, I take a slurp of Earl Grey, but if there's nothing at hand you can simply pay attention to how your mouth tastes (generally gross) or, alternatively, say one nice thing about yourself (never gross).

Why do this? First, grounding yourself in your senses brings you back to the here and now. If you're anticipating, 5-4-3-2-1 reels you in from the future; if you're ruminating, it gently shepherds you back from the past. Second, the countdown from five to one and working your way through your senses forces your brain to keep track, which pokes a stick in the spinning spokes of your worry wheels.

Mindful listening. This is a good one for the "nonjudgmental" part of the definition. Simply listen to whatever's happening around you. The din of a coffee shop, the hum of highway traffic, the quiet rustling of a library. Allow yourself to listen to every sound without responding. If your mind starts making a grocery list or playing back laundry detergent jingles, just bring it back to the sounds around you. Tune in to what you're hearing in the moment.

The classic: mindful breathing. The tried-and-true peanut butter and jelly of mindfulness is mindful breathing. Pay attention, on purpose, to your breath. Feel the air enter your nostrils. Note how it feels cool against the inside of your nose. Forget any "in for four counts, out for six" nonsense. Just breathe. Feel your torso expand, and then feel it contract as you breathe out. Notice that the air is warm as it leaves your nose. Then do it again. If your mind has the discipline of a cornered weasel, don't despair—the opportunities to be mindful of your breath last, oh say, a lifetime.

These are three, but there are a zillion other exercises and meditations you can try. Remember that sense of, *Oh, I'm watching a movie,* and use it to watch a flower, a raisin, or, crucially, your anxious thoughts. As Dr. Neff says, "You can't heal what you can't feel." No matter what you choose, simply pay attention, on purpose, without judgment.

HOW KINDNESS OUTSHINES CRITICISM

Okay, thus concludes our necessary tangent on mindfulness. We now return to our regularly scheduled section on Embrace. In my conversation with Dr. Neff, she noted, "We can't skip ahead and say, 'Don't believe the Inner Critic.' We need to turn toward the Inner Critic and ask, 'How are you trying to help me?' People often find their Inner Critic and self-compassion want the exact same thing."

Remember the two swim coaches? Both coaches ostensibly wanted the same thing: for the kids to learn how to swim. Even the first coach, in a way, was trying to help. When we're tempted to bail on the neighborhood cookout because we're worried we'll be awkward and the neighbors will think we're weird, we can ask the Inner Critic how it's trying to help. The answer? Almost always, it will be, *I'm trying to keep you safe.* Like a neurotic mother hen, the Inner Critic will say, *If you don't go, they can't hurt you. Just sit this one out and you guarantee you won't be ridiculed. Better safe than sorry, so why don't you just stay home this time?*

But using self-compassion, you might then tell yourself, *Oh, sweetheart, I know you're scared. You don't know the neighbors very well and this is intimidating. You're not alone—everyone feels awkward and weird sometimes and everyone was new to the neighborhood at one point. You know from experience that just showing up is the worst part. It gets better from there. You've done hard things before, and I know you can do this, too, even while you're feeling nervous.* Now, if you feel corny calling yourself sweetheart, don't. The point is to be kind and supportive and, most important, brave. Notice self-compassion didn't say, *Oh, sweetheart, I know you're scared. Why don't you stay home and eat a pint of Cherry Garcia instead?* Just as the second coach didn't offer empty praise or let the kid go on kicking incorrectly, neither does self-compassion let you off the hook. Just as the second coach gave our struggling swimmer a gentle, friendly nudge in the right direction, self-compassion can do the same for you. Self-compassion knows we all have our stuff, so why bother pretending we don't? Self-compassion sees our inadequacies and failures and not only is cool with them but also provides a safe and caring place for them. Self-compassion loves the package deal that is you, or me. When you talk to yourself with compassion, you invert the Golden Rule—rather than treating others as you would like to be treated, you also treat yourself as well as you would treat others.

Self-compassion is different from self-esteem. According to Dr. Neff, self-esteem is a label: *I'm great! I'm beautiful!* But even the positive labels we have for ourselves, if we are lucky enough to have them—*I'm smart, I'm successful*—are still just labels. The danger is that we tend to cling to positive labels and avoid trying new things that might threaten the label. There's that word again: "avoid." Indeed, a 2015 study showed that among those who practiced self-compassion even low self-esteem had little effect on their mental health, suggesting that self-compassion creates a buffer, a safety net of kindness, that keeps those on this high wire we call life from crashing down.

If you're like me, the first time you try speaking to yourself compassionately it will work for about three seconds. Then your mind will get sucked, as if by a tractor beam, back into fretting about The Reveal du Jour. This is normal. In terms of discipline and controllability, remember: toddler/puppy. It's hard to talk kindly to ourselves when we're used to being hard on ourselves. But here's where the mindfulness comes in again. The sense of, *Oh, I'm watching a movie,* can be used to watch your anxious thoughts without judgment and allow you to try again.

PUTTING REPLACE AND EMBRACE INTO ACTION

Okay, let's put Replace and Embrace together. You can use these tools separately, but like two great tastes that taste great together, they're even better and more powerful when combined.

For instance, my former client Pranav is a biotech guy who founded a startup a few years back; to get funding, he had to pitch his idea to venture capitalist firms worth billions of dollars. When he told me the story of his pitch, he joked (at least I hope he was joking) that in lieu of ice cubes his glass of water contained chilled gold nuggets. In other words, it was an intimidating mix of pressure and wealth—enough to make almost anyone nervous. But public speaking wasn't the stage for Pranav's feared Reveal, so even though pitching was intimidating, he presented with passion, clinched funding, and after treating his family to the celebratory dinner of a lifetime proceeded to work his tail off for three long years. After that, his startup was acquired by a pharmaceutical company whose drugs you've probably ingested; they made his startup into a division. Today, Pranav has fifteen direct reports and many more employees under them. He reports only to the CEO. Pranav can lead a meeting and give a presentation—no problem. Texting or emailing—no problem. But he couldn't make a phone call.

Pranav would ask his wife to make all the customer service calls for their household—calling the gas, cable, and cell phone companies. He didn't call friends or family, preferring to keep in touch by email. "Thank goodness for online ordering," he joked. "I'll go pick up the food. I'll let other people choose the restaurant or what we order. I just don't want to call it in." Why? Pranav worried the person on the other end of the line would get upset with him. If he was ever forced to call, afterwards he'd play it over in his head—*Did I say the right thing? Did I use the appropriate tone? Was the other person annoyed?* Just thinking about calls made him hot and anxious.

So Pranav walked himself through Replace and Embrace. With specify, specify, specify, he pondered. "It's hard to explain," he said. "I guess it's that I'll be a burden, will be annoying, or will be catching the person at an inconvenient time." What's the worst that can happen? "I guess whoever's on the other end of the line will think I don't have my stuff together. They'll think I'm not competent enough to know when to call or what to say." Excellent. Houston, we have our problem: "They'll think I don't have my stuff together."

Okay, so let's walk our way through the questions. First up: "How bad would that really be?" Pranav thinks for a minute. "It's not exactly a disaster," he said slowly. "It's not like I would die or something. But I picture them rolling their eyes and talking to me like I'm in preschool." He asked himself the question again: *And how bad would that really be?* "It feels bad. It would be embarrassing." But with a worst-case scenario whittled down from snarling guard dog to yappy ankle-biter, he was able to think, *Well, I've sure felt that a lot. I guess it's not* horrible. *It's like a kidney stone—feels bad, but it always passes. I guess if someone thinks I don't have my stuff together to order pad thai it doesn't mean I don't have my stuff together* in general.

Awesome. Now for *What are the odds?* Pranav thinks. He concludes: "These guys have probably heard it all. Drunken stories. Arguments. They probably don't care if I change my order midstream."

Finally, *How would you cope?* Pranav ponders. "If someone was annoyed? I guess there's nothing *to* do. I'd feel bad about it for a few minutes, but then I'd probably get distracted by the next thing: my kids, my work, something."

With this, Pranav shrunk his anxiety from Venti to Short. It didn't disappear, but it was helpful to remind himself it wasn't as bad as he first thought—plus he could handle it.

Next, Embrace. First Pranav struggled with mindfulness. It was too hard to notice the thoughts without doing something about them. The problem solver in him got tangled too easily. Then, one Thursday evening, Pranav was exhausted. It had already been a long week and the final thing on his schedule was to call a collaborator in Australia. Pranav's brain started dreading the call, but at that moment he found he could let the thoughts go. "I was basically too tired to respond. I was mindful by accident, but I was mindful. I saw the worried thoughts run and just said, 'Meh.' I got excited when I realized what had happened—it really was like realizing you're watching a movie."

He tried to replicate his accidental mindfulness the next time he ordered food. This time he was able to see his thoughts for what they were. "Wow, I'm having the thought that whoever answers the phone is going to yell at me for trying to give him my money. That would never happen."

To bolster himself even more, he thought about how he would soothe his young son in the same situation. Changing his perspective this way made him feel concerned and tender, a far cry from the "pull yourself up by your bootstraps" attitude he usually used on himself. "Okay, Pranav," he said. "Everyone gets anxious; everyone has their stuff. You're working on this; you're committed to trying." He sat up a little straighter. "Plus, you can handle feeling awkward for a few minutes. If you survived the last few years, you can make some phone calls. It's okay to feel awkward as long as you keep moving forward."

Nice work, Pranav.

Let's up the ante. Nelly is a community college student in her mid-twenties who wants to be a clothing designer and is also chasing romance. The last time she headed out to meet a guy in person after meeting online and exchanging messages, she was a nervous wreck. They'd emailed and texted back and forth. He seemed funny, actually paid attention to what she wrote, and, if his picture was to be trusted, was cute. But Nelly hated the whole process. She considered taking a swig of liquid courage before heading out, but didn't want to show up smelling like Jack Daniel's. "Not the image I'm going for," she said. Another part of her image she wanted to work on was her habit of sleeping with guys on the first date because she was worried she didn't have anything else to offer. The adult sleepover wasn't the problem, she said, it was that she did it for the wrong reasons. "Dates literally scare the pants off me," she said.

So before her date, Nelly ran herself through Replace and Embrace. First she asked herself what she was afraid of (*specify, specify, specify*) and discovered a flock of questions running through her head: *What if he doesn't like me? What if he's disappointed? What if he thinks he's wasted his time?* It's impossible to argue with questions, so Nelly changed them to statements to make them easier to contend with: *He won't like me. He'll be disappointed. He'll think he's wasted his time.* But it was even more than that. In this one first date Nelly foresaw her entire future, and in that future she saw herself alone with nine cats, abandoned by friends long since married. *I'll be alone forever,* was her worst-case scenario. Whoa, Nelly. With a thought like that running through her head, no wonder she was anxious.

But the magic questions can work with any scare-your-pants-off thought. So first she asked herself, *How bad would that be? Really bad!* she thought at first. *I don't want to be alone forever.* But something about saying the worst-case scenario out loud made her realize how extreme her phrasing was. *Alone! Foreverrrrrr!* She paused. *But I'm not going to be in solitary confinement or something,* she thought. *And this date doesn't determine the rest of my life. And even if I never found a partner, I'd survive. It's not what I pictured, but I wouldn't die.* By asking, *What are the odds?* she realized that she had control over whether she adopted nine cats or not, and that she could make the probability of that feared future exactly zero. Bringing herself back to the present, the more realistic worst-case scenario, Nelly thought, was that it would simply be another awkward date. Next, in answering *How would I cope?* she thought she would come home after saying good-bye, change into sweatpants, and watch Comedy Central. Which, Nelly realized, didn't sound bad at all.

Once she got to Embrace, she was already feeling better but still talked herself through it. "I *definitely* know what I'd say to a friend in the same situation," she said. "I think I had this very conversation last week." Nelly said to herself, "Of course I'm worried—a lot of people feel the exact same way in this situation. This is hard stuff." She told herself that looking for love is tough on anyone, that sifting through to find a partner takes time, and that it's hard to put yourself out there. She congratulated herself for being brave, despite it being uncomfortable, and reminded herself that this guy was probably nervous, too. Or he was a jerk, in which case she could come home and watch *Drunk History.* "I've got some guts just to put myself out there," she concluded. "I can do hard things. I've done lots of hard things in my life and I've always come out the other side."

In the end, Replace and Embrace didn't feel like a lie. It didn't feel like forcing herself to feel better. Instead, to her pleasant surprise, it felt like relief.

Now it's your turn. First Replace to challenge your thoughts.
Specify, specify, specify

When _____,
    (SOCIAL SITUATION WHERE I FEEL ANXIOUS)

it will become obvious that I am

_____

(WHAT MY INNER CRITIC SAYS IS WRONG WITH ME).

Now take your feared consequence and ask:
"How bad would that really be?"
Is this truly a disaster of epic proportions? Really?
If you've already talked yourself down to less-than-disastrous proportions, you can go right to "How could I cope?" If not, ask,
"What are the odds?"
What's more realistic? What is more likely to happen?
And finally,
"How could I cope?"
Think of all the resources you could gather: family, friends, self-care, health insurance, gummy bears; pull out all the stops here!

Next, use Embrace to show yourself some compassion: talk to yourself as you would to a good friend. Soothe, encourage, and support. Show appreciation for your efforts. Validate your fears. If you're really hard-core and nobody's watching, wrap your arms around yourself as you talk, literally supporting yourself. Give yourself pats on the back or an encouraging squeeze. If you hear a harsh edge creeping into your voice, forgive yourself and try again.

Best of all, Replace and Embrace are just the first steps. They give you a running start into practicing the very situations you're afraid of. Replace and Embrace won't make your anxiety evaporate, but the questions of Replace will help shrink it and the self-compassion of Embrace will help you feel comforted.

Okay, we're all warmed up. The wrap-up: The Inner Critic only wants what's best for you, but lets you know in an ineffective way. So reason with it. Tell it how strong you are. And remind it that kindness trumps criticism. Now, Inner Critic, if you'll excuse us, it's time to go face some fears.

PART 3

Heading Out into the World

7

Get Started and Your Confidence Will Catch Up

Brandon Stanton is prowling the streets of Chelsea, walking one of his estimated six miles a day—about a mile for every photo he posts to his phenomenally popular photoblog, *Humans of New York,* which as of this writing has over 20 million followers on social media. He wears well-worn chinos, a gray thermal top, and a knit beanie, perfect garb to match his penchant for laying his six-foot-four frame flat on the sidewalk to get just the right shot.

He brightens when he spots three chefs—African-American women in toques and whites—taking a break outside their restaurant, and trots over to strike up a conversation. His approach is easy and authentic. He's not unctuous, not fake. As he described it when I spoke with him, "I start talking to them as if a relationship had already been established, as if we'd known each other for a very long time." The conversation starts to flow and he asks the women if he can take their photograph. As they chat, he lifts the camera to his eye and begins to click. Magically, effortlessly, stories and images merge.

It wasn't always this easy. In 2010, after losing his job in finance, Brandon, a self-taught photography hobbyist, decided to turn his back on the financial world and bum around the country, taking photographs in cities such as New Orleans and Pittsburgh. When, a few months later, he rolled into New York—the first time he had ever been to the city—he was awestruck by the scale, the sheer volume of people. He was instantly hooked.

When he first started roaming New York City with his camera, Brandon was broke and didn't know a soul. Nevertheless, he hit the streets every single day, taking thousands of photographs. At first, Brandon photographed everything—buildings, fire hydrants, signage. He would photograph people, too, but candidly, surreptitiously. Over time, he noticed that in the albums he posted to social media for his friends and family photos of people got the most feedback. People were compelling in a way signage could never be. Therefore, never one to shirk from a challenge, Brandon set a goal to photograph ten thousand of his fellow New Yorkers and plot the results on an interactive map—a photographic census of the city. But once his plan was set, he realized, like a lightning bolt, that the project would require approaching ten thousand people. He was going to have to learn to talk to strangers.

Now, even before approaching ten thousand strangers Brandon considered himself to be pretty good with people. Even so, he said, "Those first months that I was on the street stopping strangers, I was so scared every time I walked up to somebody. There's something about approaching someone and the possibility of being rejected that inherently makes you nervous."

So how did Brandon get over it? How did he learn to approach total strangers as if they'd known each other for years?

He said, "I just had to do it so many times. There were no longer any unknowns . . . there was nowhere for my imagination to go and create this kind of anxiety in me. I had seen it all before, I knew that I could handle it, and so I got to the point where I could just approach people very comfortably without any worry or anxiety about what their reaction would be."

Click-click-click. Brandon wraps up a final few shots and warmly thanks the three chefs. As he sets off to find his next subjects, let's highlight two things he said: First, *there was nowhere for my imagination to go.* As we know, our brains are wired to jump to the worst-case scenario. The "what-ifs" start to bubble. "What if someone pulls a gun?" "What if someone tries to kidnap me?" Our brains tell us the worst is *possible,* but with experience we learn it's not *probable.* This is why the first approaches are the hardest—we don't have the experience to temper the warnings of our well-meaning but overprotective brains. In Brandon's case, the experience of approaching ten thousand strangers allowed him to confirm that most people are friendly, even in a hardened city. Of course, sometimes he would get a rejection and sometimes he would get something rude, nonsensical, or even obscene. But nothing improbable. Experience tethered him to reality, which was that most people, when face-to-face with a fellow human, are happy to help.

Second, Brandon stated, *I knew that I could handle it.* No matter what happened—a rejection, a rude remark, an attempted hustle—Brandon found, to his surprise, that he could roll with pretty much anything. Failure to get a yes didn't mean that *he* was a failure. It just meant that this time didn't work out and he could try again. Indeed, the rejections taught Brandon more about his capabilities than the acceptances. They taught him to trust himself. And that, in turn, gave him the confidence to be himself.

I asked Brandon what advice he would give someone who wanted to become more comfortable talking to strangers. "If you want to be comfortable talking to strangers," he said, "the only way to do it is to approach strangers while you're *un*comfortable. You have to earn the comfort through being uncomfortable many, many times." Indeed, that photographic census Brandon had planned never happened. But something much more important did: he grew into himself. Thousands of conversations later, he's earned every ounce of his ease and confidence.

All this may sound familiar. It's also called fake it till you make it. And it works. Why? When you see yourself doing it, you start to believe you can.

To be sure, fake it till you make it is daunting and somewhat unfair. Why do the first times have to be the hardest? When will we ever feel ready? Indeed, before those ten thousand approaches how did Brandon know he was ready? Typically, we think we're ready when we *feel* ready. If we're feeling anxious, we put it off. But here's a secret: this approach is actually backwards. Like Brandon, we're ready when we're *un*comfortable. Get started and your confidence will catch up.

When I was first introduced to this concept, I started to see it everywhere. The perception that we have to *feel* like doing something before we do it is amazingly common. Think of all the things you don't feel like doing: go to the gym, eat the salad, log off and go to bed, meditate. But once you do it, aren't you glad you did? Likewise, if you're trying to build a skill, how often do you actually *want* to practice? If you're like me, after seven years of childhood piano lessons, the answer probably barely breaks double digits. Likewise, swimmers seldom look forward to laps and violinists rarely crave scales. The idea of hitting the ice hockey rink on a dark, frozen February morning makes you want to snuggle in bed, not strap on your skates.

But how often, once you got started, did you get into it? Even if you'd never admit it to your parents or coach, did you enjoy the rhythm of the laps, the smooth glide of the ice? Despite my initial reluctance, once I finally dragged myself to the piano I usually found myself practicing longer than my required twenty minutes. Not that I ever admitted it, but it was my own resistance that made me miserable, not the practice itself.

These days, when we don't *feel* like getting on the yoga mat, lacing up our running shoes, sitting down to write (not that I know anything about that), or getting off YouTube and focusing on work (not that I know anything about that, either), we can use a little magic: we can put action before motivation. Just like Brandon, we don't have to wait until we *feel* like doing

How we think gaining confidence works

ZAP!

I'm ready for anything!

① ② ③

something before we do it. Instead, we start doing it, *and the feeling will catch up.*

Lo and behold, the exact same thing happens with confidence. There's a myth that you have to feel confident to be ready. In truth, you gain confidence by doing things before you're ready, while you're still scared. Go through the motions and your confidence will catch up.

So put action before confidence. Fake it till you make it, truly and genuinely. When you go ahead and try, your confidence will catch up as you build and learn, just like Brandon. Do the thing that scares you a little. Call it bravery. Being brave isn't *not* being afraid. Indeed, fear is a prerequisite to bravery. True bravery is being afraid and doing it anyway.

After a while, something shifts. Social anxiety becomes something that *happens* rather than something you *are.* You start thinking about anxiety as, *Eh, this happens,* rather than, *This* cannot *happen.* Rather than seeing social anxiety as a ball and chain that keeps you mired in place, you can pick up the ball and bring it along. You can do things before you feel confident. Whether it's walking into a crowded room, making more eye contact, or letting loose a little, rather than waiting until we feel ready, we can get out there to practice, and *our confidence will catch up.*

Just like Brandon talking to strangers, the first few times will be the most difficult. Experience hasn't yet balanced out our fearful imaginings of all possible worst-case scenarios. So while you're in the tough early stages, base your achievement on what you *do* rather than how you *feel*. You were anxious *and* you said hi. You were sweating bullets *and* you asked for a raise. You didn't have the perfect answer ready *and* you raised your hand. You felt like throwing up *and* you asked her out. Your anxiety isn't credible, so don't ask it for feedback. Instead, look at what you did. Let your accomplishments be the measure of your success. Your confidence is there. See? Here it comes. It's sprinting to catch up.

8

No False Fronts in This Town:
Play a Role to Build Your True Self

Pretend you're Beyoncé.

—FIFTH-GRADE GIRL AT MY LOCAL
ELEMENTARY SCHOOL, ENCOURAGING A
NERVOUS FRIEND BEFORE THE SPRING RECITAL

In a vintage episode of *The Tonight Show,* Johnny Carson welcomed guest Rona Barrett, 1970s gossip columnist and celebrity interviewer. She turned the tables on Johnny, plying him with questions about his start in show business. In their conversation, Johnny shared a memory: As a child, he performed in a play and got the audience to laugh. In that moment, he realized he liked being the center of attention. Barrett pounced. "Why did you want the attention?" she asked.

Carson answered, "Why did I want the attention? Because I was shy. Now that sounds like ambivalence, right? Onstage, you see, when you're on stage in front of an audience, you're kind of

in control. When you're off of the stage or in a situation where
there are a lot of people, you're not in control, and I felt awkward. So I went into show business thinking it would give me
a little more . . ." He paused. "I could overcome that shyness."

The young Johnny Carson intuited something that many of
us discover. For some, in order to stop reading about the bicycle
and get on the bicycle it helps to have some structure. Being left
to your own devices is overwhelming: What to do? What to say?
But counterintuitively, the structure of a task or a role can be
oddly liberating. For Johnny, the role of "Entertainer" was his
way to feel more certain of his purpose and direction.

Limitless options are overwhelming. If you've ever been faced
with a yawning expanse of a blank page with no idea what to
write or a looming white canvas with no idea what to paint, you
know the pain of trying to start from scratch. Oddly, it's much
easier to work within constraints. Give me some direction, some
structure, or a model to follow, and magically I feel much more
confident. Contrary to common sense, limitations get things
moving.

Structure works the same way in social situations. It's easier
to know what to do when you have a role or a goal that takes
away the guesswork. Indeed, a classic study by Australian researchers Drs. Simon Thompson and Ron Rapee showed that
changing a social situation from unstructured, with ambiguous
roles and rules, to structured, with defined roles and goals, results in an astonishing difference in the performance of folks
prone to social anxiety.

Thompson and Rapee asked women with high social anxiety and women with low social anxiety to take part in the study,
which, unbeknownst to them, began as soon as they stepped into
the lab's waiting room. Shortly after each woman was seated, a
male confederate sat alongside her and attempted to make small

talk. This was the unstructured portion of the study. The confederate made benign statements like, "I hope we don't have to wait too long," and then rolled with whatever chitchat ensued. If thirty seconds of silence elapsed, he made another comment, attempting to jump-start conversation again. After five minutes that might have ranged from pleasant to excruciating, a researcher entered, thanked the pair for waiting, and changed the task to one with structure. "Imagine you're at a party," the researcher instructed, "and have to get to know each other as well as possible in five minutes." More small talk ensued, but this time the women had a mission—structure.

Both five-minute interactions were videotaped, and assessors later watched the tapes and rated them for social competence, including body language, conversational skills, and more. In the unstructured interactions in the waiting room, the women with social anxiety scored, predictably, quite a bit worse than the nonanxious women, who chatted with the confederate without a second thought. But after the structure was added, the whole game changed. Once the socially anxious women had an assignment to fulfill, the gap in the assessor's ratings of social competence narrowed dramatically, with the two groups nearly neck and neck. Turns out the socially anxious women had considerable social skills; they just needed some structure on which to hang them. Even against a low-anxiety group who were *more* confidently chatty than average, the socially anxious group, once handed some structure, laid down one impressive showing in the oft-dreaded game of small talk.

Structure can be big or small and it can last for months or moments. No matter how extensive, structure gives you a purpose, a definition. It takes away uncertainty and gives you clarity and conviction. It allows you to gain confidence in your skills and, by extension, in yourself.

The structure you choose might be formal and defined. For example, at a wedding you might create structure by offering to round up guests for photos or volunteering to ask attendees to sign the guest book. If you're part of an organization, you might take on a leadership position so you have a reason to talk to every member, even if just to collect dues or verify their email address. If you're a parent, you might volunteer to work the checkout stand at your kid's school's book fair, bake sale, or auction in order to practice talking to everyone who comes through the line.

Even if there's no predetermined job, you can still create structure by giving yourself an assignment. At a networking event, assign yourself the task of introducing yourself to three people. At the company holiday party, give yourself the job of chatting with your boss, your two closest colleagues, and the office manager. Or, like the women in the study, challenge yourself to get to know a new acquaintance as well as you can in five minutes.

"But wait," you say. "I get the general idea, but if I'm just playing a role, will any of it rub off on the real me? How can I get comfortable being myself if I set up all these constraints?"

Good question. To answer, let's go back to Johnny Carson.

As a boy, Johnny was obsessed with magic—he would follow his family around the house, hounding them to "pick a card, any card!" He practiced his sleight-of-hand tricks in front of a mirror for hours. As a teenager, he started performing around his hometown of Norfolk, Nebraska, and he was good, good enough to earn three dollars—a monumental sum for a kid in the late 1930s—for his first performance at the local Rotary Club. But he wasn't in it for the money.

In another old *Tonight Show* segment, Johnny is ostensibly interviewing actress Bea Arthur. But for a moment, the roles reverse and he shares his own past. "I took up magic when I was young because I was somewhat shy and within myself," he says. "And I thought that was a good way to go to parties. I read those ads: Be the life of the party! And get girls. Mainly I did it to get girls. Neither one worked well. But lots of people do that. They like to get up and perform. You can be the center of attention without being yourself, as such."

You can be the center of attention without being yourself. As Laurence Leamer, Johnny's biographer, said in the documentary *Johnny Carson: King of Late Night,* "Johnny liked to be in control. Being a performer allowed him to do that. He was always performing, always learning, always developing his character, who was anyone but Johnny Carson."

Johnny gave himself plenty of structure—magic tricks, performing. But he never felt comfortable being himself. Even Ed McMahon, Johnny's loyal sidekick for thirty years, said of Johnny, "He was good with ten million people, lousy with ten." Why didn't structure work for Johnny? Why did he never transition to the ultimate role: himself?

The answer lies in the source of the role. For Johnny Carson, biographers theorize that Johnny's persona, Johnny Carson the Entertainer, was created to win the approval of a specific person. His mother, Ruth, didn't like boys; they were dirty and nasty, she said. Her favorite child was her daughter, Catherine. So Johnny's persona, lore has it, was created to get positive attention from Ruth. If he could just be funny enough, successful enough, famous enough, maybe she would be proud of him. He didn't do it for himself; he did it for approval that, sadly, turned out to be unattainable. Reportedly, at the height of Johnny's fame Ruth once watched his *Tonight Show* monologue in the presence of a *New York Times* reporter, switched off the TV, and pronounced, "That wasn't funny."

So here's the difference between structure that hinders you and structure that's a stepping-stone to the ultimate role of being yourself: the role should come from within, not from someone else. It can't come from your impossible-to-please mother, your boss, your current crush, American society, or whoever else. Instead, your role should be chosen and inhabited only by you.

Think of it this way: Pretend you are a building. Creating a persona chosen by someone else sets up a false front. Picture an old Wild West town: tumbleweeds rolling by, horses tied to their hitching posts in front of the buildings on Main Street. Looks like a solid settlement, right? But peek behind the imposing fronts and you'd find the buildings were often just canvas tents and a wooden floor, shoddy structures at best. Indeed, the cost and danger of hauling building materials to a town that may or may not survive the boom-and-bust economy of the Old West was prohibitive. But business owners realized they needed to project an image of success and stability to lure in customers. So they poured their resources into erecting impressive false fronts. They attended to the image but neglected the actual building.

Playing a role that is chosen for you is like constructing a false front. Your precious resources get poured into the image while the actual building—the real, authentic you—is left wanting. The false front may be impressive or even intimidating, but its intention is to fool, to deceive.*

---

* Granted, sometimes creating a false front is necessary. If your situation is dangerous or abusive, keeping the real you hidden may be a matter of safety and survival. Once you're out and safe, building your true self can begin.

By contrast, playing a role you choose yourself is like erecting scaffolding. With scaffolding, temporary structure is placed around a building in order to construct or repair it. The scaffold grants access and provides safety while you shore up the building, incorporate new elements, or add finishing touches. Then, when the work is done, the scaffolding is no longer necessary—it can be removed, but the new, improved building remains. Giving yourself some structure by playing a role you choose allows you to build up and reinforce the real you.

So how might this work in real life? How to assign yourself some structure so you can build up the real you? Meet Aisha, a physician who used to deal with hard-core social anxiety at work. She was the first in her bursting-with-pride family to go to college but always felt one step out of step at the prestigious schools and hospitals from which she built her career. She was convinced she didn't belong, not among the ivy and the prep school kids. Her education and career went beyond anything she had previously imagined, and she was sure that someday someone would eventually notice, say, "I'm sorry, mistakes were made," and politely usher her out.[†]

These days, Aisha's medical specialty—kids with autism—is hot. And despite her doubts, Aisha's skills are hot, too. She put

---

† This might sound familiar. It's known as Impostor Syndrome, which is when social anxiety goes to work and school. Impostor Syndrome whispers: *You don't belong here. They made a mistake letting you in. This isn't for people like you.* Impostor Syndrome assumes you will be revealed, with dire and humiliating consequences. So people react in one of two extremes. On one end, they overcompensate for perceived deficits: they overprepare, overrehearse, overdo. On the opposite end, others detach and devalue the experience, insisting, "This isn't for me," "What's the use?," or, "I'm not even going to try."

together a successful applied research program from scratch and toiled hard to win an avalanche of funding. All this got her noticed by the hospital higher-ups, and without quite knowing how, Aisha found herself rising in the ranks. But instead of being elated, she was terrified, convinced The Reveal of her inadequacy and incompetence was close at hand.

When Aisha came to see me, she told me she belonged in the trenches, not at the top. On the one hand, she knew patient care was where she did her best work: she genuinely enjoyed helping families with an autistic child, especially single parents trying to balance everything. But more problematically, Aisha also thought she belonged in the trenches because she wasn't competent to lead. During her first presentation to hospital leadership, she got so overwhelmed that mid-slide she passed the presentation off to a colleague. Poker face in place, the colleague graciously took over as if it had been planned that way all along, though afterwards she approached Aisha with a mix of incredulity and concern, which is how Aisha ended up in my office. During another meeting with leadership, Aisha faked an emergency phone call in order to go into the hallway, lean against the wall, and breathe. She told me she saw the power suit she wore on meeting days as a costume—a far cry from the familiar, in-the-trenches scrubs she usually wore alongside everyone else in the clinic.

But then, in one meeting, Aisha watched the hospital CFO, an elegant woman in her fifties, give a presentation about the yearly hospital budget. The CFO's style was clear and measured, and Aisha realized that she told stories—stories about patients who benefited from the hospital's investments and expenditures—in order to keep a technical presentation about hospital finances from acting as a powerful sleep aid.

As much as Aisha wanted to hightail it back to her clinic

trenches, she knew she could do more for her patients from the boardroom. She had an opportunity to make her patients—those autistic kids and their families—a priority for hospital leadership, who held the keys to funding and staffing. So, inspired by the CFO and her stories, she decided to play a role, give herself some structure, and see what happened.

Aisha decided to assign herself the role of Advocate. She would deliver the stories of her patients—kids learning to connect, families giving their all—to the height of hospital power. If the CFO could tell patient stories to keep the annual budget relatable, Aisha could tell the families' stories to keep the lines of funding and attention open to her clinic. So she made herself the families' spokesperson. She put everything through the filter of, "What would be best for the families?" When she showed up at meetings with bigwigs, it was for the families. When she spoke up at a roundtable, it was for them. When she presented, it was for them.

Inspired, Aisha kept showing up, and through sheer repetition the bigwigs got a little less scary every time. At first, Aisha only spoke up as a mouthpiece for the families. She presented only to deliver their message. But with time, little bits of Aisha's character began to leak into the role of Advocate. And interestingly, little bits of the Advocate—standing up, speaking up, raising her hand—leaked into Aisha's character. By watching herself do these things, Aisha started to believe that she *could* do them.

Johnny Carson's role was a persona—a false front erected to please his implacable mother. By contrast, Aisha's role was that of a champion—she filtered her actions through what would be best for her families. And through the safety of constraints, she was able to build her building until she didn't need her scaffolding anymore. She had outgrown the structure of her role.

She could still be an advocate. But now she could advocate as herself.

Part of playing a role is looking the part. Arrange yourself in a powerful, confident posture, sitting or standing in a way you imagine someone open, strong, confident, and solid would present. This creates two feedback loops: one to yourself and one to others. Adopting a posture of confidence sends a message of confidence to your brain. And looking confident, whether you're Brandon asking strangers in Manhattan for a sidewalk photo session or Aisha advocating for kids with autism, makes people treat you with respect.

The phenomenon of power posing, pioneered by Dr. Amy Cuddy, was built on this principle. While researchers are still slugging it out on whether or not power posing "works" biologically by changing your cortisol and testosterone, it definitely changes your mindset, as power posing's many adherents report. Indeed, you're not *pretending* to feel powerful; you're taking on the posture of someone who *is* powerful.

Traditionally, power posing is done to prepare for a big moment. Stories abound of ducking into a bathroom stall before an audition, interview, or presentation. But it can also help before, during, or after a dubious social moment. When you start to feel a cringe coming on, take a moment to arrange your body in a confident posture. Why? Our brain likes to coordinate posture, facial expression, tone of voice, and emotion like a well-matched outfit, a phenomenon known as *congruence*. Try this: sit in a slouch, cross your arms over your chest, put a frown on your face, and say, "I'm ready for a challenge." Try it. I'll wait. Not so convincing, huh? Now stand in the classic "Wonder Woman" stance—feet apart, arms akimbo, fists on hips, chin raised—and say, "I'm ready for a challenge." Different, right? Not only does emotion affect the body; the body also affects emotion. If that's not a superpower, I don't know what is.

Like Aisha, most people susceptible to social anxiety are reluctant to play a role that benefits only themselves. There's no point in being Wonder Woman or Superman if we can't use our powers for good. This is part of the package deal of social anxiety—being self-serving isn't our style. But we'll step up in service of someone we love or on behalf of a cause we believe in, like Aisha and the families from her clinic. So play the role of Host and organize a playdate in service of your toddler's social development. Play the role of Good Pet Parent by taking your dog to the dog park and assigning yourself the task of learning one other dog's (and dog owner's) name. Play the role of Icebreaker by introducing yourself to the new guy at work to help him feel more comfortable. Or, like the girl from the epigraph, pay it forward by advising your stage-frightened friend to pretend she's Beyoncé. Now, that's some fierce structure.

Speaking of making other people more comfortable, as you learn about social anxiety you'll start to see it everywhere. For example, watch someone stand alone at a party for a moment and it's almost guaranteed they'll pull out their phone to quell their internal awkwardness. So kill two birds with one stone by taking on the role of The One Who Puts Others at Ease. Indeed, the vast majority of people prefer that someone else strike up conversation and will be profoundly grateful if you initiate, even if they don't admit their relief to you. So in the service of making others more comfortable, assign yourself the task of finding someone standing alone at an event and saying hello.

Internally, they'll thank you for it, but what's more, you'll come away feeling happier and stronger.

A creative 2014 study out of the University of Chicago found that even in the culturally expected silence of the weekday mass transit commute, people who take the initiative to say hello not only brighten someone else's day but also reap rewards for themselves. The study assigned commuters the task of striking up a conversation with a stranger on their train—the longer, the better. To give them some structure, they were told, "Find out something interesting about him or her and tell them something about you. . . . Your goal is to try to get to know your community neighbor this morning." Alternatively, those randomly assigned to the solitude condition were told, "Please keep to yourself and enjoy your solitude on the train today. Take this time to sit alone with your thoughts. Your goal is to focus on yourself and the day ahead of you." Predictably, participants who were assigned to strike up a conversation were initially reluctant. They expected the experience would be awkward, unpleasant, and unproductive, but the results were exactly the opposite. Surprisingly, commuters who connected with a stranger had a significantly more positive commute than those instructed to sit in solitude. What's more, the productivity of the trip wasn't compromised—the group assigned to connect with a stranger reported a level of productivity that was nearly identical to those who kept to themselves. Indeed, assigning yourself the task of saying good morning and making a remark about the weather may end there, which is fine, but it could also lead to pleasant conversation, boosted mood, invigorated productivity, and— most important—another brick added firmly to your building.

The only word of caution: don't choose a structure that allows you to avoid. Helping with the dishes after a dinner party is generous, but if it keeps you in the kitchen while everyone else is chatting over coffee on the stoop your building goes neglected. Volunteering on the fundraising committee for your tai chi group is great structure, but not if the committee communicates only by text.

Whatever structure you choose, whether big or small, extended or momentary, as you fulfill your roles you build up your building—your true self—brick by brick. The role of Unofficial Photographer is a structure that teaches you to be politely assertive: "Everyone squeeze in closer, please! Lynda, can you take off your sunglasses?" The role of Takeout Master for your family teaches you that the guy on the other end of the line doesn't expect you to be letter-perfect and can handle your teenager's mid-order change from sausage to pepperoni.

Your structure may be in place as a guide, but ultimately, you're building yourself and discovering how strong you can really be. Indeed, after some practice, you'll find there are no false fronts in your town.

9

Mountains to Molehills:
It Gets Easier Every Time

New York City, 1942. A skinny nineteen-year-old kid named Albert is standing in the Bronx Botanical Garden, biting his nails and staring from afar at a woman with shapely legs seated on a park bench. After a moment, he squares his shoulders, marches over, and sits down beside her. He flashes a smile. "Beautiful day today, isn't it?" he asks her.

Fast-forward many decades. Turns out that same skinny kid would become a legend in psychology and his experiences in the botanical garden would form the foundation for one of the earliest forms of cognitive-behavioral therapy (CBT), the treatment on which this book is based. Why is *How to Be Yourself* grounded in CBT? In short, it works. Over the years, CBT has been shown time and again to be the most effective treatment for all sorts of mental health challenges, from depression to PTSD to capital-*S* Social Anxiety Disorder. But in 1942, nineteen-year-old Albert Ellis didn't know that contemporary clinical psychologists, when asked to name the most influential psychotherapist in history, would rank him above Freud. In

1942, the teenage Ellis only knew that he was afraid to talk to cute girls.

Ellis was an extremely shy child. Despite the prominence and unguarded eccentricities of his adulthood, as a kid he refused to take part in classroom plays and "sweated and sizzled with anxiety" whenever he had to recite a poem or accept an award. So at nineteen, Ellis assigned himself a project—some structure. He decided to talk to as many women as possible. Every day, he took himself to what is now called the New York Botanical Garden. In a 2004 interview with National Public Radio, at the age of ninety, he recalled his project as if it were yesterday: "Whenever I saw a woman sitting on a park bench alone, I'd sit on the same bench and give myself one minute to talk to her. If I die, I die. Fuck it."* Over the course of a month, Ellis talked to over 130 women. He was brave for the short time it took to approach, sit down, and say hello. And what happened? Ellis said, "I saw philosophically, cognitively, that nothing happened. Nobody cut my balls off. I had a hundred pleasant conversations."

Nothing happened. This is the ideal outcome: nothing. Nothing our imaginations can conjure. Nothing our Inner Critic can predict. Even rejection, once experienced, is seldom as bad as we imagine.

Another thing Ellis discovered is that repetition is key. Like Brandon Stanton's experience, the first approaches were the hardest. But every time Ellis approached another woman, it got a little easier. With every approach, he was a little less anxious. What's more, he recovered more quickly—the sweating and sizzling didn't last as long. Indeed, as your confidence catches up, as you choose your structure and play your roles, here's what

---

* As you may infer, Ellis, in addition to being a brilliant and pioneering theorist, had a mouth that would make a sailor blush.

you've been waiting for: your anxiety will also ebb away. But don't take it from me. Take it from none other than Albert Ellis.

THE ONLY THREE GRAPHS IN THIS BOOK

Since a picture is worth a thousand words, let's bring in some visuals to see what was happening to the young Albert Ellis. Take a look at the first graph. The x-axis is time ticking along. The y-axis is anxiety, anchored by the official scientific terms of "chillin'" at the bottom and "freaking out" at the top.

You know how it works. Social anxiety can jump out in an instant, like a bogeyman in a Halloween haunted house. In just a few seconds, it's all systems go. You're hit with the urge to leave, to dart the long way around to avoid being spotted, or to pull out your phone so you don't have to make eye contact. And avoidance works—sort of. When we avoid, the anxiety magically dissipates, leaving us with not only a sense of relief but also the unfortunate confirmation that whatever we just avoided—small talk with your kid's classmate's mom, a break room discussion of last night's game with your co-workers, or a conversation

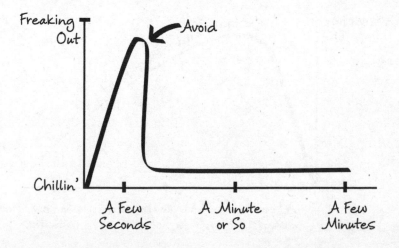

on a park bench with a 1940s cutie—was really and truly a danger. What's more, avoidance leaves us with the nagging feeling that we couldn't have handled it anyway.

By contrast, take a look at what happens in the second graph. This is what happens when we hang in there—when we're brave for the few seconds it takes to join the group at the party, raise our hand in class, or for young Albert to sit down on the bench. The anxiety shoots up, but then, when we stick with it, after we reach the summit of the mountain it's all downhill from there. What goes up must come down. When we go over the summit instead of avoiding, we learn a very different lesson. Rather than reinforcing the idea that the girl on the bench is a threat to be avoided, we learn she's polite, even if she already has a boyfriend. We learn that while we're uncomfortable, sitting there doesn't kill us—we can handle this, even if what we blurt out isn't exactly smooth and witty. Of course, the anxiety goes down more slowly than if we ducked out, but the trip down that long, slow slide teaches us exactly what Brandon Stanton and Albert Ellis figured out: one, we are much safer than our imaginations would have us believe, and two, we can handle it.

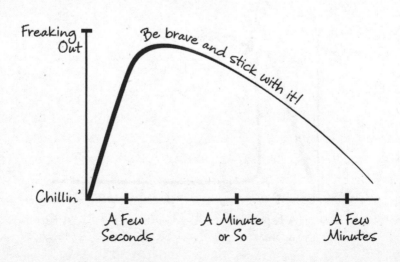

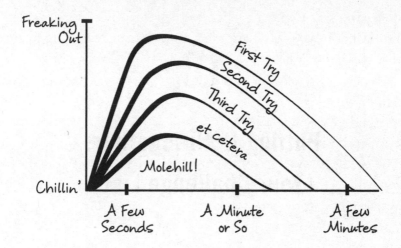

Now let's zero in on the hardest part—the tippy-top of that peak. This is where Jim hid behind a bush. This is when Aisha faked her phone call. This is where I may or may not have crossed the street to avoid well-meaning but aggressive nonprofit sidewalk fundraisers with their clipboards and smiles, even if it meant forgoing the taco salad I'd been craving. I'll never tell. That peak might be high, but it's actually a skinny little thing. To climb the peak and go over the top doesn't actually take that long—maybe ten seconds to a minute. So commit to being brave for one minute. Once you do that, it's all downhill from there. As we stay with it, it gets easier. Plus we get a taco salad.

Thankfully, you don't need to be as thorough as Brandon or Albert. You don't need to approach 130 attractive women, much less ten thousand strangers. The first approaches are the hardest: the first conversation, the first book club, the first softball practice. But don't stop at one. At your next opportunity, do it again. And again. Each time, both the intensity and duration of your anxiety will lessen. Your mountain of anxiety will erode into a molehill. And your confidence will grow into a mountain.

10

Putting It All Together: Your Challenge List

My life has been filled with terrible misfortune, most of which never happened.

—MONTAIGNE

Look in the dictionary for the "American Dream" and you might find a smiling picture of Jia Jiang. At the age of sixteen, Jia came to the United States from China with big ambitions: he wanted no less than to be the next Bill Gates. But as often happens, time passed quickly. High school, college, a first job, business school, marriage. Before he knew it, Jia was thirty, with a mortgage, a wife, and a baby on the way. Jia knew if he didn't take the leap soon middle age and middle management would calcify around him. So with his wife's blessing, he took a chance, quit his six-figure corporate job, and chased his lifelong dream: he founded a startup.

Jia was in heaven. It was exactly as he had hoped: creative, social, fast-paced. He was brimming with energy and hope. But four months in, just as major funding was about to make Jia's dream a reality, the funder bailed, leaving Jia with four employees, a family to support, and exactly zero income. Jia was crushed. He knew he had to find a new backer fast but was flooded by doubt. *The investor is an entrepreneurial veteran,* he thought. *If he thinks my company is not worth investing in, there must be some truth to it.* Jia's doubts snowballed. *You're a wannabe,* his Inner Critic sneered. He was paralyzed by the idea of casting around for more funding—the prospect of rejection was too frightening.

Jia realized his anxiety was getting in the way of fulfilling his startup dream, so he decided to crush it with a boot camp–style project he called 100 Days of Rejection that, to his great surprise, resulted in a book, *Rejection Proof: How I Beat Fear and Became Invincible Through 100 Days of Rejection.* Each day, he tried his hardest to get rejected. He made ridiculous requests to complete strangers: "Wanna have a staring contest?" "Can I take a nap in this mattress store?" "Can you ship this package to Santa Claus?" "Can I slide down the fire station's pole?" "Can I be a live mannequin at this Abercrombie store?" A lot of people said no, but given that he was trying to get rejected, getting a no made Jia's project a success.

While many people said no, to Jia's surprise way more people said yes. "Yes, you can use my backyard for soccer practice." "Yes, you can sit in the driver's seat of my police car." "Yes, you can give a lecture to my college class." "Yes, you can make an announcement on this Southwest flight." "Yes, this dancing Santa will teach you how to Dougie." "Yes, I can make the Olympic rings out of Krispy Kreme donuts for you in fifteen minutes flat."*

---

* See Jia's videos of all of these rejections and non-rejections at fearbuster .com/100-days-of-rejection-therapy

Now, you don't have to ask a dog groomer for a haircut, as
Jia did. But just like Jia, it's important to take action—to face
your fears. So pick a few things that scare you. Not pee-in-your-
pants scare you, just things that scare you a little. In technical
speak, facing your fears is called *exposure,* which sounds like either
a misdemeanor or something that happens at latitude, but really,
it's just a fancy name for practice.

Ali was a client of mine many years ago, but in my mind he remains the king of social anxiety exposure. The first time we
practiced together, he was reluctant. So we started out with
simple tasks at the hospital where I worked. First I asked at the
information desk for directions to the cafeteria. Next it was Ali's
turn. Then we each stopped a hospital volunteer, identifiable by
their salmon-pink blazers, and asked directions again. Within
half an hour, Ali was getting into it. As we were walking down
the busy main corridor, without any prompting he stopped a
complete stranger and asked for directions to the parking garage.
He thanked her and let her walk on. But then he started improvising, riffing on his own practice. He stopped another stranger
to ask for directions, but this time, when the young man directed
him to head one way down the corridor Ali walked the opposite way. The young man jogged after him: "Hey, man, no, this
way." Ali feigned sudden comprehension and thanked him as the
man smiled and wished him a good day. I hung back and watched
in proud astonishment. Ali was like an exposure DJ, remixing
the best of them and having fun with it. Then he asked a third
stranger for directions and, with a twinkle in his eye, asked the
stranger which way was "left." The stranger didn't even blink.
"That way," he said, pointing. No one raised an eyebrow. Ali
was elated. "I could stand on my head and no one would care!"

he exclaimed. As we parted after our session, I peeked out my office door, half-expecting to see him standing on his head in the middle of the waiting room.

So ask yourself what you would be doing if you had faced down your fears and were on the other side. Not *How would I feel?* but *What would I be* doing? What would I be doing if I felt confident? For Brandon Stanton, the answer was: *If I wasn't uncomfortable, I'd be asking strangers if I could take their picture.* For Albert Ellis, the answer was: *If I wasn't anxious, I'd be chatting with cute girls.* For Jia, it was: *If I was confident, I'd face rejection, dust myself off, and try again.*

How about you? Would you say yes to more invitations? Introduce yourself to more people? Show up even though you're worried about blushing? Whatever your answer, haul out the concrete mixer and make your goals concrete. You'll know you're on the right track if you can check off your goal on a list: "Ask the professor a question after class." Check. "Look at the audience the majority of the time while I give this presentation." Check. "Call Customer Service without rehearsing what I want to say first." Check. "Go to Jaime's party and talk to two people." Check. Why should your goals be so defined? With a vague, squishy goal like "Be confident," "Make a good impression," or "Act normal," it's impossible to know if you've achieved it. I know I could always be more confident, and my Inner Critic would snort with laughter if I asked it if I made a good impression or acted normal, no matter how things actually went. By contrast, with a concrete goal you'll know when you've accomplished it. You get the payoff of The Moment.

Dreaming about your post-social anxiety life is the start of your Challenge List. A Challenge List is similar to a bucket list in that it's a list of things to conquer.

When I introduce the Challenge List to my clients, I promise I'll do their scary things right alongside them. I can't in good conscience ask them to do something I'm not willing to do myself. In the service of conquering other people's social anxiety, I've asked strangers for the time, pushed the wrong button in a crowded elevator on purpose, gone jogging with a client, spilled my coffee in public, knocked rolls of paper towels off a display (and picked them up; don't worry—my mother raised me right), walked up and down a hallway with toilet paper deliberately stuck to my shoe, and done lots more. I can do these fairly easily because they're not my little fears. But these are:

1. Go my normal speed when someone is waiting for my parking space, rather than getting all stressed and rushed
2. Join the conversation when my kids FaceTime relatives
3. Tell a story in a group of people where I don't know everyone well
4. Initiate introducing myself to people I see all the time but don't know by name

These things scare me a little. And I'd be hypocritical if I asked you to do things that scare you a little and didn't do the things I was scared of. Believe me, I considered faking it, but for you, dear reader, I'll face my fears.

Let's take the first one. I *hate* it when someone is lying in wait for my parking space. I feel pressured, imagining the person is growing impatient with me. I worry they'll honk in disapproval or give me the finger as they floor it and roar away. So for my own practice, I decided I would simply go at my normal pace the next time someone was waiting for my space. What happened? Nothing. The guy waited. It was such a nonissue I felt like it didn't count. But it did. That was an easy Moment. A few days later, it happened again. That time, the driver slowly drove away after it became obvious I had a cart full of groceries and two wiggly boys unwilling to get in their booster seats. There were no honks or fingers. He just rolled on to someone who might vacate her space before, say, sundown.

But even if he had honked or given me the finger? Remember Replace from chapter 5? *How bad would that really be? What are the odds? How would I cope?* Being on the receiving end of a honk or finger from a stranger would be a little alarming, but I could handle it. I could text my husband and say: "Can you believe this guy?" I could turn it into a teachable moment for the kids about the importance of being patient. All in all, it would be fine.

Speaking of giving the finger, for your own Challenge List practice things that scare you, but don't practice being a jerk. Practice being the *authentic* you, not a pissed-off, unhinged you. Even though the prospect of telling off your boss makes you anxious, it's not something you want to practice. Use common sense. Just because the thought of indulging in some road rage makes you anxious doesn't mean it's a good choice.

Instead, choose things that will build a more authentic you. In fact, one might even call this Challenge List an Authenticity List. Think of it this way: What would you be *doing* if anxiety weren't standing in your way? What do you want to do without overthinking? What would the you-without-fear do? Put those things, big and little, on the list.

Now it's your turn. Let's start with things that scare you a *little*. List some small, concrete things that buy you an express ticket to the land of (a little) social anxiety.

1. _____

2. _____

3. _____

4. _____

Then, at the next opportunity, try out the things on your list. Spoiler alert: you will feel far worse anticipating your challenges than actually completing them. This is so common it has a name: the *worry mismatch*. It's called a mismatch for a reason: just like my experience with the parking space, the consequence of intentionally trying something outside our comfort zone is, typically, nothing. Sometimes we get a raised eyebrow or an incredulous stare, but it's nothing we can't handle. Jia learned that even though the dog-grooming ladies giggled as they explained they don't do human haircuts, they were nice about it. Nothing catastrophic happens. No one calls the police. No one asks why we're so stupid. No one gets angry. But we have to experience it to believe it. Indeed, when I talked to Jia about his anticipation versus his experience he said, "That mismatch gets corrected really quickly. Do it a couple of times and your calibration changes pretty fast. When I started, everything I was thinking about was the worst-case scenario: the person would pull out a gun, call the cops, or cuss me out. My mind was treating this as a foregone conclusion. But by the end, I could ask anything of anyone, anywhere."

So it's okay if you feel a little leery before you try the things on your Challenge List. Pranav *will* feel anxious when ordering food. Nelly *will* get the jitters before heading off on a date. Ali didn't want to ask for directions. I felt nervous introducing myself to parents at my sons' schools. But I did it anyway and that's what matters. Whether or not you get the raise, her number, or even a smile doesn't matter: it's that you did it. The success of your task is independent of the outcome. The only bar: Did you do it? Yes? Gold star for you.

Of course, not everything has to be officially on your Challenge List—you can do little challenges on the fly, too. Recently, my four-year-old's backpack somehow got left at his preschool.

Later that night, realizing it wasn't in the house or in the car and not wanting to face a thermos of moldering spaghetti the next morning, I zipped over to the school to get it. As I pulled into the unusually crowded parking lot, through the school's big plate-glass windows I could see there was an all-staff meeting going on. I realized I would have to walk past the entire staff of the school, including the director and all my son's teachers, in order to get his backpack. I sat in the car for a moment with a strong urge to head back home. But I muttered to myself, "Do it before you're confident," and got out of the car. I went in, walked past everyone with a wave and a smile, grabbed his pack, and started to head out. His favorite teacher was sitting by the door. She smiled and waved. *I forgot this,* I mouthed. "No problem," she whispered. "See you tomorrow." In short, totally anticlimactic. I even forgot to tell my husband about it when I got home. Challenge by challenge, I keep learning that consequences are never what they seem. And even if something went wrong, I could handle it. And guess what? You could, too.

THE CHALLENGE LIST, PHASE TWO: LETTING GO OF THE LIFE PRESERVER

As you work through your Challenge List, don't worry if you start to feel a little stuck. Many others, including me, have been there. They're doing everything right—they'll go all in and be brave. They'll sit on their front stoop and play guitar until they run out of songs. They'll walk into that networking event with their head held high. They'll stick it out at the party until they're the last woman standing. But then they'll go home disappointed. "I did it, which I know is what counts, but I felt lousy the whole time," they'll lament. "My anxiety didn't go down at all."

Don't fret; this happens all the time. You're willing to climb the mountain, so why don't you slide down the other side? The answer: you may be hindering yourself without even realizing it. How? Enter Dr. Lynn Alden of the University of British Columbia. Dr. Alden has been studying social anxiety for almost forty years. With her former student Dr. Charles Taylor, now on the faculty at the University of California, San Diego, they are a dynamic duo of social anxiety research. When I spoke with them, Dr. Alden told me a story about a female client she once worked with. Let's call her Beth. "Whenever a man Beth found attractive was in the vicinity, she would leave the room. And imagine what you would think if you were that man—if you walked in a room and Beth immediately stood up and left, every time."

Leaving the room was Beth's *safety behavior.* Yours might be to chug down a couple of drinks as soon as you walk into a party, cling to your close friend throughout lunch with new acquaintances, look at the floor, or hover on the edge of groups. Safety behaviors are the actions we take to conceal our perceived inadequacies—those things the Inner Critic says are wrong with us. But they are the very reason our fear remains. The things we're doing to save ourselves are keeping us mired. It's ironic, like being held underwater by a life preserver.

Why do we keep using safety behaviors? When we do, there is a sense that we are hiding, which makes us feel safer. But instead of truly hiding, we are hiding in plain sight. Even though we feel like we are concealing our flaws, people can see us. I know that sounds obvious, but while we're busy trying to keep ourselves safe we're actually sending an entirely different message. We rehearse what to say in order to come across as well-spoken but end up appearing preoccupied. We pepper others with questions to avoid talking about ourselves but leave our conversational partner feeling interrogated. We agree with everything our boss says, which makes her wonder if we're even listening.

As Dr. Alden puts it, "Every behavior sends a message to others. People with social anxiety can forget that; they think they're erasing themselves." But in reality, safety behaviors send a loud and clear message, and it's exactly the opposite of what we're trying to do. We accidentally send the message of *I'm aloof, I'm distant, I'm snobby, I'm prickly,* when nothing could be further from the truth. Dr. Alden's client Beth thought that by leaving the room she'd be safe from her crush. But of course he could see her. And she realized that it came off as cold and stuck-up. With Dr. Alden's help, Beth learned to stay in the room, where she got the chance to realize not only was her crush friendly, but also she was safe without her safety behavior after all. Her life preserver had indeed been keeping her underwater.

Through the years, Drs. Alden and Taylor have seen this happen again and again. Their clients' greatest lightbulb moments come when they start to see their safety behaviors from the point of view of others. Indeed, imagine how you might respond to someone wearing sunglasses indoors, scrolling through their smartphone, looking at the floor with their arms crossed, or vamoosing whenever you walked in the room. You would assume they didn't want to talk with you or, worse, that they didn't like you. I remember my own lightbulb moment: in high school, one particularly tactless but honest boy signed my yearbook with the comment that he found me "aloof but likable," which jump-started my growing comprehension that working hard to keep my anxiety at bay was also keeping others at a distance.

How to fix this? As Dr. Taylor puts it, "We want people to be scientists. First you need to have a good understanding of what safety behaviors you are using. Then you can do some experimental testing and see what happens if you remove the safety behavior."

Here's the good news: letting go of the life preserver that's actually keeping you underwater not only is doable; it also gets results. How do we know? Over the past decade, Alden and Taylor have run a series of groundbreaking studies where they asked people to do just that. And in those studies, they told me, 92 percent of people could identify right away what safety behaviors they were using. I certainly know what I used to do: I avoided eye contact and avoided introducing myself, preferring, oddly, to pretend that I already knew the person, which led to confusion on their part and awkwardness all around. But once I realized that's what I was doing, I stopped. And in their studies, Alden and Taylor found their participants could stop, too.

In several studies, Alden and Taylor asked socially anxious participants to have a five-minute conversation with a lab confederate—a getting-to-know-you chat that is the prerequisite for any potential new friendship. Beforehand, the participants were asked what they were afraid might happen during the conversation. In other words, what Reveal was their Inner Critic predicting? Answers ranged from, "I will say something stupid," to, "My partner will think badly of me," to, "They'll think I'm weird," and everything in between.

Next, participants were asked about their safety behaviors: What did they do to try to make themselves feel safer or to prevent The Reveal from occurring? Again, answers ran the gamut:

"Think really hard about getting my words out right."
"Put my hand in front of my mouth when I talk."
"Rehearse what I'm going to say next while the other person is talking."
"Smile, smile, smile."

"Focus on my enunciation."
"Continuously monitor what I'm saying."
"Think about taking deep breaths to calm myself down."

Then half the participants got the following instructions, with their personal fears and safety behaviors filled in the blanks, like so:

> *In order to help overcome your anxiety, it is important to discover whether what you fear can actually happen. To accomplish this, you should try not to do the things you normally do to prevent the person from <u>thinking you're stupid.</u> For example, during the conversation, do nothing to save yourself, do not <u>avoid eye contact.</u> Just think that you want to discover what will happen when you don't <u>avoid eye contact</u>. By doing this, you will be better able to see if your expectations are confirmed.*

The other half were told nothing about safety behaviors. They were told to wait it out—that getting over anxiety was like getting into a bath of hot water: at first unpleasant, but after a while they'd get used to it and feel better.

Then each person was sent forth into their own one-on-one five-minute conversation. What happened was nothing short of amazing: First, participants who dropped their safety behaviors looked *less* anxious. Indeed, when they stopped trying to conceal, rather than all that unconcealed anxiety spilling out, they looked *more* comfortable.

Next, when Alden and Taylor asked the confederates about their experience, guess whom they enjoyed talking to more? The group who dropped their safety behaviors. Who would they like to spend more time with? Ditto. Who did they want as a friend? You guessed it.

But most interesting is that participants who dropped their safety behaviors thought the confederates liked them because they seemed less anxious. But in reality, the confederates said they liked them because they were friendlier, talked more openly, conveyed interest, and were actively engaged. In other words, the participants thought their partners liked them because they did *less of the bad stuff*, but in reality the partners liked them because they did *more of the good stuff*. Once all the bandwidth used for rehearsing sentences or managing their appearance was freed up, authentic friendliness—the good stuff—naturally filled in the gaps.

There's that word again: "authentic." In other words, being yourself. Indeed, when we use safety behaviors we know we're coming off as fake. We know it's not our true self that we're presenting to the world—instead, it's a filtered, highly managed version. Safety behaviors are designed to hide your true self, the one your Inner Critic says is flawed. But instead, safety behaviors keep us stuck in the idea that we're unlikable or deficient. We never get the chance to prove those ideas wrong. Ironically, when the study participants stopped trying to save themselves they could be themselves. And that, in turn, made them connect on a genuine level. Plus, unsurprisingly, they had a much better time than the participants who were simply told to hang in there.

For Jia Jiang, the difference between his first two attempts at rejection illustrates the difference between concealing with safety behaviors and leaving them behind. For his inaugural rejection attempt, Day One, he decided to ask a stranger—the security guard in the lobby of his office building—if he could borrow a hundred dollars. In the video of the encounter Jia filmed on his phone, the security guard is sitting at his desk, hunched over a computer screen. Jia approaches. Before he even gets to the desk, he blurts out, "Excuse me, do you think I could borrow a hundred dollars from you?" The guard looks puzzled and says no. But then a hint of a smile crosses his face. He looks up at Jia. "Why?" But Jia is too freaked out to hear him. "No? All right. No. Okay, thanks," and he scurries away.

What safety behavior did Jia use? How is he trying to keep the guard from thinking he's a total nut job? In this case, it's speed. Jia moves in quickly, chatters his words, and gets out, as he put it, "like some sort of small animal running away from a predator." As for the rest of us, we might avoid eye contact, speak in a low, mumbling voice, or hover a few steps away. This all makes sense—we're trying to keep ourselves safe.

But later, when Jia was editing the video of the encounter, he saw what he had missed. The security guard wasn't hostile in the slightest; he was just perplexed. Jia also realized the guard's "Why?" was an offer to extend the conversation. Jia could have been honest and said, "I'm trying to overcome my fear of rejection, so I am forcing myself to make absurd requests." Or he could have offered to leave his driver's license as collateral and promised to repay him. But Jia let his safety behaviors get the best of him and skedaddled.

Jia vowed to do better the next day.

On Day Two, he went to a burger joint for lunch. As he was filling his cup with soda at the dispenser, he saw a sign that said: "Free Refills." Jia's eyes lit up. After finishing his bacon cheeseburger, Jia approached the counter. In his phone video, a young guy with glasses, a red apron, and an armload of tattoos strides up to help him. "What can I do for you?" he asks. This time, Jia looks the guy in the eye, smiles broadly, and stands up a little straighter. "Yeah, your burger is really good. Can I get a burger refill?"

"A what?" says the cashier.

"A burger refill."

"A burger refill," the cashier repeats, trying to wrap his head around the question. "What do you mean?" He's not unfriendly. Like the security guard, he is merely perplexed and curious.

"Like a free refill. Do you have free refills for burgers?"

The cashier gets it. "Uh, no free refills for burgers," he says.

"How come you have it for drinks but not for burgers?" asks Jia. He asks this with a steady confidence, as if his request were totally reasonable.

The cashier chuckles. "That's the way it is, man," he says with a shrug.

Jia smiles, thanks him, says he'd like the place even more if they offered burger refills, and saunters off.

What a difference. Even though he still got a no (a triumph—his goal, remember, was to get rejected), he doesn't feel the panic he felt with the security guard. The *way* you ask makes a big difference, Jia discovered. Even though he was still anxious, without his safety behaviors Jia appeared as if he were not anxious. He stood up straight, looked directly at the guy instead of at the floor or over his head, smiled, and used his normal volume and speed. He slowed down and took his time. And lo and behold, this looked the same as confidence. After just two experiences, one with safety behaviors and one without, Jia had discovered a major secret: you set the tone. Act as if you were not anxious, drop your safety behaviors, and not only will you feel better; you'll also get a better response. And guess what? No one can tell you're acting. Guess what else? Eventually, you won't be.

When I talked to Jia about this discovery, he said, "I realized that *what* I was asking was out of the realm of the social norm, but the *way* I was asking was not. I didn't blow a horn or do a dance. I came in being very respectful. And people usually respond in kind."

My first inkling of how this worked occurred in college. My junior year, I was a "Resident Counselor," an upperclassman who lived in a freshman dorm, not necessarily to enforce rules but to act as a resource for first-years as they transitioned to college life. As a public health measure, all Resident Counselors had help-yourself envelopes of safer-sex supplies—condoms, lube, dental dams—taped to the outside of our doors. I was usually conscientious about refilling them, but in the late spring I got caught up in the rush of finals, leaving wilting, empty envelopes hanging sadly on my door.

At the very end of the year, on move-out day, I was packing books in boxes in my room. My door was open—I was hoping friends would pop in to distract me. But then a student I didn't recognize—glasses, spiky hair—knocked and stuck his head in my doorway. "Hey, do you have any condoms?" he asked. I was impressed with his boldness. "No, sorry, I'm out—but there's another counselor's door down the hall and to the right. Try there."

"Thanks," he said, and trotted off.

Almost twenty years later, I still remember this guy's chutzpah with admiration. He needed a condom, urgently, which implied what he planned to do as soon as he found one. But he wasn't afraid to reveal all this to a stranger *and* ask for help—two things that are usually one-way tickets to social anxiety. He could have easily thought, *She's going to think I'm creepy/weird/perverted,* and snuck away, but instead he knocked, showed his face, and asked like it was no big deal.

Like Jia, what I learned is this: you get to set the tone. The guy at my door made his request with an air of confidence, and I followed suit. Now, you may ask, what if he was faking it? What if he psyched himself up beforehand with an internal chant of, *Act casual. Act casual*? Quite honestly, it doesn't matter. Either way, my roll-with-it response underscored that if you approach something as if it's totally reasonable, it will be. Or you can just pretend you're Beyoncé. Or, in this guy's case, Trojan Man. To this day, I'm indebted to that guy, who inadvertently taught me one of my earliest lessons about social anxiety. For everyone's sake, I really hope he found a condom.

Despite the lesson of Trojan Man, I hung on to some of my own safety behaviors for years. Whenever my words went out to an audience of strangers—as a guest on a podcast or during a radio interview—the old anxiety would come rolling back. So for a long time, safety equaled having scripted responses in front of me— sometimes, I admit, word for word. I knew I'd be more natural and give a better interview if I wasn't clinging to my life preserver of pre-prepared answers, but with lots of people watching and listening, letting go and loosening up didn't feel like an option.

Unfortunately, that meant that's exactly what I had to do. If I wanted to graduate from social anxiety school, I had to do interviews with no notes. I'd still give the interview the respect and preparation it deserved, but I needed to trust myself to remember the points I wanted to make. So when the opportunity to do a live radio interview came along, I let myself cringe for a minute (or an hour), then said to myself, "Do it before you feel confident and the confidence will catch up." (Thanks, chapter 7!)

This was the next phase of my Challenge List, sans safety behaviors:

5. Smile and start conversation with people I think don't like me (several grumpy moms, one grumpy teacher, several grumpy co-workers). Do this repeatedly.

6. Be a guest on a pre-recorded podcast where mistakes can be edited out, but without my usual notes. Do this as often as is offered.

7. Do a live radio interview (ack, no do-overs!) without my usual notes (but whew, no camera!).

Over time, I did all of these and they turned out just fine. I was anxious for each of them, but I went over the mountain. That's important: *I was anxious*. You will be, too. You won't stop feeling anxious. You'll feel anxious, square your shoulders, and do it anyway.

Okay, your turn. So let's add to that Challenge List again. Now that you've done some smaller-scale stuff with your brave pants on, nudge yourself along to some things that scare you a little more, and this time get rid of the very things you think are keeping you safe. If you're worried that your hands shake, your life preserver might be to drink only from a bottle, not a cup that might shake and spill. If you're worried about blushing, you may wear one of your many turtlenecks. If you're worried about running out of things to say, you may only go to parties with your partner. So drop the life preserver, pour your beer in a glass, and leave the bottle behind. Put on a V-neck shirt, blushing be damned. Go stag to a party. Or all three. Whatever your life preserver, leave it at home and see what happens. Try it out. Or as a wise, short-statured social anxiety therapist once said, "Do. Or do not. There is no try."

Below, fill in some new challenges, along with the safety behaviors you'd like to drop. Then, as Dr. Richard Heimberg, the aforementioned father of social anxiety research, said to me when I asked the secret to overcoming social anxiety, "Go forth and do."

5. My challenge (what I would be doing if I weren't anxious): _____

Safety behavior(s) I want to drop: _____

6. My challenge (what I would be doing if I weren't anxious): _____

Safety behavior(s) I want to drop: _____

7. My challenge (what I would be doing if I weren't anxious): _____

Safety behavior(s) I want to drop: _____

Nice work. As Dr. Seuss might say, you're off to great places; you're off and away! We're almost up to the hardest stuff on your list. As you cruise into the home stretch, you may wish to psych yourself up with a pep talk—perhaps some self-affirmations. But affirmations often get a bad rap, evoking cheesy, overly earnest sessions with the bathroom mirror. The interweb makes fun of affirmations: "I become better each day in every way. Unless there is a *Golden Girls* marathon on, and then I'm not leaving the house." Or, "I honor and express all facets of my being, regardless of state and local laws." We make fun of affirmations because they feel tacky and dumb. But worse, they feel like a lie.

If we try, in desperation, to psych ourselves up for our Challenge List with affirmations—*I got this! I'm gonna be awesome! Yeah!*—we are left feeling deflated. Why? Because we don't believe them.

Instead, try this: affirm yourself with the values you are 100 percent rock-solid sure about, even if they have nothing to do with the task at hand. You heard that right. Even if it has nothing to do with your Challenge, affirm yourself with what you know is true about yourself. *As the sun rises and sets, I am a loyal friend. I value being a good listener. I'm a really good mom. I've accomplished more than I ever thought possible through my own hard work.* It may seem silly to affirm your love for your family or your commitment to your religious faith when you're about to walk into a quarterly sales meeting, but it works.

Likewise, you can gain strength by affirming your own courageous acts. A 2017 eye-tracking study from a group of Dutch researchers found that when participants brought to mind a memory of their own integrity—the time they stood by a friend when no one else did, the time they could have thrown a colleague under the bus but didn't—they were able to look pictures of angry faces square in the eye. So affirm your truths. Affirm the times you did the right thing. Remind yourself of your best and your best will show up.

THE CHALLENGE LIST, PHASE THREE:
TAKE IT ON HOME

Here we are, the home stretch. What are some things that scare you a lot? Don't move on to these until you're done with the things that scare you a little, then the things that scare you a little more, and you've experimented with dropping your safety behaviors. Even though we're almost at the deep end, we're still inching into the pool.

Something you may notice is that as you nudge yourself through the things that scare you a little and the things that scare you moderately, these biggest things may not scare you as much as they used to. They may still curl your toes, but there may be a tiny flame of willingness where there wasn't one before. Why? As you move through your small and medium challenges, you may be incrementally resetting your social anxiety set point. As Dr. Richard Heimberg so neatly summed up the process when I talked with him, "Good exposures set in motion a success spiral."

So let's bring it on home. What are your big stretches? Think of some concrete things that make you want to hide behind the curtains. If you start planning an escape route, you know you've found your last big challenges. Here are mine:

8. Contact and interview psychology luminaries for this book (breathe)
9. Do a live, on-camera interview with minimal notes (ack!)
10. Send a real book out into the world containing my own story of social anxiety (double ack!)

For me, these definitely fit the bill. Cold-contacting academic titans and telling them I'm not only presumptuous enough to write a book about a topic they've spent their lives researching, but also they should volunteer their time and expertise to help me do it made my hair stand on end. I waited until embarrassingly close to the book due date to email them, afraid they would see me as a two-bit interloper who didn't know what I was talking about. But in reality, they couldn't have been more agreeable. Eighty percent of them emailed me back and were delighted to be interviewed. They opened their schedules and their minds, and they couldn't have been nicer about it.

Next, I was momentarily pumped but mostly terrified when I got an offer to do a live online interview. It was high time to vanquish my lifelong but irrational fear of video cameras, but that didn't mean I wanted to do it in front of an online audience of thousands. I admit I overprepared and overrehearsed, though it seemed vital in the moment. The night before, I had a hard time sleeping. The day of, I locked myself in my office and tried to work but instead fretted for hours in a haze of adrenaline. At the appointed time I logged on, and in ten minutes it was over. The host was friendly, actually laughed at my jokes, and invited me back anytime. I even got some complimentary emails from people who had seen me on the show. I had stared down the little green light on my laptop and lived to tell the tale.

A few months later, the same show invited me back again. That round was a thousand times easier. My fear-of-cameras mountain wasn't a molehill yet, but the erosion was dramatic. The little green light seemed less like a laser into my soul and more like a porthole to a world where I could share nerdy psychology research and maybe even be helpful in the process.

Finally, there's the book in your hands. For years, I've wanted to be a writer. Writing a book was a lifelong goal of mine, but when I decided to write about social anxiety I realized I would have to write about myself. And that's not something those of us familiar with social anxiety do easily. To be sure, I am much more open today than I was five, ten, and especially twenty years ago, but sending bits of myself out into the world between hardback covers was the biggest stretch out of my comfort zone to date.

These were my demons to slay. I could have listed "sing karaoke" or "do improv comedy," but even though these make me want to play dead, they weren't the things that were holding me back in life. However, my unwillingness to cold-contact experts in positions of authority, speak live on camera to an unseen audience of thousands, and make myself vulnerable to criticism and lousy reviews by sending a book with my name on it into the world was definitely holding me back. These were the things that, if I didn't do them, would most definitely get in the way of living the life I wanted to live. I was torn between the gauntlet of facing down fears (which, rationally, I knew were overblown and distorted) and the specter of regret.

Now it's your turn. If you're not ready, that's totally okay. Go back to the beginning or middle of your Challenge List and knock off a few more of those. Getting a running start can bolster confidence and make the scariest stuff a little less toe curling. So what are the things that scare you a lot? What is holding you back? Ask him out. Dance at your daughter's wedding. Change your job. Move out. Speak up. Show up. Fill them in below. Do these and your confidence will catch up. Move forward *by* living your life.

8. _____

9. _____

10. _____

What will working your way through your Challenge List be like? Most of the time, it will be tough but well worth it. You'll find that your confidence catches up. You'll discover what you never knew was in you all along. But other times it may not go so well. You'll disappoint yourself. You'll pull out all the stops of your bravery, and nothing will change. You'll feel like trying to stretch your range is futile. Your Inner Critic will tell you to sit down, shut up, and keep your head down. *This isn't for you,* it will say. *You weren't built to have confidence.*

Plus, once in a while, something bad *will* happen. People are judgy; people talk. There are haters out there. But if your practice doesn't go as planned, ask yourself who was acting inappropriately. For her Challenge List, Camilla asked a stranger for the time, but the stranger ignored her. Who was out of line, Camilla or the stranger? Julio asked a question in a meeting and his boss blew him off. Again, who acted poorly, Julio or his boss?

Remember Replace and Embrace from chapters 5 and 6? They're not just a running start; you can use them as cleanup, too. Ask yourself how *truly* horrible was the experience? It feels cringe worthy now, but who will remember in a few days? (Probably no one besides you.) How often do things like this happen to people? (Probably often.) How many people has this happened to? (Lots—chalk one up for the human experience.) For example, for his Challenge List, Dante asked a question in class, but the professor didn't understand what he meant. Dante tried to explain but tripped over his words. The professor looked perplexed and gave an answer that didn't match the question. Dante felt embarrassed, but looking around, he saw none of the other students seemed to care. And a couple weeks later, when Dante went to office hours, the absentminded professor didn't even seem to remember him. Clearly, it was no biggie.

Finally, ask yourself a question that should sound familiar by now: *How can I cope?* For example, Winnie would always leave church as soon as it was over to avoid lingering and getting stuck in conversation. One Sunday, for her Challenge List, she stayed, determined to face her fears. But before she could say good morning to anyone, she got cornered by the church's resident eccentric—a harmless but oddball elderly lady who smelled strongly of mothballs and sported dried toothpaste at the corners of her mouth. Winnie endured for twenty minutes before she excused herself and ran to her car. After calming down, she asked herself what she could do. How could she cope? She called her mother and told her the story. Instead of being horrified, she thought it was hysterical, and Winnie realized she had a good story to tell at work the next day.

Now, you certainly don't have to cope by sharing with your mother—you can cope in any healthy way that works for you. But Winnie discovered something: practice gone wrong is often great fodder for conversation. Everyone loves embarrassing stories; it humanizes you, shows you have a sense of humor, and you might even get an embarrassing story in return. And guess what? That's part of how closeness develops, which I'll cover in depth in chapter 16.

So make your Challenge List. Then talk your way through with Replace and Embrace. Give yourself some structure—play a role that you choose. Be brave for the time it takes to get over the summit. Take on your challenges, a little at a time. And leave your life preservers at home. The mountain is all downhill from there. Slide down the hill and into your life. The more you practice, the easier it gets.

Finally, remember the confidence myth. You don't gain confidence in a vacuum and then go off and conquer the world. Instead, you learn to be confident, to have courage, to get over anxiety, to live your life authentically, *by* doing challenging things. And an authentic life includes some rejection, some awkwardness, and some embarrassment. But guess what? It also includes deep satisfaction in your accomplishments, even when they don't turn out exactly as you pictured them. And with ongoing practice, you'll find it also includes many Moments and even some elation. By practicing, you'll learn that even if bad stuff happens, you can keep moving forward, keep being brave. You can handle it.

But don't take it from me; take it from Jia, who said to me: "It was surprising how easy it was to get a yes. I realized how many opportunities I missed because I was afraid of people rejecting me, but I was just rejecting myself." He paused. I've learned to recognize that pause in client after client, as well as in myself. It was The Moment. Then with wonder in his voice he said, "The world is a lot nicer than I thought."

PART 4

Busting the Myths
of Social Anxiety

11

How (and Why) to Turn Your Attention Inside Out

Wah-wah, wah. Wah wah wah wah. Wah wah. To Diego, the medical resident sounded like Charlie Brown's teacher. She was reviewing with him how to perform a testicular exam while their alarmed-looking patient looked on, but Diego was too busy trying to look calm and doctor-like to hear much of what she said. Then she stopped *wah-wah*-ing and looked at him expectantly. With a start, Diego realized he was supposed to do something, which, given the circumstances, was probably a testicular exam.

Diego was a third-year medical student, but so far this year felt more like being on the wrong end of a sniper's rifle. During the first and second years of med school, he had largely buried himself in a study carrel or worked long hours in the anatomy lab, determined to excel. But this past July, when he and his classmates made the shift from classroom to hospital, he fell headlong into culture shock. He found himself in a whole new world of responsibility, helping to care for real, living patients—not the dead ones of the anatomy lab or the imaginary ones of his textbooks' case studies.

But the biggest change was the scrutiny. Given that the residents and attending physicians didn't trust the med students to do much besides breathe without supervision, Diego was observed by someone in authority all the time. He was supposed to take vitals, take histories, conduct physical exams, but he always felt as if he were play-acting. His Inner Critic would whisper to him, *They can tell you don't know what you're doing. You don't belong here. You look stupid.*

The worst, Diego said, was when he had to do a physical exam and actually touch someone's body. "And the absolute worst is when I have to do a Pap smear, a breast exam, a testicular exam, or anything like that," he said. Between being observed by supervisors and having to touch patients, Diego said, "I'm anxious all the time."

So Diego worked hard to cover himself. When he spoke, he monitored himself to ensure he was using his "doctor voice" and sufficiently impressive vocabulary. While other people were talking, he thought about what to say next, weighing and rehearsing to make sure he didn't say anything impolite, insensitive, or stupid.

But all Diego's impression management—focusing on his anxiety and monitoring what he said—was royally screwing up his work. He often missed what was being said to him—by patients, attending physicians, his resident. He had to ask people to repeat themselves. He would get distracted and lose his place while taking a history or forget the entire circulatory system while performing a physical. During bedside teaching sessions, he didn't answer the attendings' questions unless they asked him directly, and then his mind would go blank, unable to remember the lines he had just been rehearsing in his head.

But after a couple of months in the hospital, his midsemester evaluations, to put it lightly, left room for improvement. He was distracted and unfocused, said the residents. He seemed preoccupied, said the attendings. Diego was discouraged and unnerved. He wanted nothing more than to do well, to be a good doctor. Something had to change.

As you know by now, social anxiety is fundamentally a *distortion:* it's a mistaken belief that something is wrong with you and everyone will notice. That you'll be Revealed. But that's not the only lie social anxiety tells. In this section of *How to Be Yourself*, we'll put the myths of social anxiety in the hot seat.

Diego is a classic example of the first myth of social anxiety: *I must always monitor myself and my anxiety.* He plans and rehearses what he says, ensures his voice isn't squeaky or cracking, and weighs his words to ensure he simultaneously sounds smart, doesn't offend anyone, and generally avoids criticism. But all this impression management is exhausting, plus in the end, it actually hinders his performance and keeps him mired in social anxiety.

Like fossil fuels or political capital, attention is a limited resource. We have only so much we can allocate before it is used up. For Diego, all his attention is focused on himself and the management of his anxiety, a phenomenon aptly called *self-focused attention.* Self-focused attention eats up our bandwidth by focusing on our bodies (*I look weird, don't I?*), emotions (*I'm freaking out here*), performance (*Why did I say that? I sound like an idiot*), or management (*I should smile at her. But maybe that looks creepy. But not smiling is creepier, isn't it? Argh, I probably look like I want to stuff her in my car trunk*). Thus, we come away from social encounters with very little information about how things actually went. And where do we look to fill in the gaps? Unfortunately, we ask our anxiety, which is about as credible as asking the used-car sales-man which model we should buy. Or we ask the Inner Critic, which is even worse. In short, we look *inside* to see how things *outside* are going.

Whether at a high school dance or our annual performance review we use our discomfort to determine how we are com-ing off to others. This is called the *felt sense*. We *feel* like an idiot, so we must be spouting nonsense. We *feel* like a loser, so everyone must be secretly signing an *L* on their foreheads when we turn around. Again, it *feels* true, so we ask our anxiety, arguably the least credible source of information, for reassurance. No won-der it's not working.

To top it off, this self-absorption reverberates far beyond just our anxious moments. Researchers from Wilfrid Laurier Uni-versity in Ontario asked socially anxious undergrads to have a five-minute getting-to-know-you conversation with a lab assis-tant (as you probably noticed by now, social anxiety researchers love the five-minute getting-to-know-you conversation). In order to induce self-focused attention, half the participants were instructed to pay close attention to their own feelings, thoughts, actions, and body sensations during the conversation. By con-trast, the other half were asked to pay close attention to their partners' words and facial expressions. After the conversation, the researchers let them stew for twenty-four hours. The next day, the self-focused group reported lashing themselves with crit-icism more harshly and more often than the partner-focused group. Indeed, the first myth of social anxiety—*I must always monitor myself and my anxiety*—set in motion a twenty-four-hour-long ripple effect of negativity.

For Diego, the myth kept him trapped in the closed circuit of social anxiety as well. He desperately wanted things to go well, which made him anxious, which made him monitor his performance. But all the management limited his attention and, ironically, made things go poorly. His Inner Critic's forecasts about poor performance became a self-fulfilling prophecy.

So if monitoring is getting in our way, what do we do instead? How do we get out of our heads? The answer is your next tool: turn your attention inside out.

Remember the children's song "Head, Shoulders, Knees, and Toes"? Sing it silently to yourself; you don't have to do the accompanying hand motions (unless you want to, which would be pretty awesome). Bring your awareness to your head. Then shift your attention to your shoulders. Let it linger for a moment, then move on to your knees, then your toes. Notice how it feels to shift your attention from one body area to the next. To an observer, your actions are invisible, but internally your attention is active, shifting from one place to another to another. The same concept applies to turning your attention inside out. You choose where your attention goes. We can shift from focusing inward on our internal commentary to focusing outward on what's currently happening around us. We can focus on our conversation partner's words, which for Diego means she won't sound like Charlie Brown's teacher anymore. We can focus on their face. We can focus on what's happening right here, right now. And, most important, we can focus on the task at hand, which is called, appropriately enough, *task-focused attention*.

To help us with this, we have Dr. Susan Bögels of the University of Amsterdam, a creative researcher who teaches how to turn away from the internal commentary and tune into the people around us. Dr. Bögels encourages us to build our task-focused muscles much like actual muscles—one workout at a time. And by "focus," I don't mean stare people down like a WWE wrestler. Instead, simply aim for the majority of your attention to be on task. Even 51 percent is fine.

Dr. Bögels recommends practicing shifting your attention outward by first focusing on something quiet and undemanding, like a walk through the forest, emptying the dishwasher, or petting your cat. This sounds easy, but just like with mindfulness from chapter 6, our attention will not often do what it is told. It will run around, heedless of what you want it to do. No biggie—that's just what brains do. Gently lead it back.

When you're able to focus a majority of your attention on your quiet task, up the ante. Try focusing on a TV show, radio program, or podcast for a few minutes. Afterwards, summarize what you heard.

Next, move on to focusing on real, live people: phone conversations and then face-to-face conversations. Turn your attention to the task at hand: listening or speaking, rather than the running commentary of your Inner Critic. When you're speaking, focus on the message, not the delivery. After some practice, when you catch yourself trapped in a closed circuit of anxiety during a conversation you'll be able to shift your attention back to the tasks at hand: talking and listening with your conversation partner.

One note: bring your focus back to your task, not just any random thing. Putting your attention on something other than the task at hand ("Maybe if I focus on my breathing I'll feel better" or "Must. Check. Twitter.") is *distraction* and not what we're aiming for. Instead, redirect your focus to what you're supposed to be doing.

To further drive home the power of turning your attention inside out, try an experiment suggested by Dr. David Clark of

Oxford. Have two separate conversations, he suggests, with store clerks, co-workers, whomever. The first time, focus your attention inward on your performance, your body, your anxiety. Monitor what you're saying and work hard to manage their impression of you. Focus on *you, you, you*. Then, in the second conversation, turn your attention outward. Look at your conversation partner's face. Listen closely to what they're saying. Focus on *them, them, them*. This is a fundamental shift. Which conversation is more productive? Which is more pleasant? Where do you get the best response? I'll bet you a rockin' rendition of "Head, Shoulders, Knees, and Toes" it's the second. Says Dr. Clark, "It helps people discover through experience that what they've been doing to manage their social anxiety is not helping; it's actually part of the problem. Try this courageous and challenging thing—changing your behavior—so you can learn something new."

Diego did exactly this. He practiced shifting his attention away from monitoring and weighing his words. With all the freed-up bandwidth, he focused on his tasks: taking vitals, listening to his patients' questions, and yes, performing Pap smears and testicular exams. As he practiced, he felt a palpable difference. He realized so much of his attention had been focused inward, which he thought had been helpful but had left little for his job. Now he doesn't let himself get sucked into a whirlpool of self-absorbed prophecies. By turning his attention inside out, far from coming across as stupid, he's made room for the attentive, responsive doctor who is anything but.

Sometimes when we're feeling socially anxious, we do focus outward, but we tend to focus on what might be going wrong. Our conversation partner looks away and we think he is scanning desperately for an escape route. Our colleague shifts in her seat and we decide she thinks we're a weirdo. We fear judgment but then, oddly, twist ourselves into a pretzel to find it. This is called *attention to threat*.

Once we feel threatened, we lock in and see threat everywhere. It makes sense—the rabbit keeps an eye out for the fox at all times. But it costs us. To illustrate, look around you and scan for things that are blue. The blue sky, your blue jeans, perhaps a bluebird outside or a blue book on your shelf. Done? Okay, now try to recall what you saw that was *red*. Exactly. When our attention is directed elsewhere, we miss out. There are probably plenty of red things around you, but since you weren't attending to them, you didn't see them. So it is with threat. When we selectively zoom in on turned backs and grumpy scowls, we miss the nodding heads and smiling faces surrounding them.

Ah, faces. We particularly find threat in faces. Pictures of angry and disgusted faces have been used in innumerable social anxiety studies to send participants' threat-o-meters spinning. Even smiling faces get interpreted as a threat to a socially anxious brain. And while it might make sense to avoid angry faces, avoiding smiling faces doesn't seem useful to anyone. But a research group in the Netherlands led by Dr. Mike Rinck of Radboud University Nijmegen created an ingenious method of training a socially anxious brain to feel comfortable with smiling faces. In the study, Rinck and his colleagues showed participants pictures of faces on a computer screen and equipped them with a joystick. Pulling on the joystick zoomed in on the face, making it grow until it abstracted and disappeared, while pushing on the joystick zoomed out on the face, shrinking it until it vanished. Enlarging the face mimicked approach, while pushing away mimicked avoidant retreat. Over hundreds of trials, half the participants were instructed to pull a crowd's worth of smiling pictures toward them, while the other half pushed the pictures away, shrinking them until they disappeared into blackness on the screen. Joystick pull by joystick pull, the participants who pulled the smiles toward them, the researchers hoped, would rewire their brains to see smiling faces as just that—friendly faces safe to approach.

To test whether the training spilled over into real life, the team asked each participant to give a one-minute speech on camera, plus they were told their video would be evaluated on attractiveness, friendliness, competence, and more. In the face (pun intended) of impending judgment, the group who had practiced approaching smiling faces was less anxious (not to mention happier) after the speech than the group who pushed smiling faces away. In short, it worked.

Of course, we don't travel the world armed with a joystick that allows us to push unwanted sights away and pull others close (though someone should totally invent that). So how to adapt the findings of the lab to the real world?

One way is to play a game with yourself. When you're out and about, count how many people you see wearing glasses. Then count how many people are wearing earbuds. Or count how many people have facial hair. The counting is conscious, but it unconsciously teaches you to shift your attention to faces. In the end, the number of glasses, earbuds, or mustaches you count doesn't matter, but the fact that you're looking at human faces matters a lot. This will feel weird at first. Looking directly at people, even if they're not looking back, might seem odd. But keep going. I do this myself when I'm in a crowded subway car, at the mall, or on the playground with my kids after school. When I deliberately look at faces, I feel more grounded and relaxed. It turns my attention outward, which gives me accurate information about what's happening—I'm surrounded by bored commuters, weary shoppers, or energetic kids. As one of my clients, Anthony, exclaimed after we stood on a subway platform for an hour of looking at faces, "But wait, these are just *people!*"

As for Diego, now he looks at faces at the hospital—patients, residents, attendings—not to scan for signs of contempt but in order to pay attention to what they're saying. Instead of focusing inward on his worries and management strategies, he focuses on people and the tasks at hand. As a result of busting the first myth of social anxiety, he's a better doctor, not to mention less anxious.

Even better, by the end of that first year in the hospital, by turning his attention inside out Diego also turned his evaluations around. The residents found him attentive and focused. The attendings wrote that he was observant and responsive. He had mastered taking histories, doing physicals, and yes, performing testicular exams, but he knew the key to being a good doctor wasn't any of those things—instead, it was paying attention to his tasks, not his anxiety.

12

Seeing Is Believing: How You Feel Isn't How You Look

I hate presentations," said Mei as she took a sip of her latte. "I loathe them with the fire of a thousand suns."

It was early spring, and as Mei sat in my office for her first appointment, she told me she was scheduled to give a presentation in August to five hundred people, with two thousand more watching via webcast. Although it was five months away, she was already petrified. "I can't feel like this for months," she said. "I'll die. I will absolutely die." Death sounded like a lousy option. So instead, we busted the second myth of social anxiety: *How I feel is how I look.*

Mei is a director at a footwear company you've definitely heard of. With a pixie haircut and hipster glasses, she looks way cooler than most moms in their early fifties. She is warm and gracious, with a dedication implied by her striding pace and the *venti*-sized Starbucks she carries at all times. She likes her job and the close-knit team she supervises, but whenever she is called upon to present, Mei either begs her co-worker Yaser to take her place or insists on emailing the slide deck around and explaining it by conference call so no one can see her. A couple of times, when there was no other option, Mei called in sick.

Why does a smart, capable woman like Mei turn to Jell-O when faced with a PowerPoint deck? Let's ask Mei: "I just feel like a babbling idiot. I'm worried I'll lose it and that everyone will think I'm an anxious freak."

Mei isn't alone in this. When we're anxious, we think we wear it on our sleeve. No matter our worry—we'll look stupid, seem incompetent, lack personality, or anything else—we assume that it's written all over our face. For Mei, it all boiled down to: "I must look like what I fear."

This second myth is unbelievably common. But why? What's to blame for the idea that how we feel is how we look? For the primary culprit, look no further than your body. To explain, let's take a quick tour through the physiology of anxiety.

All emotions are physical: sadness is heavy and slow; anger is a roiling rush of adrenaline and bared teeth; disgust is a shudder of revulsion. Anxiety? Finely honed by millennia of evolution, all systems work together in service of sending oxygen to your lungs and shunting blood to your large muscle groups, readying you to come out swinging or to turn and flee. The result is the physiological signature of anxiety: Blushing is the dilation of blood vessels. Sweating is a natural consequence of raised body temperature. Shortness of breath and dry mouth are explained by your muscles' increased demand for oxygen and water. Cold hands and feet? Victims of the sudden diversion of blood to your biggest muscles. Shaking hands or lips? Blame the adrenaline that floods the body, leaving us trembling like a revving motor. Muscles get fatigued from being coiled like a spring. And finally, the gastrointestinal system discharges any, uh, extra weight, thus lightening the load so we can run faster or fight more nimbly.

None of this is particularly pleasant. Prolonged anxiety leaves us exhausted, with knots in our shoulders, back, and stomach. Plus, it's hard to think through adrenaline, which makes it difficult to concentrate, think of what to say next, or remember what you were talking about—not exactly the impression you're aiming for during, say, a job interview, a date, or, in Mei's case, a presentation before a packed auditorium.

But it's not just the physical signs of anxiety that trip us up; it's how closely we pay attention to them. You probably know someone who's the exact opposite of the princess in *The Princess and the Pea*—someone who can't tell if she's hungry or has no idea how he got that bruise. On the flip side, you probably also know someone with a remarkably clear sense of their own internal workings. This person may even be you. This awareness of one's own body (or lack thereof) is called *interoceptive awareness*.* Interoceptive awareness, unsurprisingly, is more sensitive in individuals with any kind of anxiety. Indeed, when those of us attuned to our bodies feel ourselves blush, sweat, tremble, stammer, or tear up that's when things start to get all meta and we get anxious about our anxiety. Indeed, if our bodies spark the myth of *how I feel is how I look,* our brains fan the flames.

This happens due to a quirk of thought called the *illusion of transparency,* which is exactly what it sounds like: We think our internal state is visible and will give us away. In normal, nonanxious life, we generally assume that others share our experience.

---

* An easy way of measuring your own interoceptive awareness is try to detect your own heartbeat. You can try it now: sit up straight, scoot forward so your back doesn't rest against anything, put your hands in your lap, and breathe normally. Can you sense it? If you can't, don't despair. Either way is considered normal, but studies have found that folks with social anxiety are particularly accurate at noticing and estimating changes in their heart rate, which suggests a well-practiced ability to monitor their bodies.

Indeed, most of the time people can see what we see, hear what we hear. But in moments of high anxiety, we seem to forget that what goes on inside our bodies and brains is actually private. We feel our heart pounding, our panic rising, our thoughts racing, and think everyone can see through us like a jellyfish. But when reminded, we remember we are not jellyfish. One study even found that simply telling participants that, hey, guys, there's this thing called the illusion of transparency, allowed them to strengthen their un-jellyfish-like spines and give a better speech performance. What's more, when the participants' speeches were viewed, raters agreed, meaning the reminder didn't just lead to feeling better—it led to performing better.

Okay, now it's time for a pop quiz! Is your refrigerator handle on the right or the left? What color was your childhood home? Did Einstein have a mustache? Got your answers? Nice work. To answer these questions, you probably conjured up a picture in your head. You "saw" your fridge, the home you grew up in, and Einstein's mustachioed face. You created and held these images in your mind's eye. Our brains do the same thing when we get anxious, which perpetuates "how I feel is how I look."

When we're stuck in social anxiety, we often see ourselves in our mind's eye. But it's not the reflection we see in our bedroom mirror. Instead, we see our image as if in the funhouse mirror of the House of Social Anxiety. And this awkward image is what we think others see. For example, in high school I was asked to emcee a small talent show at the last minute. To be nice, I agreed, but without time to (over)rehearse, I was frozen onstage, a Cheshire cat–like smile plastered on my face as I "ummmed" my way through the show and tried to appease a bored and disappointed audience. Or at least that's how it felt.

When I truly think about it, I'm pretty sure it wasn't that bad. But when I bring the memory to mind more than twenty years later, I picture myself onstage, as seen from the audience, which, interestingly, *is a view I never actually saw.* I'm "seeing" myself looking lost and scared, as if this is how things actually played out. But the pictures in my head are all my imagination.

On what information am I basing my memory? Remember the *felt sense* from chapter 11? I'm basing it on how I *felt* the show went. I *felt* scared and awkward, so I assume I *looked* scared and awkward. Since I can't travel back in time, I'll never know. But even though it's totally made up, that's how I remember the situation in my mind's eye. And now the view I never even saw has worked its way into my memory.

This tendency to remember our anxious moments in our mind's eye, even if we never saw that perspective, is common. But it's also the key to busting the *how I feel is how I look* myth. So how to do this? Look no further than the phone in your pocket.

A tried-and-true method to replace your imaginary mind's eye movie is to make an actual movie. Have someone you trust make a video of you having a conversation, giving a presentation, or doing whatever it is that sends you into social anxiety. I know, I know: "But I hate watching myself! I hate it even more than listening to my own voice on voicemail!" You may hate this, but the payoff is huge. You can finally see yourself as others see you.

Once you make the video, before you watch, ask yourself what exactly you think you'll see. Close your eyes and form a vivid, internal movie of how you *think* you will look. Will you spout random, incoherent words? Tremble like a Shake Weight? If we ask Mei, she might say, *I'll look stupid, which means I'll pause a lot, jump from topic to topic, say "um" every few words, and have an expression on my face straight out of* Dumb and Dumber.

Then gather your courage and hit "play." For the first few seconds, you will have a visceral reaction—"Is that what I *look like*?" Everyone experiences this—it's totally normal. But then watch as if you were watching a stranger. Watch as objectively as possible and ask if your fears came true. Does *this person* look stupid? Does *this person* jump from topic to topic? How many times did *this person* pause? Taking a neutral perspective allows you to see and hear yourself for real. Chances are that bits of visible anxiety leak out here and there, but not nearly as much as you think. How you feel inside and how you appear outside don't match.

Then watch again and take a look at the other people in the video—your conversation partner, your audience. Find a point in which you remember feeling a surge of anxiety—a mistake, a pause, a point where your mind went blank. Then ask yourself, *Do other people seem to have noticed? Are the other people reacting as if there was a big mistake? If a stranger walked in would they think one of these people looked really odd?* (Probably not.) If it's a conversation, compare each side. *Is the other person pausing and tripping over their words at all?* (Probably a little—welcome to the human race.) But more important, welcome to evidence that how you feel isn't how you look.

When I'm watching videos with a client in my office, sometimes I'll take a screen shot of the moment they felt worst—self-absorbed and brimming with anxiety. Then we'll take another from a moment they felt pretty good—attention focused outward, feeling calmer. We'll put the screen shots side by side. I got this technique (as well as the following picture) from a team at King's College London and the University of Oxford. Take a look. On the left is this gentleman's worst moment during a conversation. He remembers feeling anxious, turning his attention inward, and was sure his face looked weird. On the right,

he reported focusing outward, feeling much less anxious, and that he wasn't thinking at all about his face. What's the difference in how he looks? Exactly nothing. The only difference was in how he felt. Not only did his face not look weird, but also his feelings weren't even visible.

But sometimes people watch their videos and notice they *do* look weird. In the same study, the King's College and Oxford team describes two clients they worked with. One man was worried his colleagues might see his hand shaking while he was drinking a beer, so he turned his back to them each time he took a sip. He thought this was a great way to hide his anxiety until he saw himself on video. He realized it looked odd to turn around with every sip and may have conveyed to everyone at the bar that he wasn't interested in them when the exact opposite was the truth. A woman the team worked with was worried she'd seem stupid, so she ran through a pre-prepared list of topics when she talked with people and mentally monitored how she thought she was coming across. This made her feel better inside. On video, however, she looked like she was giving a lecture rather than listening to what others were saying and responding accordingly. Again, the exact opposite of what she intended. She experimented with listening and just saying what came into her head, which on video, she was pleased to discover, came across as being open and friendly. Bingo.

By the same token, if you see something you don't like—you talk too fast, make no eye contact, wring your hands incessantly—don't panic. All of these are safety behaviors—they're what you're doing to try to save yourself and make yourself less anxious. Remember letting go of the life preserver that keeps you underwater? Once you identify your safety behaviors, you can let them go.

The next time Mei gave a presentation to her group, she asked Yaser to record her with his phone. He emailed it to her, and after locking her office door, she watched it peeking through her fingers, as if it were a horror movie. At first, she cringed. It was so hard to watch herself on camera. *Does my hair really look like that? I say "um" so often!* she thought. But then she remembered what she was supposed to be looking for. She had predicted that she would look like a nervous wreck, a babbling idiot, an anxious freak. She thought she would fidget, move jerkily, spout incoherence. She took a deep breath and tried her best to watch it objectively. *Is* this person *fidgeting? Is* this person *jerking around? Is* this person *speaking incoherently?* But other than thinking, *This person's "umming" is kind of distracting,* she was surprised. She just saw a person, a woman talking about her work and sharing what she knew. She knew how she felt inside during that presentation, but she was astonished to find that how she felt—nervous, babbling, stupid—wasn't at all how she looked. Instead, she just looked a little tense. She paused a few times. At one point, she tripped over her words, but what she remembered as a huge blunder internally was just a blip when viewed from the surface. It reminded her of a nature documentary she once watched—deep-sea volcanoes might erupt on the ocean floor, but the surface hardly shows a burble.

And of course, what happened with Mei's big presentation? With five hundred people in the auditorium and thousands more via webcam, she was nervous beforehand, to be sure, but appropriately so. She didn't call in sick. She didn't beg Yaser to take her place. Beforehand, she imagined herself as she had seen herself on video—a capable woman sharing what she loved about her work—and made that happen onstage. She called me afterwards and told me, with a triumphant sip of her Starbucks, that her talk had been met with applause and congratulations.

The take home? Huge discrepancies exist between how we *think* we look and how we *actually* look. What we imagine in our mind's eye—the funhouse mirror—is distorted. So don't ask your anxiety how you look. Instead, remember that seeing is believing.

BRING IT ON

Jake was running as fast as he could. He pounded away on the treadmill, gasping for air. But he wasn't trying to get fit, lose weight, or train for a race. Instead, he was trying to get his face as red as possible before the end of his lunch break so he could go back to the electronics store and see if his colleagues noticed.

Huh?

I promise this will all make sense shortly. Sometimes we *do* show visible symptoms of anxiety. We do actually blush, sweat, or shake. But in this next myth, we think that everyone will not only see us, but also criticize us harshly. In other words: *people will judge me.*

For Jake, he knew he flushed when he exercised, when he had more than one beer, when he felt embarrassed, and, most important, when he got anxious. He could see it in the mirror, in photos, and sometimes people would comment. In the summer he could blame his blushing on the heat, but in cold weather his story didn't hold up. "Sometimes I turn red, and then I turn redder because I'm embarrassed about turning red, and then I turn even redder because I think people notice me turning red," he said. "It's a disaster."

When he feels the heat start to rise, this is what flashes through Jake's head: *If I blush, I look like I'm hiding something. And then people will think something's wrong with me—that I have a disease or that I'm a pervert.* He was convinced that people would see his blushing and think, *Wow, Jake has* problems.

Has that ever happened? Jake reports: "The worst was once when there were these two teenage girls I was helping at the store and one of them was like, 'What's your problem?' That time I turned purple." For weeks afterwards, Jake hid out in the appliances section, where most customers—especially teenage girls—never ventured.

Here's how the vicious cycle works: first, have a bodily reaction (that part's easy—anyone with a body qualifies), but then, and this is the crucial part, identify the body reaction as shameful. *People will think something's wrong with me if they see my hands shake. It would be horrible if I got dizzy and fainted in public. People will notice my eye twitch and bad stuff will ensue.* For Jake, it was, *If I turn red, everyone will think I have problems.* For the final step, anticipate situations where your body might betray you and try to hide it, like Jake hiding among the vacuum cleaners and toaster ovens to avoid The Reveal. Voila: a perfect recipe for a torturous result.

Some people go to great lengths to try to hide their symptoms. Once I had a client named Jocelyn for whom the cycle started with sweat. She was a big woman who happened to run hot, and she was convinced the beads of sweat on her brow and the spots under her arms would lead people to wonder, with barely concealed expressions of disgust, *What's wrong with* her? She felt self-conscious in public, so she religiously applied prescription-strength antiperspirant, not just to her underarms but also to her forehead, every hour, which took away from her ability to commit to anything for more than sixty minutes. Once she even tried stitching sponges in the underarms of her work uniform, but they bunched and shifted and just made things worse. Managing her sweat had hijacked her attention, her time, and, with it, her life.

Like Jake or Jocelyn, when we get stressed about our bodies our bodies react accordingly, which is the opposite of what we're aiming for. For Jake, he went from blushing because he was stressed to being stressed because he was blushing. It was the *fear* of blushing—and worrying that others would notice and disapprove—that fueled the act of blushing itself.

This myth of inevitable judgment gains great momentum from the *spotlight effect*. The spotlight effect is a phenomenon in which we overestimate the extent to which our actions and appearance are noticed by others. This phenomenon strengthens when we feel particularly exposed or vulnerable. Studies show that whether we're having a bad hair day, wearing a conspicuous T-shirt, screwing up a volleyball game, or sucking at old-school Nintendo (how awesome are these studies?), we consistently overestimate the amount of attention paid to us. When we feel weird, odd, or stupid, our felt sense of others' scrutiny shoots sky-high, but in no case is the social spotlight nearly as bright as we think. This idea isn't new: way back in 1936, in his classic *How to Win Friends and Influence People,* Dale Carnegie wrote that the person you are talking to "is a hundred times more interested in himself and his wants and his problems than he is in you and your problems." We're each at the center of our own worlds, but we forget that every other person is in the same position. The process by which our brains process ambiguity provides the finishing touch for the people-will-judge-me myth. In order to keep ourselves safe, we fill in any ambiguity with the worst-case scenario so we can be prepared and not caught off guard. Consider the following sentences:

Your boss calls you into his office.
People laugh after something you said.
A friend doesn't text you back.
An old friend comments on how you look different now.

Did you immediately assume your boss was going to ream you out about something? Or could it have been that he wanted to compliment you or simply assign you a new project? Were the people laughing because you said something embarrassing? Or funny? Was the non-texting friend mad? Or distracted? And was your old friend throwing some shade your way? Or implying that you looked good?

This is what's happening when Jake senses people looking at him. He assumes the worst—that they see his blushing and think he has some serious problems. So what's the solution? When Jake confided in his friend Charles, his advice wasn't what Jake was hoping for. "I've got one for the ladies," said Charles. "How about this: 'I'm not blushing—you're just so hot I got sunburned.'" Jake rolled his eyes. Being a smart person, Jake's not about to try that one. Like, ever.

Here's where we circle back to Jake on the treadmill. Rather than provide him with one-liners, our goal is to make blushing less of a big deal. Notice I didn't say our goal was to *stop* the blushing. Instead of being afraid to turn red, Jake said to his blushing, "Bring it on." It was time to bust the myth and discover not only do most people not notice, but also noticing doesn't necessarily equal judging.

Over his sessions on the treadmill, Jake became an expert at flushing red. Exercise feels a lot like the pesky sensations of anxiety: a pounding heart, sweating, shortness of breath, and, of course, turning red.[†] Push-ups or a good weight-lifting session can make you shake. Run up and down stairs or knock out some burpees to make your heart pound. Even a good session with a stress ball can make your hands a little trembly, if that's what you're trying to get bored with.

You can get creative, too: breathe through a coffee stirrer to feel light-headed, sit with your head between your knees for a minute and then quickly sit up to feel faint, or spin around in a swivel chair like a five-year-old let loose at Mom's office to get dizzy, all in the service of getting bored with those sensations. I once had a client who, terrified of the tight space and restriction involved in getting a head-and-neck MRI, readied himself by lying on the floor with his head under his bed. When that got boring, he upped the ante by lying under the bed with his head duct-taped to the floor. The only problem was that he neglected to warn his wife about his practice and when she found him taped to the floor she had to be coaxed out of calling 911.

But I digress. The point: your goal is to get accustomed to

---

† Bonus: I've been blown away by the research on the mental health benefits of exercise. Study after study finds that exercise improves depression, PTSD, ADHD, panic—pretty much any challenge you can name. Plus, it's been used to help people quit smoking, sleep better, improve energy, sharpen cognitive functioning, and increase libido. If you could bottle it, you'd make billions. And what do you know? It works for social anxiety, too, not just for pesky sensations or turning red but also to blow off nervous energy. A good workout before any event calms your nerves.

the hijinks of your own body, whether it sweats, trembles, qua-
vers, blushes, or what have you. Remember *exposure* from chapter 10? This is the same thing. "Exposure" is simply the word
for going through your fear, not around it, and realizing not only
is it not so bad, after some practice, it's boring.

After a few treadmill sessions, Jake felt ready to try out the
next step. He powered down the treadmill and headed to the
locker room, where he took a hot shower for good measure and,
as soon as he could throw on his clothes, strode out of the gym
and across the parking lot to the electronics store. It was working—he felt hot and flushed, which, for the first time ever, was
exactly what he wanted.

The automatic doors whooshed open as he entered the store
for his grand showdown with his fear of judgment. He walked
down the aisles, through the home theater section, through the
video games where, on slow days like that one, many of his colleagues hung out. As he walked, he greeted people, trying to
catch their eye. A few said hi. One of his co-workers commented
on the latest Red Sox loss but didn't say a thing about Jake's face.
Jake actually felt a little miffed. All this work to make himself
red—he could tell his legs would be sore tomorrow—and no one
even cared.

I once worked with a client, Leslie, who was worried about
people noticing her pauses in conversation. So we said "bring it
on" to awkward pauses and staged an experiment where she had
a conversation in session with one of my colleagues. Unbeknownst to my colleague, Leslie deliberately trailed off mid-
sentence and left the conversation hanging while she silently
counted off five seconds, then started talking again. In the de-

briefing afterwards, we asked my colleague her reaction. "It was a little odd, but I figured you just lost your train of thought," she said. "To be honest," she admitted sheepishly, "while we were sitting there not talking, I just started thinking about the things I had to do today. I didn't really think about you."

This is typical. Think of the last time you noticed someone who paused, said, "Um," had a strange expression, or an unusual appearance. Were you evil and judgy about it? Probably not. More likely, you just noticed and then moved on. For Jake, even if someone had asked, with a puzzled look, "Are you okay?" Jake could have simply said, "Yeah, I'm good." Not so bad. No judgment, just curiosity.

But what about the teenage girl? After some reflection, Jake realized he didn't even know if she had been referring to his flushing when she asked, "What's your problem?" He wondered if he had been unconsciously trying to hide his face or acting like something was wrong, all of which would have looked sketchy, prompting her question. It might not have been about the redness at all.

But what if it was? Grumpy, judgy people are out there. Heaven knows most of us are related to at least one of them. But if something rude is said, *who is acting inappropriately*? You or them? Even if your worst-case scenario comes true, let's go back to the tried-and-true tool: *How bad would that really be? What are the odds? How would you cope?*

Let's sum up our myth busting: Contrary to the feeling that we're transparent and in the spotlight, our thoughts and bodies usually get overlooked. How we feel isn't how we look, plus even if they do notice, it doesn't necessarily mean they'll judge us. Noticing usually stops with noticing. People only start to wonder when we call undue attention to ourselves by putting sponges in our armpits or hiding behind a display of wine fridges. And as a bonus, if something rude is said it says more about them than you. Being judged does not render the judgers correct.

Importantly, Jake still blushed just as often—his natural physiology didn't change at all. But his *attention* to it changed. After his treadmill experiments, Jake built up the confidence to station himself near the cell phones—the most popular section of the store. Over the next few months, he doubled his commissions and earned a "Rising Star" sales award at the next all-team meeting. As he accepted his certificate, Jake blushed, but this time it was with pride.

13

"I Have to Sound Smart/Funny/Interesting": How Perfectionism Holds Us Back

Rosie stood in a circle of six other conference attendees, growing increasingly quiet as the talk volleyed back and forth above her head. As she picked absently at the name tag stuck to her shirt she thought of things she'd like to say, but by the time she worked it out in her head the topic had changed. She felt her resolve shrinking. When she had walked up and joined this circle, she had felt brave. But now she felt invisible.

So far during the conference, Rosie hadn't felt brave very often. She arrived at presentations just as they started and left as soon as they ended, feeling unable to face the small talk before and after. She worked on her own presentation during lunch breaks. It had been ready for days, but the fiddling made her feel like she was doing something productive while avoiding the lunchtime gatherings. At a networking session for fellow grad students, she approached a couple of groups but immediately felt overwhelmed and intimidated, eventually stealing away under the pretense of going to the bathroom, getting an urgent alert on her phone, or suddenly remembering she had to be somewhere. Worse, Rosie could feel everyone around her connecting—people hugged old colleagues and fell into easy conversation.

She had come to present her graduate work and to network for her next position—maybe a postdoc, maybe an instructorship. She was acutely aware of how few positions there were in academia, so she told herself exactly how she wanted to come off to potential future colleagues: witty and charming, funny but also sensitive, competent and smart, but not overbearing or bossy. It was a tall order, and standing silently in the circle absently shredding her name tag, she felt utterly unable to rise to the occasion. "I remember actually thinking to myself, 'I have no idea how to be a normal person,'" she said, remembering the conference. "I felt that awkward. I was convinced something was wrong with me."

Soon after the conference, Rosie came in for an appointment, asking me to put her through a social boot camp. "I never figured out how to be normal," she said flatly. But there are no social skills deficits in social anxiety (I'll talk more about this in chapter 16), so I knew something else was going on. Rosie talked about the conference, about feeling increasingly dispirited as easy groups formed around her. "It's like not knowing how to speak the local language," she said of her brushes with social anxiety. To compensate, she said, "I'll spend hours planning my approach to something social. But if it doesn't go as planned, I get really mad at myself. I'll analyze things afterwards to see what went wrong so it doesn't happen again. I'm twenty-five. I should really know how to have a conversation, right? So there's really no excuse for making any mistakes. Talking should go smoothly. I shouldn't be offending anyone, make anyone feel bad, and I should be smart, confident, and sensitive. Oh, and witty. I need to be witty. And don't say, 'Be yourself.' I hate that. If I was myself, I'd act all awkward, weird, and pretentious."

Welcome to the stratosphere of perfectionism. No wonder we can't breathe. Here we find the fourth myth of social anxiety: *I have to perform perfectly.* We've crossed a line into unrealistically high standards, rigid and relentless adherence to those standards, and, most important, a belief that one's self-worth is contingent upon the results. Indeed, in a culture that places the standard at "flawless" it's no wonder we're anxious. But "perfectionism" is actually a misnomer. Few of us expect our lives— social or otherwise—to be truly perfect. Instead, perfectionism is about never being good enough.

As Rosie talked about the conference, as well as other social situations she'd found herself in since then (lab meeting, showing a visiting scholar around the lab, and one excruciating bar hop with her classmates), she let the rules she'd been holding herself to slip.

I must always sound intelligent.
I should always have something interesting to say.
There should never be gaps or silences in conversation.
I should always project an air of easy confidence.
I am responsible for keeping my conversation partner interested at all times.
I have to be entertaining.
I have to perform well.
I have to make a good impression.
I must connect with everyone.
People need to like me.
If I am not funny or cool, people will not want to be around me.

Feeling pressured yet? Perfectionists have unrealistic criteria for success and broad criteria for failure. Just listening to her rules made me feel hopelessly inadequate, which made total sense; I'd be hard-pressed to find anyone who could excel under those expectations.

In an illustrative study, leading social anxiety researcher Dr. Stefan Hofmann of Boston University investigated the link between sky-high standards and social anxiety. He and his colleagues asked individuals with and without social anxiety to give a speech (just like making people have five-minute conversations, social anxiety researchers also love making people give speeches). Prior to their speech, all participants watched the same video of a person giving an exemplary speech—smooth, articulate, confident. However, the commentary they got along with the model speech varied greatly. In the high-standards condition, they were told, "Truthfully, most people have performed quite a bit better than the individual in the video that you will now watch." In the low-standards condition, they heard: "Truthfully, most people have not performed quite as well as the individual in the video that you will now watch."

Afterwards, everyone was asked how well they thought their own speech went. Participants without social anxiety thought they did pretty well regardless of what example they had seen. But among participants with social anxiety, the example speech made all the difference: Those in the high-standards condition who thought they had to top a near-perfect speech rated their own speech as an abject failure. But in the low-standards condition, where they had essentially been told that most people sucked and the video was of some overachieving outlier, their opinion of their own speech was indistinguishable from the opinions of the non-anxious group. In other words, when the social standard was low, people with social anxiety thought they did well. When it was high, they assumed they blew it, *regardless of how they actually performed.*

If one side of perfectionism is bookended by sky-high expectations, the other is anchored by lower-than-a-worm beliefs in one's ability. Indeed, Rosie's beliefs about her social skills were as dire as her expectations were outlandish.

I have no social skills.
I don't know how not to be awkward.
I don't know how to behave normally.
I never come across the way I mean.
Something is wrong with me.
I'm a big loser.

This is textbook perfectionism: there's a gap between perceived expectations and your belief in your ability to reach them. The bigger the gap, the more we freak out. Rosie's rules for interaction and her appraisal of her own skills show what psychologists call *dichotomous thinking,* better known as all-or-nothing thinking. No matter what you call it, it means we think if something didn't go perfectly we failed. What's more, we personalize it: if we don't breeze through a conversation with witty, intelligent repartee, we're a total loser.

But we're the only ones who think that, it turns out. It's a little odd to ask friends and acquaintances for feedback, but a study out of Washington University did just that. The researchers asked individuals with and without social anxiety to bring a friend to the study and then asked them both for the honest truth. The pairs of friends were asked to rate the quality of their friendship, how much they liked each other, and more. Overall, the individuals with social anxiety rated *themselves* negatively, but their friends rated them positively, just as positively as the friends of people without social anxiety.

What's going on here? First, we hold ourselves to strict, near-impossible standards but are understanding and compassionate to everyone else. As if that double standard weren't bad enough, we also try to see the best in others, but assume others will see the worst in us. When you think about it, our assumption that others will be judgmental and rejecting is actually quite ungenerous of us.

The most damaging perfectionistic mind-set, however, is when our worth becomes contingent upon our social performance. Anything less than perfect isn't good enough, which in the land of dichotomous thinking lands closer to "totally incompetent." When a perfectionist like Rosie inevitably fails to live up to her unattainable social standards, she takes it personally. "I suck at this; therefore, I suck," is the conclusion.

But for other perfectionists, the conclusion is that everyone else sucks. Case in point: my client Vivian.

Sitting across from me in my office, Vivian grumbled, "Everybody is so judgmental. My generation is so entitled and petty. The world is full of stupid people. I mean, what makes you think you can walk around not contributing to the world?"

The "you" threw me. This was my first meeting with Vivian, who was twenty-four years old, socially anxious, and, as I was learning, very, very angry.

"I don't know how to socialize, and anyway, everyone my age is really back-stabby and immature and superficial. I expected these people to be intelligent and sensitive and mature, but all they do is gossip and back-stab and walk around with this entitlement and arrogance." "These people" were her co-workers. Vivian had just gotten a new job in the fundraising division of a nonprofit. Vivian liked the work well enough; it was meaningful and rewarding. It was the people she hated. She was miserable—she craved acceptance but couldn't stop being judgy and critical. Online was even worse. Whenever she scrolled through Instagram, she couldn't stop herself from leaving cutting little comments on pictures of parties, hikes, or get-togethers. She devalued group pictures because they made her feel so alone. Both online and in person, Vivian knew she was turning people off and alternately felt guilty for being ridiculous, as she called it, and blamed everyone else for being petty, entitled, or stupid. It was like watching a tennis match: guilt, blame, guilt, blame.

As Vivian spoke, sometimes the volume of her rants would rise until she was yelling. That, combined with her tendency to speak in the second person—"You walk around like you deserve to be here. You walk around like you're contributing something to society. Or like you deserve to be alive. Unless you've made a great contribution or you're really worthwhile as a person, you don't deserve to be here"—made me scoot my chair back a little. It took me a few sessions to realize she didn't mean me personally; she was yelling at the world at large.

I left our first meeting reeling a little. After Vivian was on her way down in the elevator, the receptionist motioned me over. "Can you book a room at the end of the hall next time?" she whispered. "We could hear her from the waiting room."

Just like Rosie, Vivian's standards were so high, so rigid, that in her eyes she herself barely made the cut of even deserving to be alive. She had fully bought into the myth of *I have to perform perfectly.* Her anxiety and discomfort ate away at her self-esteem and made her feel worthless. But she saw others, as she said,

"walking around like, 'Of course I deserve to be here,'" which
to Vivian made them seem entitled and arrogant. And that made
her angry, at both herself and others. But in reality, other people
were simply normal. For Vivian, the gap between her ability and
her expectations was huge, not because her abilities were low
but because her expectations were too high. How dare others
have confidence! They weren't struggling nearly as much as
Vivian.

While classic social anxiety might mean hanging back rather
than approaching, taking the long way around so we don't run
into anyone, or refraining from raising our hands, that's not the
only way. Judgment, anger, and hypersensitivity to criticism
don't look like the stereotype of social anxiety; instead of the
wolf in sheep's clothing, it's the sheep in wolf's clothing, baring
fangs when we feel cornered by potential judgment or humiliation. Vivian had it all. She was one of the approximately one
out of five socially anxious individuals whose anxiety manifests
as irritability and anger. Rather than cowering in the corner, she
came out swinging.

The manifestations may be different, but the goals are the
same: Avoid being rejected. Avoid feeling anxious. Be accepted.
There is a fundamental human need to belong. Anger is thought
to be the result of an impeded goal. So if feeling anxious is standing in the way of being accepted, we get royally pissed.

To illustrate, if Rosie, our classically inhibited grad student,
had been invited to a party, she probably would have stayed at
home. For good measure, she probably would have let all her
calls go to voicemail just in case someone called to persuade her
to go. By contrast, Vivian would go to the party, but she would
be overbearing and controlling during her conversations, changing the topic if it didn't suit her and always being the one to
walk away first. She would make snarky comments about other

people and might jump to correct others if they were so unfortunate to get a fact wrong: "No, actually, people use way more than ten percent of their brain—that's just a myth." "I think you mean Labor Day, not Memorial Day." She'd be aggressive and off-putting, but by deciding whom to reject before they could reject her she would feel less anxious, the same result Rosie would have achieved by staying home.

This all makes sense when you think about it. The relationship between rejection and anger is strong. If we're wired to see ambiguous social cues as rejection—a smile as mocking rather than friendly, a lapse in conversation as boredom rather than a pause—our brains will find what we're looking for. The innocuous becomes rejecting. And what does our lizard brain do with a threat? Fight or flight. Hiding in the bathroom stall is flight. But if we think our acceptance is being thwarted, we might get angry. Then it's fight all the way.

But despite frequent *anger experience,* folks prone to social anxiety have less *anger expression* than their non-anxious compadres. Which means what? It means sometimes we suppress our anger. But inevitably, it leaks out, perhaps as hostility, irritability, or passive-aggressiveness. Or it might leak inward, leaving us with GI problems, back or neck pain, or a sore jaw from gritting our teeth.

What to do with all this hot-blooded indignity? Vivian might say, "Outlaw stupid people," but given that we can only change ourselves, we might as well start there.

Let's start with our beliefs. We all carry around beliefs—guiding knowledge and values that we've picked up over the years. They may come overtly from our parents or classmates, or we may absorb them by osmosis from society in general. Some of them are helpful: *If I practice, I usually get better at something, Most people are good,* or *Don't get a tattoo when drunk.* But some beliefs are less helpful, especially when they act as the perfect kindling for a social anxiety fire.

For example:

> *Everyone has to like me.*
> *People will think less of me if I make a mistake.*
> *My happiness depends more on other people than it depends on me.*
> *I can't be happy unless most people I know admire me.*
> *If people saw the real me, they wouldn't want to be around me.*
> *Emotions must be kept under control.*
> *Expressing emotion is a sign of weakness.*

Vivian carried around most of these. But under all the prickles, she knew what was really going on. "People write me off because I don't interact easily with them," she said. "And then I write them off because I'm mad they didn't give me more of a chance. This is not how I want things to be."

Why has social anxiety surged in the past few years, especially among young adults like Rosie and Vivian? Ask a dozen experts and you'll get a dozen answers. One might say our confessional culture has reduced stigma, so people feel safe sharing their anxieties. Another might say helicopter parenting has left millennials unprepared to handle the social interactions of adulthood. There are many answers, but a huge piece of the pie is social media. In Vivian's case, she sees a picture on Instagram of people from work grabbing tacos and beers without her and feels her insecurity (and resentment) rise.

All this social-media-induced social anxiety has less to do with the specific platform—indeed, the MySpace and chat rooms of yesteryear inspired the same anxiety as the apps *du jour*. But no matter the platform, social media is a *performance*. And performance pulls for perfectionistic self-presentation. To be sure, individuals have cultivated a public image since the dawn of time (Ponytailed or curly powdered wig? Fedora or derby?), but now, armed with smartphone cameras and filters, we can manage others' impressions as never before.

In addition, the depth and breadth of access social media allows into one's life is unprecedented. Some choose to present their messy, imperfect lives with more honesty than others, but with a combination of scrutiny and an ability to control our impression management, the pull to present ourselves in just the right light is strong. Indeed, approval is quantitative— your Likes, friends, and followers are enumerated. How-to sites warn: "One photo that doesn't fit with your Instagram feed is all it takes to lose followers forever." It's hard to resist the pull of perfectionism, which beats at the heart of social anxiety. Remember Rosie's internal rules? *Everyone has to like me* has morphed into *Everyone has to Like me. Or follow me. Or retweet me.*

Perfectionism also lies at the heart of another social-media phenomenon so pervasive it was added to *The Oxford English Dictionary* in 2013: fear of missing out, or FOMO. FOMO is "a pervasive apprehension that others might be having rewarding experiences from which one is absent," which may not, at first glance, look particularly perfectionistic. But the result? We feel inadequate, rejected, or that something is wrong with us. And those black-or-white conclusions lie at the heart of perfectionism. For Vivian, scrolling through Instagram late at night, seeing pictures of gatherings she missed—yesterday's homebrew-tasting party, a night out at the hot new bistro downtown—any merry-making felt like an indictment of social failure.

As the concept of FOMO has evolved over the years, it's become apparent that it comes in different flavors. To find yours, ask yourself, "If I *did* miss out, what would that mean about me?"

The first is *I made the wrong decision*. This links right back to perfectionism. The decision in question might be as small as the last restaurant you tried or as big as what career you've chosen, but whatever the decision, it undermines confidence in your judgment. It wasn't the right choice. It wasn't good enough. This type of FOMO feeds the unanswerable, anxiety-provoking phrases of "if only" and "what if?" Indeed, a 2013 study showed that those who experience higher levels of FOMO also reported lower levels of overall life satisfaction.

The next FOMO flavor is *Other people are having a better time than me*. This is essentially envy, which is a mix of inferiority and resentment. This type is closest to what the term "FOMO" actually implies: that you've been left out, either unthinkingly or deliberately by others, or because you weren't in the know, didn't have access, or couldn't muster the guts to go. Regardless, this type links directly back to *I'm not good enough*.

Finally, the last answer to the question "If I did miss out, what would that mean about me?" is *I suck*. Or, for Vivian's version, *They suck*. You get the idea. This screams "perfectionism" and manifests as insecurity.

So what's the cost of FOMO, besides feeling anxious, envious, and insecure? It turns us inward, which also lies at the heart of social anxiety. But when we turn inward, like Diego at the hospital, we miss what's going on around us. And that's the biggest cost of FOMO: *actually* missing out. Hear me out on this one: Pretend you're at home having a perfectly relaxing evening.

But then you check your alerts and updates and find a party you're not at, and your mind stops enjoying and starts comparing. *Did I make the wrong decision? Are they having a better time than me? I suck.* The result? We end up discounting and being distracted from the most important moment: the one we're actually in. Our brains aren't wired for multitasking, so when we toggle back and forth between the present moment and status updates we end up with a series of skips and interruptions—again, actually missing out.

There are two ways for Vivian, or any of us, to resist the pull. First, remember that people put their best foot forward on social media, posting only the highlight reel of their lives. We tend to post when things are going well—vacations, accomplishments, kids doing cute things, photos in which we look hot. No one posts cleaning the cat litter, picking up tampons on sale, or a bad hair day. Everyone experiences these things just as often as you—it's just that those moments aren't on display. Resist comparing their filtered image to your everyday, unfiltered reality.

Another remedy: JOMO, or the joy of missing out. JOMO is the deliberate choice to enjoy the moment one is actually in. Sometimes JOMO is celebrated as an escape—all sweatpants, unwashed hair, and Nutella with a spoon—but it's more about intentionally focusing on wherever you actually are. A constant stream of technological connection makes people crave and value space, so a deliberate decision to stay home with a book, to cuddle with your sweetheart instead of painting the town, or to simply have a cup of tea and go to bed early can be a perfect antidote for the perfectionistic pull of constant social connection.

Now, this is where I have to point out it's easy for avoidance to masquerade as JOMO. We socially anxious types are perfectionists, after all, so it's easy to get into an all-or-nothing mind-set—hit every party or stay at home with the shades drawn. But all-or-nothing isn't the answer to perfectionism.

What is instead? In 1980, Dr. David Burns, now emeritus faculty at Stanford, published the first research-based self-help book for depression, which is now a multimillion-selling classic, *Feeling Good: The New Mood Therapy*. In it, he penned a chapter on perfectionism titled "Dare to Be Average," where he tackled perfectionism using a topic close to Rosie's heart: scientific papers. He writes that, as a young trainee, he took two years to polish his first scientific paper. It was an excellent paper and he's proud of it to this day, but he noticed that his colleagues churned out a lot more papers in those same two years. He reasoned that his first paper was really good, worth ninety-eight "units of excellence." But he reasoned that he could probably churn out ten papers each worth eighty "units of excellence" in the same time period, with a net result of eight hundred units, which would be way better than the mere ninety-eight conferred by his two-year masterpiece.

Rosie, our grad student, ever the scientific mind, jumped at the concept of daring to be average. A black belt in karate, she deliberately put herself through some mediocre workouts. She polled her colleagues about how many times they rehearsed their lab meeting presentations (the average: one or two run-throughs, maybe one more for highly technical slides) and tried to do that herself rather than overpreparing and overrehearsing. But even better, Rosie decided to experiment with having some conversations that met 50 percent of her standards. It was instant relief. She only had to be funny, confident, or smart to a level of 50 percent: "It was like the opposite of Lake Woebegone," she said. "I was *trying* to be average."

What happened? Because she felt less pressure, Rosie acted more naturally, which got a better response from her conversation partners than when she felt so uptight and miserable. She left conversations feeling pretty good, which raised her confidence. Before, when she dove in thinking she was responsible for carrying the exchange and that she had to be witty and smooth at all times, she never reached her goal. By aiming for mediocrity—a few gaps in conversation, carrying some but not all of the interaction, maybe saying something witty, but maybe not—she not only met her goal, but was also willing to try again, which created a virtuous cycle. It was not only more productive— she was racking up a lot of practice—but also way more pleasant.

As for Vivian, it took a lot of practice to talk to herself and others with less anger. The hard-core perfectionist in her thought being hard on herself was more effective. "It's tough love," she protested. But gradually, she was able to see that being so critical was keeping her stuck. Daring to be average was helpful, but so was daring to be kinder to herself. When a co-worker named Anna was friendly to Vivian, at first she told herself Anna must have nothing better to do and must not have many friends. Then she caught herself and allowed herself to think Anna might actually enjoy her company. A few days later, when Vivian had a nice time chatting with a new hire, she figured he must be desperate to meet people but then allowed the thought to sneak in that she could be friendly and likable without being so guarded. And for the first time, she believed it.

Sometimes the highest of standards get you a long way. Many of the most successful people attribute their accomplishments to a touch of perfectionism. But sometimes we find ourselves trying to apply our new knowledge about perfectionism a little too perfectly. One client, Josh, was a chef at a San Francisco restaurant. After I introduced the concept of perfectionism, he returned the next week, flummoxed and angry. "Coming to see you is the worst decision I've made in a long time," he said, to my alarm.

"I'm questioning my high standards. I almost fired a cook after a long line of his screw-ups but then thought maybe I was being too perfectionistic and let him stay. But the next evening that idiot poured out the veal stock I spent two days making. Then I had a meeting with my marketing guy about the branding and direction of the restaurant, and I laid down in front of every idea he had because I thought I was being too perfectionistic." The take home: perfectionism is only a problem if your high standards are *getting in your way*. If a high ideal is working well for you in other areas—in Josh's case, high standards for his restaurant—you're fine. This is the nontoxic version of perfectionism called *positive striving*. As opposed to feeling like a failure after inevitably falling short of perfectionistic standards, positive striving involves high but not unattainable standards, plus the striver feels satisfied and happy when those standards are reached (insert Snoopy-style happy dance here).

Eventually, Rosie was showing up to activities sponsored by her program and even initiated a few get-togethers. But she skipped out on anything that wasn't a movie or dinner. No pub crawls— there might be darts or pool involved. No bowling. And she would rather have died than gone to karaoke. She had worked her way into the periphery of grad school social life, but because she was afraid of making a fool of herself she hadn't ventured to the center. "I didn't want to be the idiot," she said. "I thought meeting people was like a laser maze: one screw-up and alarms would go off all around me."

    This belief isn't new. In the mid-1960s, the psychologist Elliot Aronson tested it in one of my favorite studies of all time. "This is a study about impression formation," participants were told. "You'll be listening to a tape recording of a student trying out for the College Quiz Bowl team." The participant was randomly assigned to listen to one of four tapes. Each tape consisted of the "contestant" answering fifty quiz questions and then talking a bit about himself and his background. The difference? On one tape, the contestant is solid. He answers most of the questions correctly. In another tape, the contestant flounders, answering fewer than a third of the questions correctly. But here's where it gets more interesting: The third and fourth tapes are identical to the first two, except for the very end. There is a sudden clatter, the scraping of a chair, and you hear the contestant exclaim, "Oh my goodness, I've spilled coffee all over my new suit!"

After listening to their assigned tape, participants were asked about their impressions of the contestant. Who was best liked and most respected? The same contestant wins every time: the competent guy who ends up wearing his coffee.

Usually, we assume making mistakes is bad. We go to great lengths to avoid screwing up. But assuming we're generally solid and competent, it actually works the other way.* The blunder has the magical effect of enhancing the attractiveness of the competent contestant. Why? Aronson and his colleagues conclude that the coffee incident made the contestant more human, more approachable. He's still impressive but no longer intimidating. It takes him from being superhuman to human, and therefore more attractive. We like people more when they're imperfect. This is why self-deprecation is so charming and why celebrities who trip on the red carpet come away looking adorable.

No one likes feeling embarrassed, but evolution has us covered. Embarrassment is thought to have evolved as a non-verbal apology and gesture of appeasement—plus it actually fosters trust. People

---

* The very fact that you're worried right now about whether you qualify as solid and competent means you're totally fine.

who are more "embarrassable" are nicer, more trustworthy, and more generous. Remember: social anxiety is a package deal.

Slowly, Vivian learned to go easier on herself, both online and in real life, and as she relaxed her own standards she became more forgiving of others. When Anna invited her and some colleagues to an overly loud restaurant with a serious lack of parking, she let it go rather than complain to the group. Rather than steering the conversation with white knuckles, she tried listening and following the natural flow and found, to her amazement, that she enjoyed herself more. Previously, Vivian felt she had been walking an acceptable social line thin as a tightrope, but as she continued to soften, to her relief, she found the line to be wide and forgiving.

And Rosie? She gathered all her courage and showed up at a bar with pool tables. She reluctantly joined in, hoping no one would notice if she skipped a turn or two. But to her surprise, a lot of other people sucked, too, and those who were skilled didn't care that she wasn't. She didn't have to buy into the myth; she didn't have to perform perfectly. It wasn't even about the pool. Emboldened, a few weekends later she went bowling, threw gutter ball after gutter ball, ended up with a low double-digit score, but had a great time. How many people cared about her bowling score? Exactly zero. But how many people, for the first time, felt happy just being her (imperfect) self? Exactly one: Rosie.

14

Why You Don't Have a Social Skills Problem (You Heard That Right)

Nothing so much prevents our being natural as the desire to seem so.

—FRANÇOIS VI, DUC DE LA ROCHEFOUCAULD,
MAXIMS, 1665

The high cinder-block walls of the brand-new boxing gym were brightened with murals—one wall with a huge logo of the gym, another with the painted likenesses of local boxing champions. Industrial shelving was neatly stacked with physioballs, jump ropes, and boxing gloves of every color. Around the two regulation-sized rings, punching bags hung from the ceiling, waiting to be pummeled. It was a perfectly equipped gym. There was only one problem—it was empty. That is, except for the owner, Derrick.

Derrick came to see me after the gym opened, asking me to put him through a social skills boot camp. And given Derrick's profession, he didn't take the term "boot camp" lightly.

Derrick's father, a local fighting legend back in the day, had owned another boxing gym south of town for the past twenty years. Derrick, who had just turned thirty, described the original gym: "There are world-class fighters training next to students, blue-collar guys, corporate execs, soccer moms, and street punks. It's basically the United Nations of boxing." The new gym was their first attempt at expansion. Derrick's dad put him in charge of the new location.

But Derrick blamed himself for the sparse attendance at the new place. "My dad knows everyone who's anyone. He can talk to anybody. Legend has it a local Mob boss came into the gym when Dad was first starting out, tried to shake him down, and Dad sweet-talked him into a workout." Derrick laughs. "The man's social skills are second to none. He makes Bill Clinton look like a wallflower."

But then Derrick's smile fades. "I didn't inherit that. Don't get me wrong, I love being at the gym—there's an energy. It's in the air. It's just when my mind starts going that everything goes wrong." Derrick explains: "Put me in front of a class and I'm good. I can teach Fighter Basics and Fighter Circuit no problem. I can give a tour to a prospective new member—that's fine. It's when things are unstructured that I get all weird." He drummed his fingers on the table, giving me an eyeful of tattooed forearms the width of my leg.

"I want people to have the best workout experience of their lives at our gym. I want them to walk away saying, 'Wow, that place is amazing.' So I try to talk to people after class, to turn on the charm like I see my dad do all the time, but it never comes out right. I either come on too strong or my mind goes blank. Something is wrong with me. I don't have the right social skills," he concluded. "I have the best mentor in the world, but I just can't seem to make it click. If I could do what my dad does, the new gym would be crawling with people."

It only gets worse when he's out with friends, Derrick adds. His friends will egg him on, tell him to go talk to a girl at a bar. "So I'll go try to introduce myself," he said, "but then I'll second-guess what I wanted to say and back off." He'd try again, but then his mind would go blank. All the indecisive hovering made him worry he looked creepy, which made him question himself even more. "These girls probably think I'm coming over to apologize rather than hit on them." He sighs. "I'm not a huge Tinder fan, but it's better than the bar. I mean, at least you know it's a match."

But the gym was his primary concern. It's his family's legacy; according to Derrick, their reputation is on the line. "I need you to beef up my social skills," he said. "I need a social skills boot camp so I can get some customers. I'm not like my dad. I don't have it in me."

This is important: Derrick assumed the empty gym was the result of his social skills. And indeed, when self-consciousness gets the best of us we may think our empty weekend, empty calendar, or empty bed is the result of our lack of social skills. We think there's some rule we don't know, some magic we're not privy to.

This brings us to the fifth myth: *I have lousy social skills.* Getting sucked into social anxiety makes us say things like "I don't know how to make conversation," "I'm not very good at small talk," "I have nothing to say," "I always end up doing something stupid," or, like Rosie, claim not to know how to be normal. Skill is *part* of the equation, but it's small. There are basic rules that Western culture has created, like greeting with a smile and a firm handshake or, say, not giving unwanted shoulder rubs to female world leaders at a G8 summit. Now, it is possible your skills are underdeveloped due to avoiding social situations. You may be rusty, but you're not hopeless. As with Derrick, it's not *I don't have it in me.* If anything holds you back, it's anxiety, which simply keeps you from accessing your skills.

Think how you behave around those with whom you are comfortable. Are your social skills still lacking? Probably not. As with Derrick, most often the apparent disappearance of our social skills is the fault of the Inner Critic. If you're actively worried about coming across as creepy or weird or awkward or idiotic, the Inner Critic is going to berate you into a lot of false positives. Or, like Derrick (or Rosie or Vivian, for that matter), if you put a lot of pressure on yourself for things to go perfectly, you're guaranteed to feel stifled. Then the resulting inhibition *feels* like you don't have skills. It feels like we have no idea what to do, feels like we have nothing to say, feels like we're going to screw up or do something stupid. But the feeling that we have no social skills is the result of anxiety, not the other way around.*

Having nothing to say or feeling conspicuous is a problem, to be sure, but it's not a skills problem; it's a confidence problem. Interestingly, most people who experience social anxiety actually have excellent social skills, but when we're feeling inhibited we apply them in a way that keeps us from gaining confidence. We might keep other people talking so we don't have to talk. We might deftly steer the conversation so we don't have to talk about ourselves. We ask lots of questions. We act in a way that researchers call *innocuously social*. We nod a lot. We agree. We tend

---

* The difference between social anxiety and social awkwardness is that social anxiety is a distortion perpetuated by the Inner Critic, while social awkwardness is a true (though often correctable) skills deficit. Take away the fear and inhibition, such as with trusted friends or family, and our social skills are totally adequate. For people who are socially awkward, however, there is indeed a mismatch between their ability and society's expectations— it's not a distortion.

For more, see Dr. Ty Tashiro's excellent book *Awkward: The Science of Why We're Socially Awkward and Why That's Awesome.*

not to interrupt. We use what linguists have labeled *back-channel responses* like "uh-huh" or "wow, really?" to show that we're listening and interested. And you know what? *All this requires stellar social skills.* We're masters at reading a group, being agreeable, paying close attention, keeping the peace, and encouraging others to take the lead without their even realizing it.

Even after we think we've screwed up, committed a faux pas, or said something unintentionally offensive, we bring in more good social skills by apologizing or explaining. Lack of such skills would get us in real trouble, which in turn would lead to isolation. Indeed, a 2012 study out of Berkeley found that even though it's uncomfortable to feel embarrassed, it serves a vital social function by acting as a prosocial gesture. In short, we're not poorly socialized; in fact, quite the opposite. Instead, we're simply inhibited. So why does it feel like we have no social skills?

Because I always end up doing something embarrassing, you might say. Or, *I always cause awkward silence.* Or, *People look at me funny and I can't tell whether they didn't hear me or they think I'm an idiot.* Okay, here's what's happening: social anxiety only strikes when there is a fear of judgment, a fear of The Reveal. You're probably open, relaxed, or funny with your partner, your family, or close friends. But with strangers or people you don't know well, you get inhibited and think you have no skills.

And you're not alone: meet Harris.

Harris O'Malley is a self-described geek, but he's not straight out of *The Big Bang Theory*†—he's open, confident, and today happily married. But back in college it was different. Back then, in addi-

---

† Who are nerds anyway, not geeks. Most oversimplified distinction ever: nerds=STEM, geeks=genre fiction.

tion to possessing ready opinions on the semiotics of *Gattaca* and *Dark City* and, as he says, "a Three Wolf Moon T-shirt worn completely without irony," he also held a raging sense of inhibition.

His pigeonhole was "the guy who wasn't good with girls." And for Harris, whenever he was friendzoned or got the "I think of you like a brother" talk, he felt like he was losing a game where he didn't know the rules. One night, frustrated, he concluded he must be doing something wrong. Like Derrick, he decided it must be his skills. He opened his laptop and searched online for "how to get better with girls."

Harris's Google search that night took him on an ill-fated multiyear journey deep into the pickup artist scene. Harris thought it was his social skills that had stymied his love life and assumed "how to" rules would improve them.‡ Instead, it left him vulnerable to a rigid system that viewed women as algorithms at best, targets at worst. "The seduction scene," Harris said, "basically taught me to be manipulative and controlling, and if a woman did something outside the flowchart, something was wrong with her. I had wanted to get better socially, but it was more like really high-pressure sales tactics. It was really toxic."

Fast-forward fifteen years. Today, Harris is the creator of *Paging Dr. NerdLove,* an award-winning blog that manages to be practical, hilarious, and insightful all at once. With the pickup scene long behind him, he dispenses love and dating advice to nerds, geeks, otaku, and gamers "without all of the toxic parts—what works *and* is healthy."

As Harris says as Dr. NerdLove, "Geeks have the worst su-

---

‡ This may sound like playing a role from chapter 8, but it's definitely a false front. The rules and algorithms of the pickup artist scene create a persona with the intention to deceive—the exact opposite of being your authentic self.

perpower in the world—we can anticipate the worst possible outcome to anything. We can tell you exactly how walking up and saying hi to someone is going to end with us going to jail." But it's not just geeks—anyone experiencing social anxiety feels as if their social skills are slipping from their grasp.

And sometimes they do slip-slide away. Our worries become a self-fulfilling prophecy. But it's not just you. It's so common it has a name: *anxiety-induced performance deficits*. This is when, precisely because we're anxious, we start to act oddly. We go blank. We spill our drink. We fall, and not in an adorable Zooey Deschanel kind of way. In a cruel twist of irony, this sets off other people's alarm bells and creates awkward moments.

Because we're sending signals that something's off, it sets off the threat-o-meter of people around us—the lizard brain at its most basic. Whether it's a deer's white tail bounding away, a cloud of ink where the octopus once was, or Derrick or Harris approaching women with a vibe of, *It's okay; I wouldn't want to talk to me, either,* when we send out signals of threat others look at us so they can react accordingly and keep themselves safe. But everyone looking at us at our most awkward is the last thing we wanted, not to mention the thing we most feared.

When we're feeling inhibited, we're already overthinking. We can't access our skills unconsciously anymore, so sometimes we have to remember them consciously. Big asterisk: *you already know how to do all these,* but when we feel intimidated and inhibited we magically forget. Here's a reminder for the next time you feel on the verge of releasing your own cloud of ink.

Eye contact. Aim to make eye contact between one-third and two-thirds of the time you're talking with someone. Less than one-third signals anxiety, avoidance, or submission; more than two-thirds gets too intense. You don't have to drill into them eyeball to eyeball. Connect, look away, reconnect, look away.

Volume. Oddly, speaking too softly is often tied to eye contact. When we're anxious, we often talk to the floor, which directs our voice the wrong way and compresses our vocal cords, muffling whatever we're saying. Instead, if you look the person in the eye they'll likely hear you, too.

Body: Face the same direction as your attention. Point your feet, body, and gaze toward whoever you're speaking with or toward the center of the group.

Approaching an individual or joining a group. As Dr. NerdLove, Harris recommends the Three-Second Rule: when you see someone you'd like to talk to, you have three seconds to approach and say hello. This is especially true for men, for whom silent hovering quickly gets creepy. Saying something within three seconds also works when you join a group: you don't have to contribute the perfect joke or even anything substantial—remember, we're not aiming for perfection. "Hey, how's it going?" or "I couldn't help but eavesdrop," is more than sufficient. Then, once you're in, simply listen. You don't have to say anything more until you're comfortable. But do two things, and you'll feel comfortable much sooner. First, drop your safety behaviors. What are you doing to try to tamp down your anxiety? Are you on the outskirts of the group? Move closer. Are you on your phone? Put it away and look at whoever's speaking. Remember Jia's discovery at the burger counter—you get to set the tone with your behavior. Second, turn your attention inside out. Remember Diego? Shift your attention away from your Inner Critic or your pounding heart and focus on what each person in the group is saying. You don't have to be outgoing; you just have to be curious. After listening through a few rounds of conversation, you may find yourself with a strange urge—the urge to say something. Which leads us to . . .

Breaking in to a conversation. I used to struggle mightily with this. I'd be paying attention, have an idea pop into my head, but be unable to find a lull in the conversation. By the time I did, the topic would have changed or someone else would have verbalized my idea first, leaving me feeling indignant at them and frustrated with myself. It took a long time, but I learned to take a quick intake of breath through my mouth and perk up my comportment a little. This signaled to the group that I was about to say something: open mouth, heightened posture. The first time it worked, I was so startled at all the heads swiveling toward me that I forgot what I was going to say.

When you're feeling like your social skills have evaporated, you can consciously think of these rules, but your goal, as Harris discovered, is to outgrow the rules, not to cling to them.

"But what if I screw up?" you ask. You will. I have. I still do. *Everyone does.* Everyone makes a joke that falls flat or inadvertently gives a compliment that comes off as inappropriate. Everyone holds a hand up for a high five that never gets noticed. We try for one result and get one we didn't intend at all. But it happens to us all. If you accidentally offend, apologize.**

But also remember you don't have to be perfect. Like Rosie

** Harris points out something important: sometimes, *actual* creeps will co-opt the "socially awkward" label as an excuse to step over women's boundaries. Then the fake apology of, "Sorry, I'm socially awkward," is invoked to imply that the woman is overreacting and should allow the infraction, even if it creeps her out. (If you are now wondering if this is you, I can almost guarantee it's not—the very fact that you're worried about it means you don't do this.) Someone who is *actually* socially awkward or socially anxious might cross boundaries by accident, but will almost always realize they made a mistake and will backpedal and apologize. By contrast, a creep will cross the line on purpose and use "I'm socially awkward" as an excuse, assuming his right to let it all hang out is greater than her right to feel safe and trust her instincts. See Harris's excellent full column at www .doctornerdlove.com/socially-awkward-isnt-an-excuse/.

and Vivian, dare to be average. If we wait until we're guaranteed to lob a perfectly timed, wittily incisive comment, we'll probably stand there silently. We're scared of getting a negative reaction or creating an awkward moment, so we don't do anything. So lower your sky-high standards. Aim to say hi rather than waiting to drop a perfectly timed joke. Ask two questions rather than waiting until you've thought up a clever monologue. Listen with 51 percent genuine curiosity to whatever's being said.

Ever been stuck in a room with a young man reeking of too much cologne? Here's why: The final reason we know anxiety is a confidence issue, not a skills issue, is because of the placebo effect. A study out of the University of Liverpool found that using a scented spray, as opposed to an unscented control spray, makes heterosexual young men act more confidently. In an ingenious design, the researchers demonstrated that sprayed-on confidence spilled over into behavior.

In the study, each man first had his photograph taken and then made a short fifteen-second video imagining he was introducing himself to an attractive woman. Heterosexual female raters were recruited to judge the pictures and videos on attractiveness but were not told whether the men were using the scented or unscented spray. In the photographs, the women found no differences in attractiveness between the fragrance-using and non-fragrance-using men. But on video, the women judged the fragrance-using men as more attractive, *even though they couldn't smell them,* suggesting a difference in the men's *behavior* rendered them more attractive. Call it the AXE Effect. Indeed, that stuff makes my eyes water, but the placebo effect it has on teenage boys is why AXE, which promises to "help make the right first impression," is a multibillion-dollar brand that dominates the market. A fragrance doesn't magically confer attractiveness. Those young men in the study had skills all along. The placebo effect just gave them the confidence to put their skills to use.

To sum up, when we feel awkward we're quick to blame our skills. And while sometimes our skills seem to escape us, it's inhibition that gets in our way, but that can be changed. In an old study from 1976, researchers asked forty socially anxious undergrads to role-play situations where they had to be assertive, like asking for a raise or requesting a neighbor turn down their stereo. Half the participants were instructed to respond as they would in real life, while the other half were asked to respond as assertively as they believed the most assertive person would. (Stage whisper: *Hey, that sounds like playing a role from chapter 8.*) Participants were able to improve their performance on demand, turning their assertiveness up and down like a dimmer switch.

Again, counter to the myth of *I have lousy social skills,* we don't need more skills, we just need less inhibition. But guess what? You already know what to do to lower your inhibition: Like the assertive study participants, play a role—give yourself a mission. Dare to be average. Fake it until you *are* it. And finally, drop your safety behaviors. Step away from the body spray.

Looking back, Derrick realized the new gym wasn't full on opening day for the simple reason that businesses don't get up to speed overnight. After a while, he also realized business success wasn't just a cult of personality, as he had assumed. His father's success wasn't due only to his social skills. Instead, it was a combination of location, marketing, hard work, time, and luck. The problem wasn't Derrick's social skills at all. If anything held him back, it was his anxiety, which kept him from accessing his skills.

A year or so after the empty opening, Derrick surveyed

the no-longer-new gym one Saturday morning. The place was packed. Guys in long athletic shorts drubbed the punching bags. Two blond women, one with pink gloves, sparred nearby. A dozen people gathered in the central ring for the start of a fundamentals class. The kids' class Derrick had started was under way. The kids' program was Derrick's pride and joy. "Shy kids learn confidence. Cocky kids learn to tone it down. There's a wait list for this class." Just then a prospective member walked up to the desk, and Derrick went over to greet him. Derrick didn't try to be his father. He didn't try to have someone else's skills. He could be himself. As Derrick discovered, he already had it in him.

15

The Myth of Hope in a Bottle

Many of us find another way to feel less awkward and less inhibited. Someone really did bottle it, and it really does make billions. It's liquid courage, survival juice, awesome water. Indeed, for the socially anxious among us, alcohol has many names and, surprisingly, just as many functions. It's not just a way to feel less inhibited ("Hey, whiskey says I can dance!") or less awkward ("Must. Grip. Beer bottle. For dear life!"). While the science of the complex relationship between social anxiety and alcohol is still emerging, I've encountered at least four types of socially anxious drinkers.

Let's call the first the Pre-Gamer. Meet my client Nia. She's an administrative assistant with a wide smile. She can handle pretty much anything as "office manager Nia," but if she has to show up somewhere as "just plain Nia," like a party or a fundraiser, she needs a drink or two to steady her nerves. "It's cliché," she says, rolling her eyes at herself, "but it really does take the edge off." Nia wouldn't be caught dead with an actual flask, but she's been known to fill an empty water bottle with a couple of shots of vodka and stow it in her purse. When she gets to an event, she'll park her car, slug the vodka down, wait a few minutes, then head in. "It works right when I need it," she says, "arrival and settling in."

Then there's Mateo, a boat salesman who loves nothing more than being out on the water. We'll call him the After-Drinker. He dreads going to trade shows and networking events, but they're all inescapable parts of his job. He always feels awkward at events and tries his best, as he says, "to act like a normal human being," but gets stuck afterwards in post-event processing. He can't help but play interactions over in his head, focusing on jokes that fell flat or the things he wishes he had said or done differently. "I dwell," Mateo says simply. He doesn't drink much, if at all, at events, but when he gets home he'll open beer after beer, trying to drown out his own ruminating. "Basically, I drink when I'm kicking myself," he says.

Then there's David, the Supersized Social Drinker, who manages a food service warehouse. He's not much of a drinker, except on the rare occasions when his friends manage to drag him out. Inevitably, he ends up drinking way more than he knows is good for him. "My friends say I'm a unicorn: I'm both a lightweight and a party animal," he says. "I get really, really social. I admit it's fun, except for the hangover. I probably wouldn't have a social life at all if not for Jack and Cokes. I know that's lame, but if there's no booze, I don't go. If I can't drink, I can't be social."

But not everyone with social anxiety uses alcohol to manage feeling judged. Sometimes our social anxiety makes us so afraid we'll be judged that we don't trust ourselves to drink at all. Take Karla, a student going for her master's in education. Call her an Almost Abstainer. Typically, she doesn't drink any alcohol. "I wouldn't want to do anything stupid," she says. "I'm just afraid I'd end up all staggerific." At parties or weddings, she says, "I'll walk around with a drink, but it's mostly a prop." If she's feeling really safe or really daring, "I might sip it, but I can make one drink last for hours. I used to not drink at all—I didn't touch a drop until I was twenty-two and almost done with college." And now? "I still only drink light stuff—wine spritzers, stuff like that. I don't like the idea of losing control and saying or doing something I'll regret."

The takeaway? If social anxiety and alcohol updated their relationship status, it would definitely be "It's Complicated."

Indeed, one study found that individuals with higher social anxiety consume *less* alcohol than folks who aren't anxious, but have *higher* levels of hazardous drinking. Huh? We also have more of what the researchers called alcohol-related negative consequences, like missing work, getting injured, and having unwanted sexual experiences. It's counterintuitive, but here's how it makes sense: Those who get socially anxious often avoid social situations like parties or get-togethers. But when they're forced to go, like David, they may drink relatively more in an attempt to "self-medicate" but have lower tolerance and less practice pacing themselves.

If you're one of the seven in ten Americans who have had a drink in the past year (which means that three out of ten haven't—millions of people are on your side if you choose not to drink), to paraphrase the great philosopher Homer Simpson, alcohol can be not only the solution to but also the cause of your social anxiety problems. Why both? On the one hand, alcohol "works," at least in the short term. One study found that for every drink, social anxiety declines by 4 percent. It's an easy way to magically feel more fabulous. Two glasses of pinot for an 8 percent reduction of feeling like a fool? Sign me up.

But over the long term, it can be a different story. First, while drinking may take away social anxiety, over time many people start to drink *in response* to social anxiety. Indeed, another study found that in individuals with both social anxiety and a problem with alcohol the social anxiety almost always came first. Second, folks experiencing social anxiety are more likely to drink alone to drown out negative emotion, like Mateo ruminating into his beer as he kicks himself. Finally, we might associate alcohol and confidence, like Nia and her parking lot swigs. We listen when vodka makes the promise: *I alone can make you a good conversationalist!* Any way you slice it, capital-S Social Anxiety Disorder more than quadruples the risk of developing an alcohol use disorder.

Why do we keep looking for hope in a bottle? Remember the perceived gap between standards and ability: we simultaneously think that social expectations are sky-high ("I must always have something interesting to say," "I should hit it off with this guy right away") and that we are too hopelessly awkward, weird, or inept to ever reach those standards. Alcohol then artificially closes the gap. Herein lies the final myth of social anxiety: *I need alcohol to feel comfortable.* Sure, alcohol makes us less inhibited, but then it steals the credit for conferring social skills. We don't realize we had those skills all along and were just too inhibited to use them. Alcohol becomes like Dumbo's magic feather; take it away and we only think we can't fly.

So tone down your sky-high standards, thank the Inner Critic for trying to keep you safe, but then challenge it and be kind to yourself. Turn your attention outward and tune into conversation rather than letting your internal dialogue drown it out. Be brave and go over the mountain. In short, instead of giving all the credit to liquid courage, nurture your own courage. Raise a glass because you *want* to, not because you *need* to. And that's way better than any awesome water.

PART 5

All You Have to Be Is Kind

16

The Building Blocks of Beautiful Friendships (They're Not What You Think)

It is a luxury to be understood.

—RALPH WALDO EMERSON

Maddy turned the key and opened the door to her apartment, where another long evening stretched before her. She felt deflated. She was a year into living in San Jose, having moved there from her tiny hometown in the Sierra Nevada. Jobs were scarce there, so when she got an offer to manage payroll for a shipping company in San Jose she took the chance, even though she didn't know a soul in the city. Overall, the move had been a success. The only problem, according to Maddy, was that she had yet to make any friends.

"It's been a year," she said to me. "Everyone at home said to give it a year, that it takes time to get to know people, but I don't think it's supposed to be *this* slow. I know I have some bad habits: after work, I mostly just stay in, get online, watch TV. I'm scared to put myself out there. Everyone said I was brave to move here, but now I'm wondering if it was stupid." She blinked back tears. "Why can't I find people I can connect with?" she said. "It's embarrassing, but I even Googled 'how to make friends' and everything just says to go to meetups or join a book club. Or volunteer. *Everything* says to volunteer. I'm not an idiot. I know that stuff. And that's not it. I can find a book club. It's walking into the book club and trying to think of things to say for an hour that's hard. What am I supposed to *say* to these people? I run out of things to say after, 'Hi, I'm Maddy.'"

Nora, by contrast, knows lots of people. Nora is a stay-at-home mom with two kids and knows all the other moms by name from school, scouts, or soccer. She waves and says hi, exchanges small talk, and though the other moms are friendly, Nora notices they're a bit formal with her, unsure of how to respond. "No one knows me," Nora says. "I'm always the person who is the last to meet everyone. People always say, 'Oh, I didn't realize you didn't know each other.' I know a lot of people on a shallow, acquaintance level, and I have a couple of close friends, but I'd like to branch out. I have lots of friends on Facebook, but I know that's not real. The only person I'd really be okay confiding in is my husband. I'm always the outsider, and I'm not sure exactly how that happens. I see people talking easily about random stuff, and it's such a mystery. I'm not sure how to get to that point."

Even without social anxiety, making friends as an adult is hard. A meta-analysis of 177,000 participants in the prestigious journal *Psychological Bulletin* found that social circles expand until early adulthood and then shrink from there. Back in 2006, a large-scale survey found that more than half (53 percent) of Americans didn't have any confidants who weren't family. A quarter of American adults—one in four—had no confidants at all. Over ten years later, I'd be willing to bet the percentage has crept even higher.

Mix social anxiety with other challenges, like Maddy's moving to a new city, the dispersion of graduation, getting clean or sober, going through an upheaval like divorce, or simply realizing you've had your nose to the grindstone so long that everyone has drifted away, and it can feel like you have to start from scratch but have no idea how this game works.

And you'd think that with so many people feeling isolated, like Maddy and Nora, everyone would be talking about it. But no one does. There's a stigma to admitting you have no friends. Or that you're lonely. To make matters worse, if you look for advice on how to make friends, like Maddy, you usually end up with a list of places to meet people. But that's not what you're looking for. "Meeting people" is really different from "making friends." One is an event; the other is a process. When Maddy searches for "how to make friends," the answer she's looking for is not "volunteer at an animal shelter." She's looking for the answer to, "What do I do once we've shaken hands and exchanged names? Now what?"

Maddy and Nora, respectively, have two problems common in social anxiety: either we feel like we don't know anyone or we know enough people but don't feel close to them. Either way, we often think, "What's wrong with me?" Nothing's wrong with you, but social anxiety magically confers filters that are getting in your way.

Sometimes it's our presumptions: we unconsciously create too stringent a filter and rule out too many people. It might be demographic: *Oh, she's married/single—that's not going to work.* It might be perception: *Oh, she's so busy—that's not going to work,* or, *She probably has a lot of friends already—that's not going to work.* Or we might just have a low tolerance for ambiguity: if she's not 100 percent unambiguously welcoming, we rule her out—*that's not going to work.*

Sometimes it's our expectations. Remember the perfectionism chapter? Those of us prone to social anxiety tend to look for an instant, capital-*F* Friend. Without even realizing it, we're looking for a ready-made BFF with whom we feel connected right away. We wish we could walk into an event and walk out arm in arm with a new buddy (or two!). But on this planet, that rarely happens.

Social anxiety tells us we should find friends instantly. The semantics are subtle, but telling. Social anxiety tells us to *find* a friend—to win someone over right away—but real friends must be *made.* Friendship is a process, not a ready-made discovery. But that's actually good news. Rather than searching for a diamond in the rough, it turns out the rough contains scores of potential friends. The raw stuff, the stardust that transforms into friends, is everywhere. Almost everyone is a candidate. Oddly, to make a friend, you don't need the "right" person. *Instead, the person becomes right over time.*

So how does this work? If friends aren't found, hunter-gatherer-style, but instead are cultivated, like advanced agriculture, how do we do this?

Here's where to start: Is someone friendly to you? Great, they're in. This is the only bar. You're not friends yet, but you're friendly with each other. Some of your friend candidates will stay at this level, but three things will move others toward friendship.

REPETITION

The first is simply seeing someone over and over again. This seems obvious, but as recently as the late 1940s it was thought that people made friends the Freudian way: that is, drawn together by a mystical intermingling of subconscious childhood memory. But three professors at the Massachusetts Institute of Technology, chief among them the pioneering social psychologist Leon Festinger, changed that in a fundamental way. In 1946, a tidal wave of World War II veterans enrolled at MIT. Seemingly overnight, some three thousand of the university's five thousand students were vets. Many, having put their education on hold to fight in the war, were at a different life stage than their fellow students. Many were married, some had kids, and MIT scrambled to accommodate them in the hastily constructed temporary housing community of Westgate West on the far western edge of campus. In total, 180 temporary apartments—two-story structures with front doors that opened to outdoor walkways, like a Motel 6—were constructed from surplus military barracks. The sidewalks outside the buildings were unpaved, the accommodations bare bones. This being MIT, however, people got creative in order to improve their apartments: one father, a mechanical engineering major, created a device out of old washing machine parts that rocked his baby's crib and, to the dismay of the neighbors, thumped and thwacked into the night.

But in addition to being creative, people were friendly, too. And it was into this environment that Festinger and his colleagues strode with a research question: Who was friends with whom? They asked residents to name their three closest friends, curious to learn if they shared beliefs, interests, attitudes, or childhood experiences. The answer, the team discovered, was much less glamorous. Far from sharing fundamental commonalities, friends often shared nothing more than a hallway. Proximity was the biggest predictor of friendship: next-door neighbors were most likely to be friends. People who lived on either end of the first floor, at the foot of the stairwells, were downright popular, presumably because everyone on the second floor had to pass by their apartment multiple times a day. At first, Festinger and his team thought proximity was the key. But proximity, they realized, was a proxy for something else: repetition. We tend to make friends with the people we see most often. Repeated contacts, like seeing your neighbors coming home with the kids, headed to the market, or on the way to mechanical engineering class, are the foundation of friendship.

In 1957, just over ten years after its construction, Westgate West was systematically emptied and demolished to create permanent housing, but the discovery the housing complex revealed lives on. Additional studies confirmed the effect, such as one where forty-four state police trainees reported their best friends were those who fell closest to them in alphabetical order of seating. We can make friends with almost anyone. Provided our potential friend is not mean-spirited, given time and repeated encounters, we can—and do—become friends with whoever's around.

So how does this apply to Maddy? To have a shot at making friends, the specific activity is almost beside the point. It's less about what or where than about *how often* and *whom*. To have the best shot at friendship, she needs to see a steady drumbeat of the same faces—*the same people, regularly*. That rules out most come-and-go situations like the gym but rules in specific gym classes where the same core people show up every week. It rules out onetime events or drop-in meetups where the people change constantly but rules in, say, dog parks at a consistent time of day. Classes can work, but only if they're interactive, like tango or a writer's workshop, not lecture-style. Forget about social media, bars, or clubs—here people bring the friends they already have and hang out together—the group is closed unless you're trying to pick someone up. When you're starting out, the best strategy is to join a ready-made community open to others: an ultimate frisbee team, a running group, a bike polo team, a choral group, community theater, a church group, and yes, a book club. In my case, preschool co-ops have twice jump-started my social life after cross-country moves.

And then? Keep showing up. Give any new social endeavor at least a season, or around three or four months, but longer is better. Lore has it that it takes six to eight conversations (not just "hi") before people consider each other a friend.

But to start, remember your only criterion: Is this person nice to me? If they grunt and stare at their phone when you say hi, then no. But if you get a smile and some basic small talk? You have a candidate. They're not going to invite you over for din-ner . . . yet. But don't stop saying hi simply because one conver-sation didn't lead to binge-watching old seasons of *Louie* together on your couch. Remember, friendship is fostered, not found.

So keep showing up. You may not be taken seriously until you've come back a few times—especially if it's a public group, they probably get a lot of one-and-dones. Distinguish yourself by showing up again and again.

Then, once you've established yourself, a well-kept secret is to take on a leadership role. Remember chapter 8? Playing a role is a blessing for the shy among us because it requires less social improvising. You'll have a set of duties and a reason to connect with everyone, even if it's just to remind them about the holiday party or encourage them to donate to the food drive.

After we discussed this, Maddy was equally fired up and frightened. She bought what I was saying about repetition but was scared. She offered that three of her female co-workers often ate lunch together in the breakroom. Usually, Maddy would eat at her desk or in her car. The setup was too good to pass up: same people, pretty much every day. They were cordial already, which, again, is the only bar.

How to approach the group was a question. Maddy dreaded what she called the "Hi, Guys" Hover, so we decided to have her get to lunch first and let the group join around her. At first, Maddy felt awkward—she didn't know the context of anything they were talking about, but she stuck it out anyway, just listening, nodding, and, to her surprise, laughing along a couple of times. She kept reminding herself—*they're friendly, they're friendly.* Before she actually sat at the table with them, Maddy realized, she had ruled them out as potential friends because two were older and one was an intern. She had thought she needed more commonality in a friend—someone her age, with her background. Looking back, she also realized she had been dying for someone else to initiate, but they all thought she just wanted to keep to herself. It was basically a big, silent miscommunication on both sides.

Maddy wasn't sure if joining lunch that first time had gone well or not, but later that night she got a Facebook friend request from one of them. "There's still a long way to go, and I'm not sure if we'll end up capital-*F* friends or not, but this isn't a bad start," Maddy reported.

Remember, if they're friendly, they're in. Think of everyone you're friendly with or could be friendly with. There. I bet you just broadened your social life substantially.

GIVE THEM SOMETHING TO WORK WITH

Next comes disclosure. This is the second step for Maddy but the first for people like Nora, who are stuck in limbo between acquaintances and friends. Like Nora, many of us have a collection of half-baked friendships and people we are friendly with, but we can't seem to get beyond that.

Sometimes this is the result of the perfectionist rearing its head again: "Nobody seems interested—everyone is so busy with life and kids and everything," Nora says. Without really realizing it, Nora is waiting for someone to seem "interested," meaning someone who unambiguously approaches her. Nora wants certainty. Without realizing it, she wants the potential friend to initiate interesting, easy conversation and invite her to do things. But because she's waiting for a friendship that materializes into clear, sharp focus, she inadvertently screens out everyone else. Despite having halfway-there friends all around her, she thinks she has to start from scratch.

How to take it to the next level? To jargonize it, we use *disclosure,* which simply means sharing what we think, do, and feel with others. This seems easy enough, but it's not intuitive. Folks susceptible to social anxiety don't often talk about themselves. We're polite and pleasant, but others often get the impression we're distant, formal, or otherwise keep the world at arm's length.

Disclosure got a lot of press when the "36 Questions to Fall in Love" phenomenon made the rounds of the interweb. Much has been made about this list of questions, with online articles like, "I Asked a Stranger These 36 Questions to See If We'd Fall in Love. And We Did," and an essay in the *New York Times* titled "To Fall in Love with Anyone, Do This." It sounded like a silver bullet for the lovelorn.

But the real story is actually quite clinical, which makes it that much more amazing. More than twenty years ago, in 1997, psychologists Arthur and Elaine Aron, and a handful of colleagues from around the country published a paper with an innocuously dry title: "The Experimental Generation of Interpersonal Closeness: A Procedure and Some Preliminary Findings." The procedure consisted of turning strangers into intimates in the laboratory by having them ask each other three sets of twelve questions. Each set became more probing and personal as they advanced. Set One included questions like, "For what in your life do you feel most grateful?" and, "Do you have a secret hunch about how you will die?" Set Two goes a bit deeper: "Is there something that you've dreamed of doing for a long time? Why haven't you done it?" and, "How close and warm is your family? Do you feel your childhood was happier than most other people's?" Set Three ups the ante again, with questions like, "Tell your partner what you like about them; be very honest this time, saying things that you might not say to someone you've just met," and, "Share a personal problem and ask your partner's advice on how he or she might handle it. Also, ask your part-ner to reflect back to you how you seem to be feeling about the problem you have chosen."

But the protocol wasn't meant to make people fall in love; instead, the thirty-six questions were simply meant to induce closeness and intimacy in a laboratory setting without the mess-iness of relationships that occur naturally in the wilds of human-kind. The questions were meant to eliminate experimental variability, not induce wedding bells, though the study team got an inkling of the power of the thirty-six questions when two subjects who had met during the study pilot ended up getting married.

Twenty years later, when the media caught wind of the

questions, it treated them like they were a secret recipe for love. But the specific questions aren't magic; instead, according to the researchers, it's the act of "sustained, escalating, reciprocal, and personalistic" disclosure that sparks liking the other person and, indeed, sparks them to like us. The thirty-six questions lead to closeness through disclosure in fast-forward.

Usually what we do when we meet someone new is small talk. Small talk is important—it's the social niceties test-track of conversation—but by definition, it stays on the surface. It's not about you; it's about other things—traffic, the weather, that your co-worker Darren is out sick and there must be Something Going Around. Disclosure, however, is about *you*. Again, it means sharing bits of what you think and do and feel. Any topic is game. Even banal small talk can be tweaked to become a disclosure. For example, talking about the weather can be a disclosure—you're happy that it's getting cooler because fall is your favorite season. Or when you were younger you used to love summer, but now you don't deal with the heat as well. Or when you were a kid, every time it rained, you and your brother would "rescue" all the worms that came out on the sidewalk and bring them home in a jar, much to the chagrin of your mother. There. You're still talking about the weather, but you're also offering up a little tidbit about yourself, which can serve as the launchpad of conversation.

When I work with the Maddys and Noras of the world about disclosure, the next question is, inevitably, "But what do I talk about?" But that's not actually their question. Just like Maddy doesn't want to be told to volunteer, she doesn't need a list of possible topics. The real question is, "How do I think through the paralyzing anxiety and come up with something that doesn't sound totally stupid?"

The answer is, yet again, to lower the bar. We think we have to be interesting, entertaining, or effortless. But that's too much pressure. Indeed, if you tell yourself you are not allowed to say anything totally stupid you won't say anything. So start with what you're doing or thinking. Say hi, ask how they are, and share some tidbit about what you're doing, what you just did, what you're planning, or what you've been thinking about recently. It doesn't have to be smart, insightful, or articulate—it just has to be about you.

Think of it this way: Remember when Facebook was new-ish? Circa 2007, Facebook prompted its users to update their status by asking: "What are you doing right now?" Circa 2009, it shifted to "What's on your mind?" Start there. "I'm fine, thanks. We're going to see my in-laws this weekend." Or, "I'm fine, thanks. I've been mulling over whether or not to take adult piano lessons." Or, "I'm fine, thanks. I've been craving barbecue for a few days. Where's your favorite place around here?" Whatever you say doesn't have to be earth-shattering—the only criterion is that it should reveal a tiny tidbit about you. "I rode my bike here and it was so much faster than sitting in traffic." "I have to buy a birthday present for my niece and I'm not sure what to get her." "Ugh, I have a song that was playing at the gas station stuck in my head."

This will feel wrong at first. It will feel like you're talking too much. It will feel selfish, like you're taking up too much space or making it about you. But this is only because you are comparing it to being reticent. Try it and see what happens. Sometimes you'll get a lame answer, "Yeah, that's cool," or, "Oh, really?" And then . . . nothing. A conversational tumbleweed will roll by. But that's fine—a lot of conversations are lame, but here's the thing: a lame conversation doesn't mean *you're* lame. Other times, you'll get a relatively substantial answer, and then you're off to the conversational races.

Too many of us have been told we're "too quiet" or that we need to speak up more. We've heard it over and over again, and it always sounds like a critique, as if something is wrong with us. Thankfully, the introvert movement has validated and empowered all of us quiet types. But stretch. If someone starts a conversation with you, gently encourage yourself to disclose a little more than usual. It's tempting to respond to, "Do you have any siblings?" with simply, "Yes, one younger brother," but stretch it to, "Yes, one younger brother, but we were five years apart, so by the time I went to college he was still in middle school and every time I came home I felt like I had to get to know him again. Now that we're both grown-ups we're buddies. He's an ER doc in Minneapolis." Likewise, the answer to "Where are you from?" can shift from, "Houston," to, "Houston, but I haven't lived there in twenty years. Though I've gone back a couple of times for the rodeo." Then? Do something you're already good at: listen. Turn your attention inside out.

Ultimately, the goal of conversation is intimacy. "Intimacy" is a word that often has sexual overtones, like "intimate apparel" or, worse, "intimate dryness," but it doesn't have to. It comes from the Latin meaning "inmost," as in sharing what is inmost—what you think and do and feel—with others.

The only note of caution is that *disclosure* is different from *confession*. In the thirty-six questions paper, the researchers define disclosure as "escalating and reciprocal," meaning that telling someone about yourself should be a gradual give-and-take. Once, at a bridal shower, I met a friend of the bride. I introduced myself, shook her hand, and before I said another word she told me she was pregnant through a sperm donor and that to prepare for the birth her doula had told her to soak a thong in vitamin E oil and hike it up to her perineum so she wouldn't tear. I wasn't sure what to say to her for the rest of the shower—I kept squirming at the mental image of her oily wedgie. I'm no prude, but as a first conversation her revelations were a tad overwhelming.

More seriously, I once had a client who would disclose in her first conversations that she had been abused as a child and had twice been raped. It was too heavy, too fast, and she was crushed when people steered clear afterwards. She thought she was speaking her truth, but as we collaboratively decided, other people couldn't handle her full truth right away. There were other truths that made up who she was and she could share those first, saving the deeper truths for later.

As for Maddy, she realized book clubs might be easier if she gave people more to work with besides, "Hi, I'm Maddy." At the first meeting, she told me, after she introduced herself in the opening go-around she had remained silent and looked largely at the floor, equally hoping that someone would talk to her and that everyone would leave her alone. Turns out a woman had approached her afterwards to see how she liked the group. Maddy had said, "It was great, thanks," with a smile but left it at that. The woman took Maddy's cue and said, "Great, hope you'll join us again," and then moved on. Social anxiety makes us masters of ending conversations. It's easy: a certain tone of finality, saying hi but not stopping to chat, or simply not saying anything more sends the message that we don't want to talk. Ending conversation is another safety behavior—we're trying to save ourselves from the anxiety. But we trade the anxiety of the moment for loneliness in the long run.

Maddy went back to the book club determined to try something new. She knew victory was not in how she felt; instead, it was in her actions: looking at people, disclosing, listening, and responding. The same woman approached and asked how she liked the book, so Maddy took a deep breath and gave her a little more to work with. "It was great, thanks. I was actually surprised at how much I liked the book—I'm not usually a genre fiction fan. I usually go for big intergenerational sagas." A short chat ensued, plus an exchange of recommendations. It wasn't a deep heart-to-heart. The earth didn't shake (though Maddy's knees did), but to Maddy it was the opening to a new world. To be sure, one conversation is a drop in the bucket, but disclosure by disclosure, conversation by conversation, over time and practice, the drops fill the bucket.

And what about Nora? She decided to combine showing up with disclosure. The next day, she surprised her daughter by suggesting they hang out at the playground after school rather than heading straight home, a change in routine that rendered Nora momentarily unable to breathe. She spotted a few women she knew, but felt overwhelmed by trying to join a group. Nora almost faked having to run an errand, looking for an excuse to leave. But then her daughter asked Nora to push her on the swings and another mom was there as well, pushing away. Nora said hi and blurted out that she was wondering at what age kids learn to pump on the swings. A conversation about developmental milestones left Nora in a sweat and her nervous energy made her push her happily squealing daughter higher than ever before, but she had a long conversation. When I saw her next, she said Neil Armstrong's moon landing quote rang through her head for the rest of that afternoon.

When you're first getting started, expect some false starts. We all get a little weird and desperate when we're lonely. If you're out of practice, you become less and less confident that you even know how to talk, much less form full sentences to which another human can respond. Worse, we also start interpreting everyone as threatening, every smile as scornful, every interaction as rejecting. But then we make it worse: we act as if the world is against us, a self-fulfilling prophecy called *behavioral confirmation*. If Maddy expects no one will talk to her, she won't say hello. If Nora expects the moms to be judgy instead of friendly, she'll make a beeline for home, not the playground.

But don't base success on the other person's response. Don't base success on how nervous you feel. *Base success only on what you do.* Did you manage to share a little bit of yourself? Great. The first times are the hardest. Try again, and try again soon—not weeks later. Keep the momentum going. It will get easier, I promise.

SHOW THEM THAT YOU LIKE THEM

The third part of crafting a friendship, besides repetition and disclosure, is *showing others that you like them.* People like those who like them. People also like those who take the initiative. In academic terms it's called *prosocial behavior,* but more simply, it's showing someone that you're pleased to be around them.

At its simplest, showing you like someone is being the first to say hi or lighting up with a smile when they say hi to you. Slightly more advanced is unnecessary conversation. I once had a colleague who would stop at every co-worker's office in the morning to say hi. "Just saying hello," she always said, or "Just checking in." She called it doing the rounds. Her efforts were thoughtful and made me like her.

Next is taking socializing out of the usual context and into another. For instance, parents from Nora's daughter's class, after connecting on the playground, may arrange a playdate, a change of context from schoolyard to home. After racking up those six to eight conversations hanging around after book club, Maddy may invite a book club buddy out for coffee, a change of context from the group to a duo. If you get invited to a get-together—someone from tai chi is having a birthday, a guy from your hip-hop class is having a Super Bowl party—go, even if just for a pop-in. People are touched when you show up to their events, and more important, it moves your friendship to another context and therefore another level.

So approach. Be the first to say hi. Once your friendship has gelled in the original context, invite them on a hike, to a book-store reading, to try the new ramen place in town. All these things are tough. Perfectionistic worry kicks in. We start worrying about the details. What if the hike is too hard for her? What if there's no parking near the bookstore and he gets mad at me? Maybe the ramen place will be sketchy. Indeed, taking the initiative is hard. But a helpful tool is to turn the tables. How would you feel if they invited you? Probably delighted. How would you feel if something went wrong? Probably understanding. Assume the same for them.

Next, be specific. Rather than, "Wanna do something sometime?" try, "The kids have been bugging me about trying that new rock climbing place—are you guys free this weekend?" Or, "Wanna grab coffee on Monday? I'm free after one o'clock." Specification shows you're sincere.

Finally, while almost everyone has adequate social skills, we are more likely to use them and reach out when we feel connected already, which isn't particularly useful if you're feeling lonely. So turn this on its head: to combat occasional waves of loneliness—a weekend with no plans, a particularly FOMO-inducing Instagram moment—use your feelings as a cue to take action. Whenever you feel lonesome, make social plans: email a friend to meet up for a movie next weekend or look at the schedule for that bocce-and-beer group you've been meaning to join. It won't make company appear in the moment, but you'll have created something social to look forward to.

To sum it all up, making friends consists mostly of overcoming inertia—both others' and our own. Assuming someone is friendly to begin with, repetition, disclosure, and taking the initiative hammer out a solid friendship that will stand the test of time.

FORGET EVERYTHING YOU KNOW ABOUT BEING POPULAR

Illinois, mid-1990s. Dr. Jennifer Parkhurst, a psychologist at the University of Illinois at Urbana-Champaign, was standing in front of an audience most others wouldn't dare to face. No, not angry mobsters or rowdy hooligans. Instead, it was a classroom full of middle schoolers. That day, classroom by classroom, Dr. Parkhurst and her graduate student Andrea Hopmeyer were reporting the results of their data collection for a study on popularity to their seventh- and eighth-grade subjects, checking in much as a congressional representative would do for her constituents. As Dr. Parkhurst stood in front of the class, braces flashed back at her. Faces studded with pimples betrayed raging hormones. A mix of awkwardness, angst, and aspirational sophistication emanated from the rows of Girbaud jeans and Reebok Pumps.

Parkhurst thanked the whole class for their participation and began her report: "So this is what we found out. In your class, the most popular kids are kind, cooperative, and trustworthy, and they don't start fights." A murmur rippled through the classroom. A girl in a pink T-shirt raised her hand. "That's not true!" she said. "Popular kids are not friendly and nice. They're mean and stuck-up."

Emboldened, other hands shot up: "Popular kids do start fights!"

"They're not kind or cooperative."

"They're mean!"

Parkhurst was puzzled. "But what I just said was based on the answers you gave us," she said.

Pink T-shirt Girl crossed her arms. "Then everyone who took your survey must have lied."

"Yeah!" echoed the class.

Parkhurst thought for a moment. To be sure, she asked, "Do you like these kids?"

What roared back was definitive: "No! We can't stand them."

The kids couldn't have known it, but in that moment they upended decades of research methodology.

Back on campus, Parkhurst and Hopmeyer, who is now a researcher at Occidental College, pondered what the kids had said. The researchers had used a well-established method to measure popularity: Each kid got a list of others in their grade. Students were asked to circle the names of the three kids they liked best and the three kids they liked least. Then they were asked to do the same for those who were "kind," "someone you can trust," "cooperates," "starts fights," "easy to push around," and "can't take teasing." It was a simple tally: You were popular if you got lots of "like most" votes and few "like least" votes. You were unpopular if you got lots of "like least" votes and few "like most" votes. Easy-peasy.

But in the face of the kids' feedback, Parkhurst and Hopmeyer reconsidered how to measure popularity. Maybe popularity wasn't just a tally of likes and dislikes. They did another study, this time with one simple tweak: they added "popular" to the list. Then they crunched the numbers again. What they found changed the game.

With the new method, being chosen as "popular" didn't actually mean a kid was well liked; it meant they were *dominant*. The kids who were pegged as "popular" did get lots of "likes," but they also got many "dislikes." These alpha dogs and queen bees were liked by some, but mostly by other high-status kids. With others, they racked up the eye rolls.

It's easy to mistake being dominant for being liked, because dominant kids get a lot of attention. Their visibility is high. The shy among us despair, thinking, *I'll never be able to do that,* or, *That's not me.* But you don't need to be someone you're not. You don't need to own the room to be liked. You don't need to be a big shot, alpha, or self-important.

True, honest, by-the-numbers popularity, as Parkhurst and her colleagues discovered, didn't come from commanding attention or gaining deference. It didn't even come from having the most confidence. Instead, the kids with the most "like most" votes and the fewest "like least" votes were those who were also rated as the package deal of kind, cooperative, and trustworthy. Dominance, it turns out, equaled *perceived* popularity. Warmheartedness equaled *actual* popularity.

This phenomenon continues into adulthood. An oft-cited study found that in first impressions of others we prioritize *warmth* over anything else, which is defined as—you guessed it— kindness and trustworthiness.

It's startling, then, to realize that the shouts and whispers of the Inner Critic are mostly about competence and confidence— we worry we'll do something stupid, look weird, seem incompetent. We work hard to increase our competence and confidence, but we're barking up the wrong tree. Competence and confidence aren't what others are hoping for in a friend—they're hoping for warmth.

Dr. David Moscovitch puts it this way: "If you try to be warm and friendly and curious, then everything else—the blemishes and foibles and awkward behaviors all of us have simply because we're human—becomes much less important to the other person because we're connecting with them." And that's what matters: connection, which is built on warmth and trust. So keep showing up. Share what you think and feel and do. Show others that you like them. These are the building blocks of beautiful friendships.

Epilogue

In 1938, researchers at Harvard wondered: What makes a good life?

This, to say the least, was an unlikely time to reflect on quality of life. In 1938, the Great Depression had been grinding on for the better part of a decade. Positive psychology and the science of happiness were developments not even on the horizon. Fulfillment was not the job of science. This was the realm of poets and priests, philosophers and ethicists. Indeed, studying what went into a good life was totally impractical, blindly ambitious, and utterly revolutionary. In 1938, it never should have been on the agenda. But thankfully, it was.

What resulted was the Study of Adult Development, also known as the Grant Study after its inaugural funder, William T. Grant. The Grant Study is the rarest among rare. It is a gem first because of its longevity—more than seventy-five years and four generations of researchers. The study has weathered wartime, social upheaval, and unimaginable medical and technological advances. It carries on in a world inconceivable in 1938.

All in all, 724 young men signed up. Given that this was the 1930s, diversity as we know it wasn't even a concept, much less a value, resulting in an all-white and all-male group. However, the study did cover both ends of the socioeconomic spectrum. The most privileged and powerful of young America signed up, including a member of the Harvard swim team by the name of John F. Kennedy, as did young men from Boston's poorest neighborhoods, most of whom lived in tenements without running water.

For over seventy-five years, the men opened up their lives to the research team. The men shared health and illnesses, successes and challenges. Everything was measured, from their bodies to their personality, intelligence, political leanings, exercise habits, alcohol consumption, and much more. The researchers asked about the young men's childhood, their relationships with their mothers (indeed, when the study opened, Freud was still a living, looming presence), and, as time rolled by, their jobs, their friends, their spouses, and the communities they built across the decades.

The study's current director, Dr. Robert Waldinger, is a psychiatrist who exudes such tranquility that it's unsurprising to discover he's also a Zen priest. In a viral TED Talk, he revealed what decades of Grant Study data have brought to light about what makes a life happy, healthy, and meaningful. He said, "The clearest message that we get from this seventy-five-year study is this: Good relationships keep us happier and healthier. Period." He continued: "People who are more socially connected—to family, to friends, to community—are happier, they're physically healthier, and they live longer than people who are less well connected." To drive the point home, Waldinger revealed that the men in the study who were the most satisfied in their relationships at age fifty were the healthiest at age eighty.

But Waldinger also points out that social connection isn't just numbers. It's not quantity. It's quality. But even more, it's not the category of social connection that matters—it doesn't have to mean being married or partnered. Instead, the biggest predictor of a healthy, happy life is the *warmth* of your relationships. From middle school to middle age and beyond, warmth, defined as being kind and trustworthy, fuels connection. And connection, the Grant Study tells us, in turn fuels not only happiness but also health and longevity. You don't have to be outgoing, extroverted, confident, or popular. As we talked about in chapter 16, all you have to be is kind. And that's something you have in you already.

Something else you have in you is all the other natural traits that come along with the package deal of social anxiety: your empathy, your ability to listen, your high standards, your conscientiousness. Combine these with the skills and knowledge you've gained in *How to Be Yourself* and you can lean in to the people around you by reaching out. Reach out to new friends, to friends you already have, to family, colleagues, and strangers. Reach out to old and young, to those who are just like you and those who are unimaginably different. Be kind. Be warm. It might change your life.

But don't take it from me; take it from someone else who's been there: Jim.

After Jim had recovered from his pneumonia, he fought his way through eight-foot-high snowdrifts to get to his weekly class at the dance studio. The weather had kept most students stuck at home, so the class was sparse that day. Afterwards, Mayumi approached him with a surprise. A regional dance showcase was coming up in June. After four years of lessons, Mayumi thought Jim was overdue to make his onstage debut.

Jim had attended the showcase before, but he had never

dreamed of participating. He was happy with his lessons and the Sunday night practice parties. Just the thought of performing made the old anxiety come roaring back, a feeling that had become much rarer and softer over the years but at times like this could still rear its head.

In the show, there were Broadway-style productions with big groups of student dancers, multicouple performances where five or six couples danced simultaneously, and a few, select performances with one couple alone onstage. There was an audience of perhaps a hundred or so, plus an actual judge who gave written feedback on each dancer's performance. Jim assumed Mayumi would recommend he join a Broadway-style group, but she didn't give him a choice. "It's you and me, Jim," she said.

Jim's eyes widened. "I just got over pneumonia and now you want to give me a heart attack?" he asked, half-joking.

But as the snow melted and the weather warmed, Jim practiced. And practiced. Before he knew it, it was June and he found himself backstage, his heart pounding beneath his tuxedo. He pulled at his collar. It was stifling backstage and he needed air. But when he peeked out from behind the curtain, he inadvertently caught the eye of the judge, who peered coolly over his glasses. Jim snapped his head back behind the curtain as if he had seen a sharpshooter. Maybe he'd have a heart attack after all. Then he wouldn't have to do this.

But then it was time. His name was announced. As if in a trance, Jim turned and walked onstage, forgetting he was supposed to make an entrance with Mayumi through the curtain. Mayumi trotted after him; after hundreds of students, she could roll with anything. And after four years of teaching Jim, she knew him well. He had told her all about his battles with social anxiety, his weekends hiding in the house, how it took him half an hour to dial the phone to schedule his first dance lesson, his hands had been shaking so badly. She knew he was nervous about this performance, but she also knew deep in her heart that he could do this, and do it well. They had practiced for months. It wasn't about the dance steps anymore. It was about being onstage, being seen, being ready for the literal spotlight. She knew he was ready.

The announcer continued, "Ladies and gentlemen, this is Jim's first performance." The applause came long and loud. "The only thing I could hear was the applause," Jim remembered. "I thought to myself, 'Is this really happening?'" The music started. A waltz, just like his surprise birthday dance. All at once, Jim felt focused. His anxiety evaporated. His body felt sharp and alert. His feet knew the steps—he didn't have to think about it. What he did think about was that his backstage panic, to his astonishment, had morphed almost imperceptibly into a very different emotion: excitement.

When the music ended and their feet slowed, Jim and Mayumi took their bows and ran backstage. Mayumi gave him a hug. "I have to go on again with another student now, but how do you feel? Would you come back and do it again next year?"

Jim looked her in the eye. "Absolutely."

She smiled. "If you had said 'never again,' I wouldn't have done my job. My job is for you to have a good experience." She squeezed his hand and disappeared to find her next student.

Jim leaned against the wall. He had done it. Yet again, he was experiencing The Moment. Thinking back, he remembers, "It was one of the greatest moments of my life."

A couple of days later, Mayumi handed him the envelope from the judge.

"Does it say I'm a mess? If he could have seen inside my brain he would have seen that I was a mess."

Mayumi looked at him. "You always assume that you're the only one who's anxious and no one else is."

"But they look so calm," he protested.

"So do you." She ripped open the envelope and put the paper in his hands. At the top of the page, in big letters, was written: "VERY RELAXED."

Jim never would have guessed that, at fifty-two, he would essentially start living a new life. He thought it was too late, that the lessons of Dorchester and decades of avoidance would have settled in irreversibly. But it's never too late to move forward. Whether you're thirteen or eighty-three, an old dog really *can* be taught new tricks.

Jim's story still isn't over. He keeps in touch with Deena, holding strong their shared connection and mutual respect from over forty years prior. It's unclear what the future will bring, but for now Jim is satisfied with the turns his life has taken. From Dorchester to the dance floor, Jim's journey over the mountain of social anxiety and down the other side is one he never knew was in him.

Just like Jim, the courage to face your fears is in you, too. You can shrink how much time you spend with social anxiety. Now you know how to question your worries with "How bad would that really be?," "What are the odds?," and "How would I cope?" You know how to talk to yourself with compassion and understanding, creating a supportive environment from which you can do hard things. You know that if you jump in before you're confident your confidence will catch up. You know that if you choose a role, a goal, or otherwise create some structure for yourself, you'll feel more certain and focused. You know that each trip over the anxiety peak erodes it. You know to drop your safety behaviors—those life preservers that do nothing but hold you under, and by doing so you'll reap the authenticity that follows. You know to shift your attention to the task at hand, the person in front of you, or even, mindfully, to your breath. You can see yourself as others see you instead of the funhouse mirror image. You can dare to be average. You can trust that your foibles and blunders make you more endearing. You know to keep showing up, to disclose bits of your life, and to show others you like them. And most of all, you know to be kind and trustworthy.

All these tools are in your toolbox, a shiny new set. Plus, they've all been shown to work again and again by some of the most brilliant research minds out there. But just like it took you time and practice to learn to ride a bike or drive a car, it will take time and practice to master these new tools. But you don't have to master all of them (remember, we're toning down the perfectionism). Choose your two or three favorites and make them your go-tos. For me, asking myself, "How bad would that really be?," turning my attention inside out, and showing people I like them are my go-tos. These get me through 90 percent of my anxious moments. And the other 10 percent? Well, either I get a good story out of it or, yes, sometimes I fold 'em and try again later.

Best yet, you can lose social anxiety without losing the good things that come along with it. The good things? Yes, remember, a propensity toward social anxiety comes as a package deal. We are empathetic—we have the ability to understand and share the feelings of others. We are conscientious—we do things thoroughly and well. Those high standards of ours propel us to success in what we do. Finally, we value getting along. And in an increasingly fractious world, the ability to get along—to be kind, to be trusted—is ultimately what will draw others to you.

But most of all, inseparable from caring what people think is, simply, caring about people. Think of the Hallmark slogan, "When You Care Enough to Send the Very Best." By caring enough, you send into the world your best efforts. By caring enough, you offer the world incredible strength and value. So while it's important to turn down the dimmer switch of social anxiety to the point where it no longer freaks you out or gets in the way of living the life you want, don't lose your care and concern for others. We care about people. We make wonderful friends and partners for the people who are lucky enough to know us.

Ironically, the individuals I work with who experience social anxiety—the same people who think they're inadequate, awkward failures—are, time and again, the most interesting, beautiful, and kind people one could ever hope to meet. I love working with people who experience social anxiety because they are invariably brave and amazing, and I am privileged to help them discover exactly that.

For the introverts among us, your true self may be quiet and contemplative. For the extroverts, your true self may be vocal and gregarious. I maintain that who you are when you're not afraid is your authentic self. Remember Gandhi's appreciation of his social anxiety? "It has allowed me to grow. It has helped me in my discernment of the truth." Go forth and do. Stretch. Grow. And in doing so, you will find your truth—your authentic self.

Author's Note

Throughout these pages, I've drawn from the experiences of clients I've had the good fortune to work with directly or whose treatment I have supervised. Because I met and interacted with them in a health care setting where confidentiality is promised and delivered, all Health Insurance Portability and Accountability Act of 1996 (HIPAA) identifiers and identifiable story details have been changed to render each person and their protected health information unrecognizable. In a few cases, I have created composite characters from several clients.

The one exception is the story of "Jim," who specifically wished for his full story to be shared in the hopes of inspiring others. Since Jim's family and ballroom dance community did not expect to become supporting characters in a book, his and other names have been changed, but locations and details are unchanged from Jim's storytelling.

Diego's story is adapted, with permission, from a case shared by Dr. Susan Bögels of the University of Amsterdam. Twenty-one-month-old Jennifer, in chapter 2, is based on my conversations with Dr. Cynthia Garcia Coll and close reading of her protocol.

Finally, for free, science-backed resources to continue your rise above social anxiety, visit EllenHendriksen.com/free-resources.

Acknowledgments

Over the past few years, as I moved away from a traditional academic career and embarked on the often-bewildering adventure of launching a podcast and writing a book, my mantra has been "I don't know where I'm going, but I'm on the right path." I know the path is right because of the generous and amazing people I have met along the way.

It is with heartfelt gratitude that I thank those who gave their time, energy, and experience to making this book a reality: Lynn Alden, David Barlow, Courtney Beard, Susan Bögels, Cara Brookins, David Burns, David Clark, Sophia Dembling, Tiffany Dufu, John Gabrieli, Cynthia Garcia Coll, Philippe Goldin, Richard Heimberg, Stefan Hofmann, Andrea Hopmeyer, Lewis Howes, Jia Jiang, Rachel Lambright, David Langer, David Moscovitch, Kristin Neff, Harris O'Malley, Jennifer Parkhurst, Ron Rapee, Mike Rinck, Peter Shalek, Brandon Stanton, Ty Tashiro, Charlie Taylor, Emma Warnock-Parkes, and Jade Wu.

I am forever grateful to the whole team at St. Martin's Press. Executive Editor Jennifer Weis believed in this project from the beginning and strengthened my belief in it, too. Assistant Editor Sylvan Creekmore was a rock (and rock star) of reason and reassurance throughout. Laura Clark, Leah Johanson, and Kim Lew opened doors I didn't even know existed. Brad Wood gave me an influx of hope when he talked up the book at launch. Barbara Wild turned the manuscript into a real book, no small task. Senior Editor Alyssa Martino is an extraordinary human. She deserves endless thanks for juggling a million moving parts and offering daily (sometimes more than daily) encouragement, reassurance, guidance, excitement, and—oh yes—editing. Alyssa, you're a superstar.

Thank you to everyone at QDT. Big thanks to Mary Beth Roche, Kathy Doyle, Joe Muscolino, Kelly Dickinson, Morgan Ratner, and Steve Riekeberg. Beata Santora got everything started when she got an unsolicited email pitch from a drifting academic with an itch to write some five years ago. Thank you, Beata, for taking a chance on me.

Early readers Doron Gan, Robbert Langwerden, Denitza Raitcheva, Juan Sanabria, and Sarah Smith Parmeshwar delivered invaluable feedback and support. Emily Jones kept things afloat and put up with my flailing. Tim Grahl's book marketing coaching was a godsend. Susan Cain, Nidhi Berry, and Colleen Quinn at Quiet Revolution were endlessly supportive. Lori Richmond, Matthew Guillory, and Claudia Scott created a gorgeous home for me on the web. Lisa Smith, David Barlow, and everyone at CARD supported the parallel universe of my writing life. Mignon Fogarty and all the QDT hosts, especially Monica Reinagel, were so generous in sharing their vast knowledge.

As a true research nerd, I say thanks to the staff of the Cambridge Public Library system, the Boston University Libraries, and the Stanford University Libraries.

To all the listeners of Savvy Psychologist: I can't thank you enough. Thank you for listening every week, sending in stupendous show ideas, and posting uplifting comments to me and each other. Without you this book wouldn't exist.

A heartfelt, humble thank-you to all the clients I have worked with over the years. It is a privilege to witness your fears grow smaller and your lives grow bigger.

And of course, deepest thanks to family, near and far. The village who supported this book opened their hearts, schedules, and houses, especially Sharon and Dan Hendriksen and Suzanne Park. Nicolas Currier had unwavering faith in me, even in those moments when I questioned the validity of this whole undertaking. He is an endless source of strength, love, and necessary silliness.

References

Prologue

the following twenty-five situations cribbed from two widely used social anxiety questionnaires.

Liebowitz, M. R. (1987). Liebowitz social anxiety scale for social phobia. *Modern Problems of Pharmacopsychiatry, 22,* 141–73.

Mattick, R. P., and Clarke, J. C. (1998). Development and validation of measures of social phobia scrutiny fear and social interaction anxiety. *Behavior Research and Therapy, 36,* 455–70.

A study out of the University of Pittsburgh

Primack, B. A., Shensa, A., Escobar-Viera, C. G., Barrett, E. L., Sidani, J. E., Colditz, J. B., and James, A. E. (2017). Use of multiple social media platforms and symptoms of depression and anxiety: A nationally-representative study among U.S. young adults. *Computers in Human Behavior, 69,* 1–9.

Cartoon courtesy of Gemma Correll.
http://www.agoodson.com/illustrator/gemma-correll/.

somewhere between the ages of eight and fifteen

American Psychiatric Association. (2013). *Diagnostic and Statistical Manual of Mental Disorders* (5th ed.). Arlington, VA: American Psychiatric Publishing.

at some point in life 13 percent of Americans

Kessler, R. C., McGonagle, K. A., Zhao, S., Nelson, C. B., Hughes, M., Eshleman, S., . . . Kendler, K. S. (1994). Lifetime and twelve-month prevalence of DSM-III-R psychiatric disorders in the United States. Results from the National Comorbidity Survey. *Archives of General Psychiatry, 51,* 8–19.

third most common psychological disorder,

Kessler et al. (1994).

21 percent of capital-S Socially Anxious folks for whom nerves manifest as anger and irritability,
Kashdan, T. B., McKnight, P. E., Richey, J. A., and Hofmann, S. G. (2009). When social anxiety disorder co-exists with risk-prone, approach behavior: Investigating a neglected, meaningful subset of people in the National Comorbidity Survey-Replication. *Behavior Research and Therapy, 47,* 559–68.

Up to 15-30 percent of the population find themselves chronically isolated.
Heinrich, L. M., and Gallon, E. (2009). The clinical significance of loneliness: A literature review. *Clinical Psychology Review, 26,* 695–718.
Theeke, L. A. (2009). Predictors of loneliness in U.S. adults over age sixty-five. *Archives of Psychiatric Nursing, 23,* 387–96.

It kills our sleep quality, our mood, our optimism, and our self-esteem.
Hawley, L. C., and Cacioppo, J. T. (2010). Loneliness matters: A theoretical and empirical review of consequences and mechanisms. *Annals of Behavioral Medicine, 40,* 218–27.

Chronic loneliness has been linked to an increased risk of heart disease, Alzheimer's disease, even mortality.
Hawkley, L. C., Masi, C. M., Berry, J. D., and Cacioppo, J. T. (2006). Loneliness is a unique predictor of age-related differences in systolic blood pressure. *Psychology and Aging, 21,* 152–64.
Penninx, B. W., van Tilburg, T., Kriegsman, D. M., Deeg, D. J., Boeke, A. J., and Van Eijk, J. T. (1997). Effects of social support and personal coping resources on mortality in older age: The Longitudinal Aging Study Amsterdam. *American Journal of Epidemiology, 146,* 510–19.
Shiovitz-Ezra, S., and Ayalon, L. (2010). Situational versus chronic loneliness as risk factors for all-cause mortality. *International Psychogeriatrics, 22,* 455–62.
Thurston, R. C., and Kubzansky, L. D. (2009). Women, loneliness, and incident coronary heart disease. *Psychosomatic Medicine, 71,* 836–42.
Wilson, R. S., Krueger, K. R., Arnold, S. E., Schneider, J. A., Kelly, J. F., Barnes, L. L. . . . Bennett, D. A. (2007). Loneliness and risk of Alzheimer disease. *Archives of General Psychiatry, 64,* 234–40.

Conscientious, with a robust inner guide
http://www.nytimes.com/2011/06/26/opinion/sunday/26shyness.html.
Kochanska, G., and Aksan, N. (2006). Children's conscience and self-regulation. *Journal of Personality, 74,* 1587–1618.

Gifted at remembering faces
Foa, E. B., Gilboa-Schechtman, E., Amir, N., and Freshman, M. (2000).

Memory bias in generalized social phobia: Remembering negative emotional expressions. *Journal of Anxiety Disorders, 14,* 501–19.
Notes: Don't be fooled by the title of this paper—it finds that those with social anxiety remember *all* faces better than those without social anxiety.

Deeply empathetic
Auyeung, K., and Alden, L. (2016). Social anxiety and empathy for social pain. *Cognitive Therapy and Research, 40,* 38–45.
Tibi-Elhanany, Y., and Shamay-Tsoory, S. G. (2011). Social cognition in social anxiety: First evidence for increased empathic abilities. *Israel Journal of Psychiatry and Related Sciences, 48,* 98–106.

"Prosocial," meaning positive to others, helpful, and altruistic
Culotta, C. M., and Goldstein, S. E. (2008). Adolescents' aggressive and prosocial behavior: Associations with jealousy and social anxiety. *Journal of Genetic Psychology, 169,* 21–33.
Note: The scientific literature is mixed on this list of characteristics, which at first surprised me while I was researching this book. In addition to the papers listed previously, you'll also find some noting that social anxiety is associated with low conscientiousness, low empathy, and other negative characteristics. In my experience working with the shy and socially anxious and in interviewing researchers and mental health professionals who work with social anxiety, I've found the positive traits on the list to be true for the majority of shy and socially anxious people. So where was all the negativity coming from? Some thoughts: the literature focuses almost exclusively on capital-S Social Anxiety, which by definition means the study sample is distressed and impaired. Social Anxiety is getting in the way of their life, not enhancing it. For instance, while most shy and socially anxious folks are eager to get along and do right by others, which hangs together with prosociality, those whose capital-S Social Anxiety is impairing may be so concerned about being judged or doing the wrong thing that they are too scared to lend a hand. Likewise, while most of the socially anxious folks I've worked with have a strong work ethic and are highly conscientious, I've also encountered some highly impaired individuals with what's called an *external locus of control,* meaning a belief that outside influences determine their future rather than their own efforts and choices, which can hamstring them in setting goals and effectively taking charge of their life. All in all, this variety makes sense: with 40 percent of the population considering themselves shy, there's sure to be heterogeneity.

Fully 40 percent of people consider themselves to be shy . . . What's more, a whopping 99 percent of people feel socially anxious in particular situations.

Zimbardo, P., Pilkonis, P., and Norwood, R. (1974). The silent prison of shyness. (Technical Report Z-17). Stanford, CA: Office of Naval Research, Stanford University.

Gandhi led a march to protest the British colonialist government's monopoly on salt,
http://www.history.com/news/gandhis-salt-march-85-years-ago.
http://www.history.com/topics/salt-march.

Not that many years later, Martin Luther King Jr. would write
King, M. L. (1958). *Stride Toward Freedom: The Montgomery Story.* New York: Harper and Brothers.

In his autobiography, Gandhi devotes an entire chapter to his social anxiety,
Gandhi, M. K. (1960). *Gandhi's Autobiography: The Story of My Experiments with truth.* Washington, DC: Public Affairs Press.

Gandhi, who earlier in life couldn't even give a toast, would, in 1947, give a speech to a live audience of more than twenty thousand people.
http://www.gandhi-manibhavan.org/gandhicomesalive/speech7.htm.

Looking back on his life, Gandhi wrote:
Gandhi (1960).

Additional References

Carducci, B. (1999). *Shyness.* New York: HarperCollins.
Crozier, W. R. (ed.) (1990). *Shyness and embarrassment: Perspectives from Social Psychology.* Cambridge: Cambridge University Press.
Heimberg, R. G., Hofmann, S. G., Liebowitz, M. R., Schneier, F. R., Smits, J. A., Stein, M. B., . . Craske, M. G. (2014). Social anxiety disorder in DSM-5. *Depression and Anxiety, 31,* 472–79.

Chapter 1: The Root of it All: How Social Anxiety Takes Hold

The story of "Jim Nolan" comes from our work together, plus personal communication, February 24, 2016.

four- to six-fold increased risk of having the same disorder.
Smoller, J. W., Gardner-Schuster, E., and Misiaszek, M. (2008). Genetics of anxiety: Would the genome recognize the DSM? *Depression and Anxiety, 25,* 368–77.

anxiety isn't controlled by a single gene . . . large effects of a few genes or
the small effects of many . . . phenotypic complexity
Smoller, J. W., Block, S. R., and Young, M. M. (2009). Genetics of anxiety
disorders: The complex road from DSM to DNA. *Depression and Anxiety, 26,*
965–95.

first described in the literature in 1966
Marks, I. M., and Gelder, M. G. (1966). Different ages of onset in varieties of
phobias. *American Journal of Psychiatry, 123,* 218–21.

and has only been a distinctly defined disorder since 1980.
American Psychiatric Association. (1980). *Diagnostic and Statistical Manual of
Mental Disorders* (3rd ed.). Washington, DC: American Psychiatric Association.

The Reveal falls into one of four categories:
Moscovitch, D. A. (2009). What is the core fear in social phobia? A new model
to facilitate individualized case conceptualization and treatment. *Cognitive
and Behavioral Practice, 16,* 123–34.

The other night, Jim was watching the TV show *Modern Family.*
http://abc.go.com/shows/modern-family/video/pl5520993/VDKA0
_mp8w14dk.

Additional References

Leitenberg, H. (ed.) (1990). *Handbook of Social and Evaluation Anxiety.* New
York: Plenum Press.

Chapter 2: Social Anxiety Is Like an Apple Tree (or, Why Social Anxiety Has Stuck Around for Millennia)

remember, 40 percent of us consider ourselves "shy" and 13 percent of us
will have capital-*S* Social Anxiety at some point in life—
Kendler, K. S. (1994). Lifetime and twelve-month prevalence of DSM-III-R
psychiatric disorders in the United States. Results from the National Comorbidity Survey. *Archives of General Psychiatry, 51,* 8–19.
Kessler, R. C., et al. (1994), Zimbardo, P., et al. (1974). The silent prison of
shyness. (Technical Report Z-17). Stanford, CA: Office of Naval Research,
Stanford University.

But if social awareness grows wild and unchecked, it distorts into capital-*S*
Social Anxiety,
Knowles, M. L., Lucas, G. M., Baumeister, R. F., and Gardner, W. L. (2015).

Choking under social pressure: Social monitoring among the lonely. *Personality and Social Psychology Bulletin, 41,* 805–21.

Washburn, D., Wilson, G., Roes, M., Rnic, K., and Harkness, K. L. (2016). Theory of mind in social anxiety disorder, depression, and comorbid conditions. *Journal of Anxiety Disorders, 37,* 71–77.

In her junior year of high school, Cynthia took a psychology course and knew, like the flip of a light switch, that she had found her life's work.
http://www.psychologicalscience.org/index.php/publications/observer/2010/march-10/champions-of-psychology-cynthia-garcia-coll.html.

When, in 1984, Cynthia published her findings from the 117 kids in the prestigious journal *Child Development*, it marked the scholarly debut of the term *behavioral inhibition*.
Garcia Coll, C., Kagan, J., and Reznick, J. S. (1984). Behavioral inhibition in young children. *Child Development, 55,* 1005–19.

even species (I'm looking at you, chimps, lions, and wolves).
Nishida, T., Hosaka, K., Nakamura, M., and Hamai, M. (1995). A within-group gang attack on a young adult male chimpanzee: Ostracism of an ill-mannered member? *Primates, 36,* 207.

The Bible, for example, is filled with stories that end in the punishment of exile, of a wrongdoer being "cut off from his people."
https://en.wikipedia.org/wiki/Banishment_in_the_Bible.

The Amish, for example, call it shunning.
Hostetler, J. A. (1993). *Amish Society* (4th ed.). Baltimore and London: Johns Hopkins University Press.

As an Amish leader in the PBS documentary *Shunned* neatly sums up, "If we lose obedience, we lose the church."
http://www.pbs.org/wgbh/americanexperience/films/shunned/.

In the early 1990s, when the kids reached the age of thirteen,
Schwartz, C. E., Snidman, N., and Kagan, J. (1999). Adolescent social anxiety as an outcome of inhibited temperament in childhood. *Journal of the American Academy of Child and Adolescent Psychiatry, 38,* 1008–15.

Personally, I remember reading Susan Cain's 2012 bestseller, *Quiet,* and feeling astonished.
Cain, S. (2012). *Quiet: The Power of Introverts in a World that Can't Stop Talking.* New York: Crown.

"There are people who cannot raise their hand or speak freely in a group," she told me when I interviewed her and recounted my story.
Cynthia Garcia Coll, Ph.D., personal communication, April 26, 2016.

think of the 40 percent of people, myself included, who refer to themselves as "formerly shy."
Zimbardo, P., et al. (1974). The silent prison of shyness (Technical Report Z-17). Stanford, CA: Office of Naval Research, Stanford University.

Dr. Jerome Kagan himself has written, "Genes, culture, time, and luck make us who we are."
Kagan, J. (2010). *The Temperamental Thread: How Genes, Culture, Time, and Luck Make Us Who We Are.* New York: Dana Foundation.

Indeed, in the constant interplay between genes and environment
http://developingchild.harvard.edu/science/deep-dives/gene-environment -interaction/

Additional References

Gazelle, H., and Rubin, K. H. (2010). Social anxiety in childhood: Bridging developmental and clinical perspectives. *New Directions for Child and Adolescent Development, 2010,* 1–16.

Gilbert, P. (2001). Evolution and social anxiety: The role of attraction, social competition, and social hierarchies. *Psychiatric Clinics of North America, 24,* 723–51.

Gilbert, P., and Trower, P. (1990). The evolution and manifestation of social anxiety. In Crozier, W. R. (ed.), *Shyness and Embarrassment: Perspectives from Social Psychology* (144–80). Cambridge: Cambridge University Press.

Maner, J. K., and Kenrick, D. T. (2010). When adaptations go awry: Functional and dysfunctional aspects of social anxiety. *Social Issues and Policy Review, 4,* 111–42.

Price, J. S. (2003). Evolutionary aspects of anxiety disorders. *Dialogues in Clinical Neuroscience, 5,* 223–36.

Tomasello, M., Melis, A. P., Tennie, C., Wyman, E., and Herrmann, E. (2012). Two key steps in the evolution of human cooperation: The interdependence hypothesis. *Current Anthropology, 53,* 673–92.

Trower, P., Gilbert, P., and Sherling, G. (1990). Social anxiety, evolution, and self-presentation: An interdisciplinary perspective. In Leitenberg, H. (ed.), *Handbook of Social and Evaluation Anxiety* (11–45). New York: Springer.

Wakefield, J. C., Horwitz, A. V., and Schmitz, M. F. (2005). Are we overpathologizing the socially anxious? Social phobia from a harmful dysfunction perspective. *Canadian Journal of Psychiatry, 50,* 317–19.

Chapter 3: Your Brain on Social Anxiety

It has been established that anything you do frequently can change your brain, from driving a taxi to playing the violin to watching porn

Hyde, K. L., Lerch, J., Norton, A., Forgeard, M., Winner, E., Evans, A. C., and Schlaug, G. (2009). Musical training shapes structural brain development. *Journal of Neuroscience, 29,* 3019–25.

Kühn, S., and Gallinat, J. (2014). Brain structure and functional connectivity associated with pornography consumption: The brain on porn. *JAMA Psychiatry, 71,* 827–34.

Maguire, E. A., Woollett, K., and Spiers, H. J. (2006). London taxi drivers and bus drivers: A structural MRI and neuropsychological analysis. *Hippocampus, 16,* 1091–101.

Münte, T. F., Altenmüller, E., and Jäncke, L. (2002). The musician's brain as a model of neuroplasticity. *Nature Reviews: Neuroscience, 3,* 473–78.

a series of studies that found that cognitive-behavioral therapy for capital-S Social Anxiety fundamentally changes connections across areas in the brain,

Goldin, P. R., Ziv, M., Jazaieri, H., Hahn, K., Heimberg, R., and Gross, J. J. (2013). Impact of cognitive behavioral therapy for social anxiety disorder on the neural dynamics of cognitive reappraisal of negative self-beliefs: Randomized clinical trial. *JAMA Psychiatry, 70,* 1048–56.

Goldin, P. R., Ziv, M., Jazaieri, H., Weeks, J., Heimberg, R., and Gross, J. J. (2014). Impact of cognitive-behavioral therapy for social anxiety disorder on the neural bases of emotional reactivity to and regulation of social evaluation. *Behavior Research and Therapy, 62,* 97–106.

Philippe Goldin, Ph.D., personal communication, April 1, 2017.

collectively known as the amygdala.

http://bigthink.com/videos/the-amygdala-in-5-minutes.

https://www.psychologytoday.com/blog/i-got-mind-tell-you/201508/the-amygdala-is-not-the-brains-fear-center.

Etkin, A., and Wager, T. D. (2007). Functional neuroimaging of anxiety: A meta-analysis of emotional processing in PTSD, social anxiety disorder, and specific phobia. *American Journal of Psychiatry, 164,* 1476–88.

Stein, M. B., Simmons, A. N., Feinstein, J. S., and Paulus, M. P. (2007). Increased amygdala and insula activation during emotion processing in anxiety-prone subjects. *American Journal of Psychiatry, 164,* 318–27.

Change the snarling dog to a snarling stranger,
Amaral, D. G. (2002). The primate amygdala and the neurobiology of social behavior: Implications for understanding social anxiety. *Biological Psychiatry, 51,* 11–17.

Phan, K. L., Fitzgerald, D. A., Nathan, P. J., and Tancer, M. E. (2006). Association between amygdala hyperactivity to harsh faces and severity of social anxiety in generalized social phobia. *Biological Psychiatry, 59,* 424–29.

the last time the Kagan lab followed up on Jennifer
Schwartz, C. E., Wright, C. I., Shin, L. M., Kagan, J., and Rauch, S. L. (2003). Inhibited and uninhibited infants "grown up": Adult amygdalar response to novelty. *Science, 300,* 1952–53.

your prefrontal cortex, the part of your brain responsible for, well, responsibility,
Miller, E. K., and Cohen, J. D. (2001). An integrative theory of prefrontal cortex function. *Annual Review of Neuroscience, 24,* 167–202.

What's more, specific areas of it can talk the amygdala down from its social freak-outs.
Etkin, A., and Wager, T. D. (2007). Functional neuroimaging of anxiety: A meta-analysis of emotional processing in PTSD, social anxiety disorder, and specific phobia. *American Journal of Psychiatry, 164,* 1476–88.
Note: A good, user-friendly article and video explaining the socially anxious brain can be found at https://joyable.com/blog/this-is-your-brain-on-social -anxiety/.

our prefrontal cortex isn't as adept as our non-anxious friends' at shutting off the alarms.
Goldin, P. R., et al. (2013). Impact of cognitive behavioral therapy for social anxiety disorder on the neural dynamics of cognitive reappraisal of negative self-beliefs: Randomized clinical trial. *JAMA Psychiatry, 70,* 1048–56.
Philippe Goldin, Ph.D., personal communication, April 1, 2017.

What's more, other studies have concluded that CBT leads to visible brain changes—Goldin's results aren't just a happy fluke.
Furmark, T., Tillers, M., Marteinsdottir, I., Fischer, H., Pissiota, A., Angstrom, B., and Fredrikson, M. (2002). Common changes in cerebral blood flow in patients with social phobia treated with citalopram or cognitive-behavioral therapy. *Archives of General Psychiatry, 59,* 425–33.
Månsson, K. N. T., Frick, A., Boraxbekk, C-J., Marquand, A. F., Williams, S. C., Carlbring, P., Andersson, G., and Furmark, T. (2015). Predicting

long-term outcome of internet-delivered cognitive behavior therapy for social anxiety disorder using fMRI and support vector machine learning. *Translational Psychiatry, 5,* e530.

Månsson, K. N. T., Salami, A., Frick, A., Carlbring, P., Andersson, G., Furmark, T., and Boraxbekk, C-J. (2016). Neuroplasticity in response to cognitive behavior therapy for social anxiety disorder. *Translational Psychiatry, 6,* e727.

the approximately 1 percent of the population who are psychopaths.
Werner, K. B., Few, L. R., and Bucholz, K. K. (2015). Epidemiology, comorbidity, and behavioral genetics of Antisocial Personality Disorder and psychopathy. *Psychiatry Annals, 45,* 195–99.

But just like a tendency toward social anxiety is a package deal, so is psychopathy.
Hare, R. D., and Neumann, C. N. (2006). The PCL-R Assessment of Psychopathy: Development, Structural Properties, and New Directions. In Patrick, C. (ed.), *Handbook of Psychopathy* (58–88). New York: Guilford.

Neumann, C. S., and Hare, R. D. (2008). Psychopathic traits in a large community sample: Links to violence, alcohol use, and intelligence. *Journal of Consulting and Clinical Psychology, 76,* 893–99.

(chili made from Scott Tenorman's parents, anyone?),
http://www.therobotsvoice.com/2011/09/cartmans_7_most_heinous_acts _of_evil_on_south_park.php.

A study by Dr. Niels Birbaumer and his team at Germany's University of Tübingen
Viet, R., Flor, H., Erb, M., Hermann, C., Lotze, M., Grodd, W., and Birbaumer, N. (2002). Brain circuits involved in emotional learning in antisocial behavior and social phobia in humans. *Neuroscience Letters, 328,* 233–36.

This, along with additional studies,
Damasio, A. R., Tranel, D., and Damasio, H. (1990). Individuals with sociopathic behavior caused by frontal damage fail to respond autonomically to social stimuli. *Behavioural Brain Research, 41,* 81–94.

Derefinko, K. J. (2014). Psychopathy and low anxiety: Meta-analytic evidence for the absence of inhibition, not affect. *Journal of Personality, 83,* 693–709.

Hofmann, S. G., Korte, K. J., and Suvak, M. K. (2009). The upside of being socially anxious: Psychopathic attributes and social anxiety are negatively associated. *Journal of Social and Clinical Psychology, 28,* 714–27.

Talati, A., Pantazatos, S. P., Schneier, F. R., Weissman, M. M., and Hirsch, J.

(2013). Gray matter abnormalities in Social Anxiety Disorder: Primary, replication, and specificity studies. *Biological Psychiatry, 73,* 75–84.

Additional References

Cremers, H. R., and Roelofs, K. (2016). Social anxiety disorder: A critical overview of neurocognitive research. *Wiley Interdisciplinary Reviews: Cognitive Science, 7,* 218–32.

Doehrmann, O., Ghosh, S. S., Polli, F. E., Reynolds, G. O., Horn, F., Keshavan, A., . . . Gabrieli, J. D. (2013). Predicting treatment response in social anxiety disorder from functional magnetic resonance imaging. *JAMA Psychiatry, 70,* 87–97.

Furmark, T., Tillers, M., Marteinsdottir, I., Fischer, H., Pissiota, A., Angstrom, B., and Fredrikson, M. (2002). Common changes in cerebral blood flow in patients with social phobia treated with citalopram or cognitive-behavioral therapy. *Archives of General Psychiatry, 59,* 425–33.

John Gabrieli, Ph.D., personal communication, May 2, 2016.

Goldin, P. R., Manber-Ball, T., Werner, K., Heimberg, R., and Gross, J. J. (2009). Neural mechanisms of cognitive reappraisal of negative self-beliefs in Social Anxiety Disorder. *Biological Psychiatry, 66,* 1091–99.

Izuma, K., Saito, D. N., and Sadato, N. (2008). Processing of social and monetary rewards in the human striatum. *Neuron, 58,* 284–94.

Krach, S., Paulus, F. M., Bodden, M., and Kircher, T. (2010). The rewarding nature of social interactions. *Frontiers in Behavioral Neuroscience, 4,* 22.

Tsukiura, T., and Cabeza, R. (2008). Orbitofrontal and hippocampal contributions to memory for face-name associations: The rewarding power of a smile. *Neuropsychologia, 46,* 2310–9.

Chapter 4: How Our Inner Critic Undermines Us

what we're really afraid of is The Reveal.

Moscovitch, D. A. (2009). What is the core fear in social phobia? A new model to facilitate individualized case conceptualization and treatment. *Cognitive and Behavioral Practice, 16,* 123–34.

It's less about fear and more about shame, a word that can be traced to the Indo-European root *skam*, meaning "to cover."

Gilbert, and Trower, (2011). The evolution and manifestation of social anxiety. In Crozier, W. R. (ed.), *Shyness and Embarrassment: Perspectives from Social Psychology.* Cambridge: Cambridge University Press, 144–77.

Hedman, E., Ström, P., Stünkel, A., and Mörtberg, E. (2013). Shame and guilt in social anxiety disorder: Effects of cognitive behavior therapy and association with social anxiety and depressive symptoms. *PLoS One, 8*: e61713. http://www.etymonline.com/index.php?term=shame.

our anxiety, our appearance, our character, our social skills—
Moscovitch (2009).
David A. Moscovitch, Ph.D., personal communication, September 22, 2016.

In 1999, Dr. David Clark, a pioneering psychologist
Mansell, W., and Clark, D. M. (1999). How do I appear to others? Social anxiety and processing of the observable self. *Behavior Research & Therapy, 37,* 419–34.

When it comes to social anxiety, bad is stronger than good.
Nesse, R. M. (2005). Natural selection and the regulation of defenses: A signal detection analysis of the smoke detector principle. *Evolution and Human Behavior, 26,* 88–105.

To use an example from Dr. David Moscovitch,
David A. Moscovitch, Ph.D., personal communication, September 22, 2016.

Think of a scenario that gives you the social heebie-jeebies.
Moscovitch, D. A., and Huyder, V. (2012). Negative self-portrayal scale (NSPS). Measurement Instrument Database for the Social Science. Retrieved from www.midss.ie on June 1, 2016.

It's there in the anticipation and in the aftermath.
Penney, E. S., and Abbott, M. J. (2014). Anticipatory and post-event rumination in Social Anxiety Disorder: A review of the theoretical and empirical literature. *Behaviour Change, 31,* 79–101.
Wong, Q. J. J. (2016). Anticipatory processing and post-event processing in Social Anxiety Disorder: An update on the literature. *Australian Psychologist, 51,* 105–13.

"snatching defeat from the jaws of victory."
Richard Heimberg, Ph.D., personal communication, September 23, 2016.

In 2003, David Clark, whose positive and negative adjective experiment we read about earlier,
Hinrichsen, H., and Clark, D. M. (2003). Anticipatory processing in social anxiety: Two pilot studies. *Journal of Behavior Therapy and Experimental Psychiatry, 34,* 205–18.
Note: I lightly edited the instructions for clarity, but the content remains true to the study.

In 2006, Drs. Judith Wilson and Ronald Rapee,
Wilson, J. K., and Rapee, R. M. (2006). Self-concept certainty in social phobia. *Behaviour Research and Therapy, 44,* 113–36.

Occasionally, I'll work with a client who is reluctant to let go of the Inner Critic.
Vassilopoulos, S., Brouzos, A., and Moberly, N. (2015). The relationships between metacognition, anticipatory processing, and social anxiety. *Behaviour Change, 32,* 114–26.

Additional References

Abbott, M. J., and Rapee, R. M. (2004). Post-event rumination and negative self-appraisal in social phobia before and after treatment. *Journal of Abnormal Psychology, 13,* 136–44.

Brozovich, F. A., Goldin, P., Lee, I., Jazaieri, H., Heimberg, R. G., and Gross, J. J. (2015). The effect of rumination and reappraisal on social anxiety symptoms during cognitive-behavioral therapy for social anxiety disorder. *Journal of Clinical Psychology, 71,* 208–18.

Brozovich, F., and Heimberg, R. G. (2008). An analysis of post-event processing in social anxiety disorder. *Clinical Psychology Review, 28,* 891–903.

Clark, D. M., and Wells, A. (1995). A cognitive model of social phobia. In Heimberg, R. G., Liebowitz, M. R., Hope, D. A., and Schneier, F. R., (eds.), *Social Phobia: Diagnosis, Assessment, and Treatment* (69–93). New York: Guilford Press.

Heimberg, R. G., Brozovich, F. A., and Rapee, R. M. (2010). A cognitive behavioral model of social anxiety disorder: Update and extension. In Hofmann, S. G., and DiBartolo, P. M., (eds.), *Social Anxiety: Clinical, Developmental, and Social Perspectives* (2nd ed., 395–422). New York: Academic Press.

Hofmann, S. G. (2010). Recent advances in the psychosocial treatment of social anxiety disorder. *Depression & Anxiety, 27,* 1073–76.

Hofmann, S. G. (2007). Cognitive factors that maintain social anxiety disorder: A comprehensive model and its treatment implications. *Cognitive Behaviour Therapy, 36,* 193–209.

Rachman, S., Grüter-Andrew, J., and Shafran, R. (2000). Post-event processing in social anxiety. *Behaviour Research and Therapy, 38,* 611–17.

Wong, Q. J. J., and Rapee, R. M. (2016). The aetiology and maintenance of social anxiety disorder: A synthesis of complimentary theoretical models and formulation of a new integrated model. *Journal of Affective Disorders, 203,* 84–100.

Chapter 5: Think Different: Replace

Antony, M. M., and Swinson, R. P. (2008). *The Shyness & Social Anxiety Workbook* (2nd ed.). Oakland, CA: New Harbinger.

Hope, D. A., Heimberg, R. G., and Turk, C. L. (2006). *Managing Social Anxiety: A Cognitive-Behavioral Therapy Approach.* Oxford: Oxford University Press.

Chapter 6: Think Different: Embrace

This is self-compassion.
Neff, K. (2011). *Self-Compassion: The Proven Power of Being Kind to Yourself.* New York: William Morrow.

"Put it in a context," she suggested. "Would a compassionate mother let her child eat all the candy?"
Kristin Neff, Ph.D., personal communication, September 29, 2016

Mindfulness, simply, is paying attention to the present moment on purpose, without judgment.
Kabat-Zinn, J. (1990). *Full Catastrophe Living: Using the Wisdom of Your Body and Mind to Face Stress, Pain, and Illness.* New York: Dell.

To demonstrate the power of mindfulness on social anxiety, a 2011 study
Cassin, S. E., and Rector, N. A. (2011). Mindfulness and the attenuation of post-event processing in social phobia: An experimental investigation. *Cognitive Behaviour Therapy, 40,* 267–78.

Indeed, a 2015 study showed that among those who practiced self-compassion
Marshall, S. L., Parker, P. D., Ciarrochi, J., Sahdra, B., Jackson, C. J., and Heaven, P. C. L. (2015). Self-compassion protects against the negative effects of low self-esteem: A longitudinal study in a large adolescent sample. *Personality and Individual Differences, 74,* 116–21.

Additional References

Arimitsu, K., and Hofmann, S. G. (2017). Effects of compassionate thinking on negative emotions. *Cognition & Emotion, 31,* 160–67.

Cassin, S. E., and Rector, N. A. (2011). Mindfulness and the attenuation of post-event processing in social phobia: An experimental investigation. *Cognitive Behaviour Therapy, 40,* 267–78.

Goldin, P. R., Morrison, A., Jazaieri, H., Brozovich, F., Heimberg, R., and Gross, J. J. (2016). Group CBT versus MBSR for social anxiety disorder: A randomized controlled trial. *Journal of Consulting and Clinical Psychology, 84,* 427–37.

Otto, M. W. (2000). Stories and metaphors in cognitive-behavior therapy. *Cognitive and Behavioral Practice, 7,* 166–72.

Note: The story about the swim coaches is based on Boston University's Dr. Michael Otto's "Coach A, Coach B" exercise, a now-classic metaphor often used in CBT.

Shikatani, B., Antony, M. M., Kuo, J. R., and Cassin, S. E. (2014). The impact of cognitive restructuring and mindfulness strategies on post-event processing and affect in social anxiety disorder. *Journal of Anxiety Disorders, 28,* 570–79.

Chapter 7: Get Started and Your Confidence Will Catch Up

Brandon Stanton is prowling the streets of Chelsea,
Kaplan, M. (2013, July 29). The man behind Humans of New York: Brandon Stanton. *American Photo.* http://www.americanphotomag.com/man-behind -humans-new-york-brandon-stanton.

As he described it when I spoke with him,
Brandon Stanton, personal communication, November 2, 2015.

It wasn't always this easy.
Stanton, B. (2013, May 3). Humans of New York: Behind the lens. *Huffington Post.* http://www.huffingtonpost.com/brandon-stanton/humans-of-new-york -behind_b_3210673.html.

Illustrations courtesy of Diana Howard. Dianahoward.com

Chapter 8: No False Fronts in This Town: Play a Role to Build Your True Self

In a vintage episode of *The Tonight Show,*
http://www.pbs.org/wnet/americanmasters/johnny-carson-king-of-late -night-watch-the-full-documentary/2093/.

Jones, P. (Writer), and Catalena, M. A. (Director). (2012). *Johnny Carson: King of Late Night* In Jones, P. and Lacy, S. (Producers), *American Masters.* USA: Public Broadcasting Service.

Indeed, a classic study by Australian researchers Drs. Simon Thompson and Ron Rapee
Thompson, S., and Rapee, R. M. (2002). The effect of situational structure on the social performance of socially anxious and non-anxious participants. *Journal of Behavior Therapy and Experimental Psychiatry, 33,* 91–102.

As a boy, Johnny was obsessed with magic—

Leamer, L. (2005). *King of the Night: The Life of Johnny Carson.* New York: Avon.

In another old *Tonight Show* segment,
Jones and Catalena (2012).

As Laurence Leamer, Johnny's biographer, said in the documentary *Johnny Carson: King of Late Night,*
Jones and Catalena (2012).

Even Ed McMahon, Johnny's loyal sidekick for thirty years, said of Johnny, "He was good with ten million people, lousy with ten."
Corliss, R. (2005, January 25). Whoooooooo's Johnny? *Time.*
http://content.time.com/time/arts/article/0,8599,1020765,00.html.

For Johnny Carson, biographers theorize that Johnny's persona, Johnny Carson the Entertainer, was created to win the approval of a specific person.
Jones and Catalena (2012).

The phenomenon of power posing, pioneered by Dr. Amy Cuddy,
Cuddy, A. (2015). *Presence: Bringing Your Boldest Self to Your Biggest Challenges.* New York: Little, Brown.
https://www.ted.com/talks/amy_cuddy_your_body_language_shapes_who_you_are.

While researchers are still slugging it out on whether or not power posing "works" biologically by changing your cortisol and testosterone,
Carney, D., Cuddy, A., and Yap, A. J. (2015). Review and summary of research on the embodied effects of expansive (vs. contractive) non-verbal displays. *Psychological Science, 26,* 657–63.
http://faculty.haas.berkeley.edu/dana_carney/pdf_my%20position%20on%20power%20poses.pdf.
Ranehill, E., Dreber, A., Johannesson, M., Leiberg, S., Sul, S., and Weber, R. A. (2015). Assessing the robustness of power posing: No effect on hormones and risk tolerance in a large sample of men and women. *Psychological Science, 26,* 653–56.
http://ideas.ted.com/inside-the-debate-about-power-posing-a-q-a-with-amy-cuddy/.

Our brain likes to coordinate posture, facial expression, tone of voice, and emotion like a well-matched outfit, a phenomenon known as *congruence.*
Meeren, H. K., van Heijnsbergen, C. C., and de Gelder, B. (2005). Rapid

perceptual integration of facial expression and emotional body language. *Proceedings of the National Academy of Sciences, 102,* 16518–23.

Stienen, B. M. C., Tanaka, A., and de Gelder, B. (2011.) Emotional voice and emotional body postures influence each other independently of visual awareness. *PLoS ONE, 6,* e25517.

A creative 2014 study out of the University of Chicago
Epley, N., and Schroeder, J. (2014). Mistakenly seeking solitude. *Journal of Experimental Psychology: General, 143,* 1980–99.

Chapter 9: Mountains to Molehills: It Gets Easier Every Time

A skinny nineteen-year-old kid named Albert
http://www.npr.org/templates/story/story.php?storyId=1921765.
Speigel, A. (2004, June 3). *Cognitive behavior therapy's controversial founder* [Radio story]. Washington, DC: National Public Radio.

Over the years, CBT has been shown time and again to be the most effective treatment
Butler, A. C., Chapman, J. E., Forman, E. M., and Beck, A. T. (2006). The empirical status of cognitive-behavioral therapy: A review of meta-analyses. *Clinical Psychology Review, 26,* 17–31.

Mayo-Wilson, E., Dias, S., Mavranezouli, I., Kew, K., Clark, D. M., Ades, A. E., and Pilling, S. (2014). Psychological and pharmacological interventions for social anxiety disorder in adults: A systematic review and network meta-analysis. *Lancet Psychiatry, 1,* 368–76.

Rapee, R. M., Gaston, J. E., and Abbott, M. J. (2009). Testing the efficacy of theoretically derived improvements in the treatment of social phobia. *Journal of Consulting and Clinical Psychology, 77,* 317–27.

Tolin, D. F. (2010). Is cognitive-behavioral therapy more effective than other therapies?: A meta-analytic review. *Clinical Psychology Review, 30,* 710–20.

Albert Ellis didn't know that contemporary clinical psychologists, when asked to name the most influential psychotherapist in history, would rank him above Freud.
http://www.nytimes.com/2006/12/10/nyregion/10ellis.html?_r=0.
Ramirez, A. (2006, December 10). Despite illness and lawsuits, a famed psychotherapist is temporarily back in session. *New York Times.*

he refused to take part in classroom plays and "sweated and sizzled with anxiety" whenever he had to recite a poem or accept an award.
Ellis, A. (1991). My life in clinical psychology. In Walker, C. E. (ed.), *The*

History of Clinical Psychology in Autobiography, vol. 1 (1–37). Pacific Grove, CA: Brooks/Cole.

In a 2004 interview with National Public Radio,
Speigel (2004).

Graphs courtesy of Diana Howard. Dianahoward.com.

Additional References

Yankura, J., and Dryden, W. (1994). *Albert Ellis.* Thousand Oaks, CA: SAGE.

Chapter 10: Putting It All Together: Your Challenge List

At the age of sixteen, Jia came to the United States from China
Jiang, J. (2015). *Rejection Proof: How I Beat Fear and Became Invincible Through 100 Days of Rejection.* New York: Harmony Books.

He made ridiculous requests to complete strangers: "Wanna have a staring contest?" "Can I take a nap in this mattress store?" "Can you ship this package to Santa Claus?" "Can I slide down the fire station's pole?" "Can I be a live mannequin at this Abercrombie store?"
http://rejectiontherapy.com/100-days-of-rejection-therapy./

In technical speak, facing your fears is called *exposure,*
Fang, A., Sawyer, A. T., Asnaani, A., and Hofmann, S. G. (2013). Social mishap exposures for social anxiety disorder: An important treatment ingredient. *Cognitive and Behavioral Practice, 20,* 213–20.

Enter Dr. Lynn Alden of the University of British Columbia.
Lynn Alden, Ph.D., personal communication, October 20, 2016.

How to fix this? As Dr. Taylor puts it,
Charles Taylor, Ph.D., personal communication, October 20, 2016.

Over the past decade, Alden and Taylor have run a series of groundbreaking studies where they asked people to do just that.
Alden, L. E., and Taylor, C. T. (2004). Interpersonal processes in social phobia. *Clinical Psychology Review, 24,* 857–82.
Plasencia, M. L., Taylor, C. T., and Alden, L. E. (2016). Unmasking one's true self facilitates positive relational outcomes: Authenticity promotes social approach processes in social anxiety disorder. *Clinical Psychological Science, 4,* 1002–14.
Taylor, C. T., and Alden, L. E. (2011). To see ourselves as others see us: An experimental integration of the intra- and interpersonal consequences of

self-protection in social anxiety disorder. *Journal of Abnormal Psychology, 120,* 129–41.

Taylor, C. T., and Alden, L. E. (2010). Safety behaviors and judgmental biases in social anxiety disorder. *Behavior Research and Therapy, 48,* 226–37.

And in those studies, they told me, 92 percent of people could identify right away what safety behaviors they were using.
Lynn Alden, Ph.D., personal communication, December 11, 2016.

In several studies, Alden and Taylor asked socially anxious participants
Taylor and Alden (2011).
Taylor and Alden (2010).
Plasencia, Taylor and Alden (2016).

In the video of the encounter Jia filmed on his phone,
http://rejectiontherapy.com/2012/11/15/the-100-days-rejection-therapy/.

Jia moves in quickly, chatters his words, and gets out, as he put it, "like some sort of small animal running away from a predator."
Jiang (2015).

In his phone video, a young guy with glasses, a red apron, and an armload of tattoos strides up to help him.
http://rejectiontherapy.com/2012/11/16/day-2-of-rejection-therapy-request -a-burger-refill/.

When I talked to Jia about this discovery,
Jia Jiang, personal communication, September 20, 2016.

Then, as Dr. Richard Heimberg, the aforementioned father of social anxiety research, said to me when I asked the secret to overcoming social anxiety, "Go forth and do."
Richard Heimberg, Ph.D., personal communication, September 23, 2016.

The interweb makes fun of affirmations:
http://chainletters.net/chainletters/funny-daily-affirmations/.
http://therumpus.net/2012/05/funny-women-78-ambivalent-affirmations/.

Instead, try this: affirm yourself with the values you are 100 percent rock-solid sure about,
Creswell, J. D., Welch, W. T., Taylor, S. E., Sherman, D. K., Gruenewald, T. L. and Mann, T. (2005). Affirmation of personal values buffers neuroendocrine and psychological stress responses. *Psychological Science, 16,* 846–51.

Likewise, you can gain strength by affirming your own courageous acts. A 2017 eye-tracking study

Van Dillen, L. F., Enter, D., Peters, L. P. M., van Dijk, W. W., and Rotteveel, M. (2017). Moral fixations: The role of moral integrity and social anxiety in the selective avoidance of social threat. *Biological Psychology, 122,* 51–58.

As Dr. Richard Heimberg so neatly summed up the process when I talked with him, "Good exposures set in motion a success spiral."
Richard Heimberg, Ph.D., personal communication, September 23, 2016.

But don't take it from me; take it from Jia,
Jia Jiang, personal communication, September 20, 2016.

Chapter 11: How (and Why) to Turn Your Attention Inside Out

To Diego, the medical resident sounded like Charlie Brown's teacher.
Note: Diego is adapted from a client of Dr. Susan Bögels of the University of Amsterdam. She discusses him in this paper:
Bögels, S. M., Mulkens, S., and De Jong, P. J. (1997). Task concentration training and fear of blushing. *Clinical Psychology and Psychotherapy, 4,* 251–58.

a phenomenon aptly called *self-focused attention.*
Spurr, J. M., and Stopa, L. (2002). Self-focused attention in social phobia and social anxiety. *Clinical Psychology Review, 22,* 947–75.
Wells, A., and Papageorgiou, C. (1998). Social phobia: effects of external attention on anxiety, negative beliefs, and perspective taking. *Behavior Therapy, 29,* 357–70.

Researchers from Wilfrid Laurier University in Ontario
Gaydukevych, D., and Kocovski, N. L. (2012). Effect of self-focused attention on post-event processing in social anxiety. *Behaviour Research and Therapy, 50,* 47–55.

To help us with this, we have Dr. Susan Bögels of the University of Amsterdam,
Susan Bögels, Ph.D., personal communication, July 20, 2016.
Bögels, S. M. (2006). Task concentration training versus applied relaxation, in combination with cognitive therapy, for social phobia patients with fear of blushing, trembling, and sweating. *Behaviour Research and Therapy, 44,* 1199–210.
Bögels, S. M., Mulkens, S., and de Jong, P. J. (1997). Task concentration training and fear of blushing. *Journal of Clinical Psychology and Psychotherapy, 4,* 251–58.
Bögels, S. M., Sijbers, G. F. V. M., and Voncken, M. (2006). Mindfulness and

task concentration training for social phobia: A pilot study. *Journal of Cognitive Psychotherapy: An International Quarterly, 20,* 33–44.

try an experiment suggested by Dr. David Clark of Oxford.
David Clark, DPhil, FMedSci, personal communication, November 14, 2016.

This is called *attention to threat.*
Hirsch, C. R., and Matthews, A. (2000). Impaired positive inferential bias in social phobia. *Journal of Abnormal Psychology, 109,* 705–12.
Perowne, S., and Mansell, W. (2002). Social anxiety, self-focused attention, and the discrimination of negative, neutral and positive audience members by their non-verbal behaviours. *Behavioural and Cognitive Psychotherapy, 30,* 11–23.

Pictures of angry and disgusted faces have been used in innumerable social anxiety studies
Amir, N., Klumpp, H., Elias, J. Bedwell, J. S., Yanasak, N., and Miller, L. S. (2005). Increased activation of the anterior cingulate cortex during processing of disgust faces in individuals with social phobia. *Biological Psychiatry, 57,* 975–81.
Buckner, J. D., Maner, J. K., and Schmidt, N. B. (2010). Difficulty disengaging attention from social threat in social anxiety. *Cognitive Therapy and Research, 34,* 99–105.
Horley, K., Williams, L. M., Gonsalvez, C., and Gordon, E. (2003). Social phobics do not see eye to eye: A visual scanpath study of emotional expression processing. *Journal of Anxiety Disorders, 17,* 33–44.

But a research group in the Netherlands led by Dr. Mike Rinck of Radboud University Nijmegen created an ingenious method
Rinck, M., Telli, S., Kampmann, I. L., Woud, M. L., Kerstholt, M., Te Velthuis, S., Wittkowski, M., and Becker, E. S. (2013). Training approach-avoidance of smiling faces affects emotional vulnerability in socially anxious individuals. *Frontiers in Human Neuroscience, 7,* 481.
Mike Rinck, Ph.D., personal communication, December 8, 2016.

Chapter 12: Seeing Is Believing:
How You Feel Isn't How You Look

To explain, let's take a quick tour through the physiology of anxiety.
Barlow, D. H., and Craske, M. G. (2007). Mastery of your anxiety and panic, (4th ed.) workbook. Oxford: Oxford University Press.

Interoceptive awareness, unsurprisingly, is more sensitive in individuals with any kind of anxiety.
Reiss, S., Peterson, R. A., Gursky, D. M., and McNally, R. J. (1986). Anxiety sensitivity, anxiety frequency, and the prediction of fearfulness. *Behavior Research and Therapy, 24,* 1–8.
Taylor, S., Zvolensky, M. J., Cox, B. J., Deacon, B., Heimberg, R. G., Ledley, D. R., . . . Cardenas, S. J. (2007). Robust dimensions of anxiety sensitivity: Development and initial validation of the Anxiety Sensitivity Index-3. *Psychological Assessment, 19,* 176–88.

This happens due to a quirk of thought called the *illusion of transparency*,
Gilovich, T., Medvec, V. H., and Savitsky, K. (1998). The illusion of transparency: Biased assessments of others' ability to read one's own emotional states. *Journal of Personality and Social Psychology, 75,* 332–46.
Gilovich, T., and Savitsky, K. (1999). The spotlight effect and the illusion of transparency: Egocentric assessments of how we are seen by others. *Current Directions in Psychological Science, 8,* 165–68.
Van Boven, L., Gilovich, T., and Medvec, V. (2003). The illusion of transparency in negotiations. *Negotiation Journal, 19,* 117–31.

One study even found that simply telling participants that, hey, guys,
Savitsky, K., and Gilovich, T. (2003). The illusion of transparency and the alleviation of speech anxiety. *Journal of Experimental Social Psychology, 39,* 618–25.

Instead, we see our image as if in the funhouse mirror of the House of Social Anxiety.
Rapee, R. M., and Abbott, M. J. (2006). Mental representation of observable attributes in people with social phobia. *Journal of Behavior Therapy and Experimental Psychiatry, 37,* 113–26.

which, interestingly, *is a view I never actually saw.*
Coles, M. E., Turk, C. L., Heimberg, R. G., and Fresco, D. M. (2001). Effects of varying levels of anxiety within social situations: Relationship to memory perspective and attributions in social phobia. *Behaviour Research and Therapy, 39,* 651–65.
Hackmann, A., Surawy, C., and Clark, D. M. (1998). Seeing yourself through others' eyes: A study of spontaneously occurring images in social phobia. *Behavioral and Cognitive Psychotherapy, 26,* 3–12.

A tried-and-true method to replace your imaginary mind's eye movie is to make an actual movie.
Harvey, A. G., Clark, D. M., Ehlers, A., and Rapee, R. M. (2000). Social

anxiety and self-impression: Cognitive preparation enhances the beneficial effects of video feedback following a stressful social task. *Behavior Research and Therapy, 38,* 1183–92.

I got this technique (as well as the following picture) from a team at King's College London and the University of Oxford.
Warnock-Parkes, E., Wild, J., Stott, R., Grey, N., Ehlers, A., and Clark, D. M. (2017). Seeing is believing: Using video feedback in cognitive therapy for social anxiety disorder. *Cognitive and Behavioral Practice, 24,* 245–55.

But sometimes people watch their videos and notice they *do* look weird.
Warnock-Parkes et al. (2017).

This myth of inevitable judgment gains great momentum from the *spotlight effect*.
Brown, M. A., and Stopa, L. (2007). The spotlight effect and the illusion of transparency in social anxiety. *Journal of Anxiety Disorders, 21,* 804–19.
Gilovich, T., Medvec, V. H., and Savitsky, K. (2000). The spotlight effect in social judgment: An egocentric bias in estimates of the salience of one's own actions and appearance. *Journal of Personality and Social Psychology, 78,* 211–22.

Studies show that whether we're having a bad hair day, wearing a conspicuous T-shirt, screwing up a volleyball game, or sucking at old-school Nintendo
Gilovich, T., Kruger, J., and Medvec, V. H. (2002). The spotlight effect revisited: Overestimating the manifest variability of our actions and appearance. *Journal of Experimental Social Psychology, 38,* 93–99.

in his classic *How to Win Friends and Influence People*,
Carnegie, D. (1936). *How to Win Friends and Influence People.* New York: Simon and Schuster.

The process by which our brains process ambiguity provides the finishing touch for the people-will-judge-me myth.
Courtney Beard, Ph.D., personal communication, September 12, 2016.
Beard, C., and Amir, N. (2009). Interpretation in social anxiety: When meaning precedes ambiguity. *Cognitive Therapy and Research, 33,* 406–15.
Note: The ambiguous sentence examples—*Your boss calls you into his office, People laugh after something you said, A friend doesn't text you back, An old friend comments on how you look different now*—are from this study or inspired by it; many thanks to Dr. Courtney Beard for sending me their study materials.

Exercise feels a lot like the pesky sensations of anxiety:
Broman-Fulks, J. J., Berman, M. E., Rabian, B., and Webster, M. J. (2004). Effects of aerobic exercise on anxiety sensitivity. *Behaviour Research and Therapy, 42,* 125–36.

Dixon, L. J., Kemp, J. J., Farrell, N. R., Blakey, S. M., and Deacon, B. J. (2015). Interoceptive exposure exercises for social anxiety. *Journal of Anxiety Disorders, 33,* 25–34.

Noticing usually stops with noticing.
McEwan, K. L., and Devins, G. M. (1983). Is increased arousal in social anxiety noticed by others? *Journal of Abnormal Psychology, 92,* 417–21.

Additional References

Amir, N., and Taylor, C. T. (2012). Interpretation training in individuals with generalized social anxiety disorder: A randomized controlled trial. *Journal of Consulting and Clinical Psychology, 80,* 497–511.

George, L., and Stopa, L. (2008). Private and public self-awareness in social anxiety. *Journal of Behavior Therapy and Experimental Psychiatry, 39,* 57–72.

Gerlach, A.L., Wilhelm, F. H., Gruber, K., and Roth, W. T. (2001). Blushing and physiological arousability in social phobia. *Journal of Abnormal Psychology, 110,* 247–58.

Chapter 13: "I Have to Sound Smart/Funny/Interesting": How Perfectionism Holds Us Back

Welcome to the stratosphere of perfectionism.
Frost, R. O., Heimberg, C. S., Holt, C. S., Mattia, J. I., and Neubauer, A. L. (1993). A comparison of two measures of perfectionism. *Personality and Individual Differences, 14,* 119–26.

Hewitt, P. L., and Flett, G. L. (1991). Perfectionism in the self and social contexts: Conceptualization, assessment and association with psychopathology. *Journal of Personality and Social Psychology, 60,* 456–70.

Shafran, R., and Mansell, W. (2001). Perfectionism and psychopathology: A review of research and treatment. *Clinical Psychology Review, 21,* 879–906.

Stoeber, J. (2015). How other-oriented perfectionism differs from self-oriented and socially prescribed perfectionism: Further findings. *Journal of Psychopathology and Behavioral Assessment, 37,* 611.

In an illustrative study, leading social anxiety researcher Dr. Stefan Hofmann of Boston University
Stefan Hofmann, Ph.D., personal communication, April 12, 2016.

Moscovitch, D. A., and Hofmann, S. G. (2007). When ambiguity hurts: Social standards moderate self-appraisals in generalized social phobia. *Behaviour Research and Therapy, 45,* 1039–52.

but a study out of Washington University did just that.
Rodebaugh, T. L., Lim, M. H., Fernandez, K. C., Langer, J. K., Weisman, J. S., Tonge, N., Levinson, C. A., and Shumaker, E. A. (2014). Self and friend's differing views of social anxiety disorder's effects on friendships. *Journal of Abnormal Psychology, 123,* 715–24.

She was one of the approximately one out of five socially anxious individuals whose anxiety manifests as irritability and anger.
Kashdan, T. B., McKnight, P. E., Richey, J. A., and Hofmann, S. G. (2009). When social anxiety disorder co-exists with risk-prone, approach behavior: Investigating a neglected, meaningful subset of people in the National Comorbidity Survey-Replication. *Behavior Research and Therapy, 47,* 559–68.

But despite frequent *anger experience,* folks prone to social anxiety have less *anger expression* than their non-anxious compadres.
Moscovitch, D. A., McCabe, R. E., Antony, M. M., Rocca, L., and Swinson, R. P. (2008). Anger experience and expression across the anxiety disorders. *Depression and Anxiety, 25,* 107–13.

But some beliefs are less helpful, especially when they act as the perfect kindling for a social anxiety fire.
De Graaf, L. E., Roelofs, J., and Huibers, M. J. H. (2009). Measuring dysfunctional attitudes in the general population: The Dysfunctional Attitude Scale (form A), Revised. *Cognitive Therapy and Research, 33,* 345.

How-to sites warn:
https://later.com/blog/how-to-curate-instagram-feed/.

fear of missing out, or FOMO.
Note: the FOMO section is adapted from a Savvy Psychologist episode I wrote previously published on quickanddirtytips.com.
5 Ways to Fight Fomo. December 4, 2015.
http://www.quickanddirtytips.com/health-fitness/mental-health/5-ways-to -fight-fomo.

Indeed, a 2013 study showed that those who experience higher levels of FOMO also reported lower levels of overall life satisfaction.
Przybylski, A. K., Murayama, K., DeHaan, C. R., and Gladwell, V. (2013). Motivational, emotional, and behavioral correlates of fear of missing out. *Computers in Human Behavior, 29,* 1841–48.

Another remedy: JOMO, or the joy of missing out.
http://anildash.com/2012/07/jomo.html.

In 1980, Dr. David Burns, now emeritus faculty at Stanford, published
the first research-based self-help book for depression,
Burns, D. D. (1980). *Feeling Good: The New Mood Therapy*. New York: Harper.
David Burns, MD, personal communication, February 7, 2016.

In the mid-1960s, the psychologist Elliot Aronson tested it in one of my
favorite studies of all time.
Aronson, E., Willerman, B., and Floyd, J. (1966). The effect of a pratfall on
increasing interpersonal attractiveness. *Psychonomic Science, 4,* 227–28.

Embarrassment is thought to have evolved as a non-verbal apology and
gesture of appeasement—plus it actually fosters trust.
Feinberg, M., Willer, R., and Keltner, D. (2012). Flustered and faithful: Embarrassment as a signal of prosociality. *Journal of Personality and Social Psychology,
102,* 81–97.

Additional References

Alkis, Y., Kadirhan, Z., and Sat, M. (2017). Development and validation of
social anxiety scale for social media users. *Computers in Human Behavior, 72,*
296–303.
Ansari, A., and Klinenberg, E. (2016). *Modern Romance.* New York: Penguin
Books.
Hawkins, K., and Cougle, J. (2011). Anger problems across the anxiety disor-
ders: Findings from a population-based study. *Depression & Anxiety, 28,* 145–52.
Kashdan, T. B., and McKnight, P. E. (2010). The darker side of social anxiety:
When aggressive impulsivity prevails over shy inhibition. *Current Directions
in Psychological Science, 19,* 47–50.
Kashdan, T. B., and Collins, L. (2009). Social anxiety and the experience of
positive emotion and anger in everyday life: An ecological momentary assessment approach. *Anxiety, Stress, and Coping, 23,* 259–72.
Kashdan, T. B., and Hofmann, S. G. (2008). The high novelty seeking, impulsive subtype of generalized social anxiety disorder. *Depression and Anxiety,
25,* 535–41.
Marder, B., Joinson, A., Shankar, A., and Thirlaway, K. (2016). Strength
matters: Self-presentation to the strongest audience rather than lowest common denominator when faced with multiple audiences in social network
sites. *Computers in Human Behavior, 61,* 56–62.
Pierce, T. (2009). Social anxiety and technology: Face-to-face communica-

tion versus technological communication among teens. *Computers in Human Behavior, 25,* 1367–72.

Sales, N. J. (2016). *American Girls: Social Media and the Secret Lives of Teenagers.* New York: Knopf.

Turkle, S. (2012). *Alone Together: Why We Expect More from Technology and Less from Each Other.* New York: Basic Books.

http://www.espn.com/espn/feature/story/_/id/12833146/instagram -account-university-pennsylvania-runner-showed-only-part-story.

https://www.theatlantic.com/education/archive/2015/01/the-socially -anxious-generation/384458/.

Chapter 14: Why You Don't Have a Social Skills Problem (You Heard That Right)

But the feeling that we have no social skills is the result of anxiety, not the other way around.
Ron Rapee, Ph.D., personal communication, November 21, 2016.
Tashiro, Ty. (2017). *Awkward: The Science of Why We're Socially Awkward and Why That's Awesome.* New York: HarperCollins.

We act in a way that researchers call *innocuously social.*
Leary, M., and Kowalski, R. (1995). *Social Anxiety.* New York: Guilford Press.

We use what linguists have labeled *back-channel responses*
Natale, M., Entin, E., and Jaffe, J. (1979). Vocal interruptions in dyadic communication as a function of speech and social anxiety. *Journal of Personality and Social Psychology, 37,* 865–78.

Indeed, a 2012 study out of Berkeley found that even though it's uncomfortable to feel embarrassed, it serves a vital social function by acting as a prosocial gesture.
Feinberg, M., Willer, R., and Keltner, D. (2012). Flustered and faithful: Embarrassment as a signal of prosociality. *Journal of Personality and Social Psychology, 102,* 81–97.

we're not poorly socialized; in fact, quite the opposite.
Juster, H. R., Heimberg, R., and Holt, C. S. (1996). Social phobia: Diagnostic issues and review of cognitive-behavioral treatment strategies. In Hersen, M., Eisler, R., and Miller, P. (eds.), *Progress in Behavior Modification* (74–98). Pacific Grove, CA: Brooks/Cole.

As Harris says as Dr. NerdLove, "Geeks have the worst superpower in the world—"
Harris O'Malley, personal communication, February 29, 2016.

It's so common it has a name: *anxiety-induced performance deficits.*
Hofmann, S. G. (2007). Cognitive factors that maintain social anxiety disorder:
A comprehensive model and its treatment implications. *Cognitive Behaviour
Therapy, 36,* 193–209.

As Dr. NerdLove, Harris recommends the Three-Second Rule: http://
www.doctornerdlove.com/2011/12/dont-be-a-creeper/2/.

Harris points out something important: sometimes, actual creeps will
co-opt the "socially awkward" label as an excuse to step over women's
boundaries.
http://www.doctornerdlove.com/socially-awkward-isnt-an-excuse/.

A study out of the University of Liverpool found that using a scented spray,
Craig Roberts, S., Little, A. C., Lyndon, A., Roberts, J., Havlicek, J., and
Wright, R. L. (2009). Manipulation of body odour alters men's self-confidence
and judgements of their visual attractiveness by women. *International Journal of
Cosmetic Science, 31,* 47–54.

In an old study from 1976, researchers asked forty socially anxious
undergrads to role-play situations where they had to be assertive,
Nietzel, M. T., and Bernstein, D. A. (1976). Effects of instructionally medi-
ated demand on the behavioral assessment of assertiveness. *Journal of Consulting
and Clinical Psychology, 44,* 500.

Chapter 15: The Myth of Hope in a Bottle

Indeed, one study found that individuals with higher social anxiety consume *less* alcohol than folks who aren't anxious, but have *higher* levels
of hazardous drinking.
Schry, A. R., and White, S. W. (2013). Understanding the relationship between social anxiety and alcohol use in college students: A meta-analysis.
Addictive Behaviors, 38, 2690–706.

If you're one of the seven in ten Americans who have had a drink in the
past year
https://www.niaaa.nih.gov/alcohol-health/overview-alcohol-consumption
/alcohol-facts-and-statistics.

One study found that for every drink, social anxiety declines by
4 percent.
Battista, S. R., MacKinnon, S. P., Sherry, S. B., and Stewart, S. H. (2015).
Does alcohol reduce social anxiety in daily life? A 22-day experience sam-
pling study. *Journal of Social and Clinical Psychology, 34,* 508–28.

Indeed, another study found that in individuals with both social anxiety and a problem with alcohol the social anxiety almost always came first.
Buckner, J. D., Timpano, K. R., Zvolensky, M. J., Sachs-Ericsson, N., and Schmidt, N. B. (2008). Implications of comorbid alcohol dependence among individuals with social anxiety disorder. *Depression and Anxiety, 25,* 1028–37.

Any way you slice it, capital-S Social Anxiety Disorder more than quadruples the risk of developing an alcohol use disorder.
Buckner, J. D., Schmidt, N. B., Lang, A. R., Small, J. W., Schlauch, R. C., and Lewinsohn, P. M. (2008). Specificity of Social Anxiety Disorder as a risk factor for alcohol and cannabis dependence. *Journal of Psychiatric Research, 42,* 230–39.
Note: This chapter is adapted from an article previously published on Quiet Revolution: quietrev.com/hope-in-a-bottle-the-link-between-alcohol-and-social-anxiety.

Chapter 16: The Building Blocks of Beautiful Friendships (They're Not What You Think)

A meta-analysis of 177,000 participants in the prestigious journal *Psychological Bulletin*
Wrzus, C., Hanel, M., Wagner, J., and Neyer, F. J. (2013). Social network changes and life events across the life span: A meta-analysis. *Psychological Bulletin, 139,* 53–80.

Back in 2006, a large-scale survey found that more than half (53 percent) of Americans didn't have any confidants who weren't family.
McPherson, M., Smith-Lovin, L., and Brashears, M. E. (2006). Social isolation in America: Changes in core discussion networks over two decades. *American Sociological Review, 71,* 353–75.

But three professors at the Massachusetts Institute of Technology, chief among them the pioneering social psychologist Leon Festinger,
Festinger, L., Schachter, S., and Back, K. (1950). The spatial ecology of group formation. In Festinger, L., Schachter, S., and Back, K. W. (eds.), *Social Pressure in Informal Groups: A Study of Human Factors in Housing* (141–61). Stanford, CA: Stanford University Press.

In 1946, a tidal wave of World War II veterans enrolled at MIT.
https://slice.mit.edu/2012/08/02/westgate-history/.

Additional studies confirmed the effect, such as one where forty-four

state police trainees reported their best friends were those who fell closest to them in alphabetical order of seating.
Segal, M. W. (1974). Alphabet and attraction: An unobtrusive measure of the effect of propinquity in a field setting. *Journal of Personality and Social Psychology, 30,* 654–57.

"I Asked a Stranger These 36 Questions to See If We'd Fall in Love. And We Did,"
http://www.theplaidzebra.com/i-asked-a-stranger-these-36-questions-to-see-if-wed-fall-in-love-and-we-did/.

an essay in the *New York Times* titled, "To Fall in Love with Anyone, Do This."
https://www.nytimes.com/2015/01/11/fashion/modern-love-to-fall-in-love-with-anyone-do-this.html.

a paper with an innocuously dry title: "The Experimental Generation of Interpersonal Closeness: A Procedure and Some Preliminary Findings."
Aron, A., Melinat, E., Aron, E., Vallon, R. D., and Bator, R. J. (1997). The experimental generation of interpersonal closeness: A procedure and some preliminary findings. *Personality and Social Psychology Bulletin, 23,* 363–77.

instead, the thirty-six questions were simply meant to induce closeness and intimacy in a laboratory setting
http://www.huffingtonpost.com/elaine-aron-phd/36-questions-for-intimacy_b_6472282.html.

according to the researchers, it's the act of "sustained, escalating, reciprocal, and personalistic" disclosure
Aron et al. (1997).

It comes from the Latin meaning "inmost," as in sharing what is inmost—what you think and do and feel—with others.
McAdams, D. P. (1988). Personal needs and personal relationships. In Duck, S. W. (ed.), Handbook of personal relationships: Theory, research, and interventions (7–22). New York: Wiley.

Worse, we also start interpreting everyone as threatening,
Bangee, M., Harris, R. A., Bridges, N., Rotenberg, K. J., and Qualter, P. (2014). Loneliness and attention to social threat in young adults: Findings from an eye tracker study. *Personality and Individual Differences, 63,* 16–23.
Jones, W. H., Freemon, J. E., and Goswich, R. A. (1981). The persistence of loneliness: Self and other determinants. *Journal of Personality, 49,* 27–48.

https://www.theatlantic.com/health/archive/2017/04/how-loneliness
-begets-loneliness/521841/.

But then we make it worse: we act as if the world is against us, a self-fulfilling prophecy called *behavioral confirmation.*
Snyder, M., and Swann, W. B. (1978). Behavioral confirmation in social
interaction: From social perception to social reality. *Journal of Experimental
Social Psychology, 14,* 148–62.

Dr. Jennifer Parkhurst, a psychologist at the University of Illinois at
Urbana-Champaign,
Andrea Hopmeyer, Ph.D., personal communication, March 3, 2016.
Jennifer T. Parkhurst, Ph.D., personal communication, March 27, 2017.

With the new method, being chosen as "popular" didn't actually mean a
kid was well liked; it meant they were *dominant.*
Parkhurst, J. T., and Hopmeyer, A. (1998). Sociometric popularity and
peer-perceived popularity: Two distinct dimensions of peer status. *Journal of
Early Adolescence, 18,* 125–44.

An oft-cited study found that in first impressions of others we prioritize
warmth over anything else,
Fisk, S. T., Cuddy, A. J. C., and Glick, P. (2007). Universal dimensions of social cognition: Warmth and competence. *Trends in Cognitive Sciences, 11,* 77–83.
https://hbr.org/2013/07/connect-then-lead.

Dr. David Moscovitch puts it this way:
David A. Moscovitch, Ph.D., personal communication, September 22, 2016.

Additional References

Cacioppo, J. T., Hawkley, L.C., Ernst, J. M., Burleson, M., Berntson, G. G.,
Nouriani, B., and Spiegel, D. (2006). Loneliness within a nomological net:
An evolutionary perspective. *Journal of Research in Personality, 40,* 1054–85.

Epilogue

What resulted was the Study of Adult Development,
http://www.adultdevelopmentstudy.org/grantandglueckstudy.
https://www.theatlantic.com/magazine/archive/2013/05/thanks-mom
/309287/.
https://www.theatlantic.com/magazine/archive/2009/06/what-makes-us
-happy/307439/.

Valiant, G. E. (2015). *Triumphs of Experience: The Men of the Harvard Grant Study*. Cambridge: Harvard University Press.

The study's current director, Dr. Robert Waldinger, is a psychiatrist who exudes such tranquility that it's unsurprising to discover he's also a Zen priest.
http://www.ted.com/speakers/robert_waldinger.

In a viral TED Talk, he revealed what decades of Grant Study data have brought to light
https://www.youtube.com/watch?v=8KkKuTCFvzI.

But don't take it from me; take it from someone else who's been there: Jim.
"Jim Nolan," personal communication, February 24, 2016.